PENGUIN BOOKS
A GREAT CLAMOUR

Pankaj Mishra is an essayist and novelist. His books include *Age of Anger: A History of the Present*, *From the Ruins of Empire: The Revolt Against the West and the Remaking of Asia*, and the novels *The Romantics* and *Run and Hide*. He writes literary and political essays for *Guardian*, *New Yorker* and *London Review of Books*, among other American, British and Indian publications.

A fellow of the Royal Society of Literature, Mishra has received, among other prizes, Yale University's Windham-Campbell Literature Prize and Germany's prestigious Leipzig Book Award for European Understanding. His new book is *The World After Gaza*.

PRAISE FOR THE AUTHOR

A Great Clamour

ENCOUNTERS WITH CHINA AND ITS NEIGHBOURS

Pankaj Mishra

PENGUIN BOOKS

An imprint of Penguin Random House

PENGUIN BOOKS

Penguin Books is an imprint of the Penguin Random House group of companies
whose addresses can be found at global.penguinrandomhouse.com

Published by Penguin Random House India Pvt. Ltd
4th Floor, Capital Tower 1, MG Road,
Gurugram 122 002, Haryana, India

First published in Hamish Hamilton by Penguin Books India 2013
This edition published in Penguin Books by Penguin Random House India 2024

Much of this book was originally published, in a different form, in *New Yorker*,
New York Review of Books, *London Review of Books*, *Guardian*, *Bloomberg* and
New York Times magazine.

ISBN 9780143423508

Typeset in Dante MT by R. Ajith
Printed at Replika Press Pvt. Ltd, India

www.penguin.co.in

For MNM

CONTENTS

LOOKING EAST:
AN INTRODUCTION

One afternoon in the summer of 1992, I was talking to my landlord and found myself asking him what lay beyond the snow-capped mountains I could see from my veranda. 'Tibbat,' Mr Sharma said, pronouncing Tibet in the north Indian way. I was startled. Was it really that close? I had only recently moved to this small village in Himachal Pradesh to see if I could be a writer; the physical isolation seemed to constantly fuel my sense of inadequacy. Now, in my imagination, that vast territory stretching from Lhasa to Hokkaido and Surabaya, an Asia even then being imprinted by the politics and economy of China, suddenly reared up as an oppressive blank—another reminder of my ignorance about the world.

Mr Sharma, a scholar of Sanskrit, didn't share this debility. He spoke naturally of Tibbat as another crossroads within an expansive Indian cultural sphere, in which Indian religions and philosophies had travelled across mainland Asia and deep into the Pacific. I envied him his Tibbat, part of his private idea of Asia, one that must have clarified the larger world, relieved the ache of incomprehension, and anchored him to the earth.

I had no such Tibbat. My own Asia was yet to be populated by specific cultures, histories, and peoples. I had read the fiction of Lu Xun and some essays by Mao Zedong, but didn't know much more about China apart from that it had betrayed India in 1962, hastening Jawaharlal Nehru's death, and was, for this reason, not to be trusted. I knew of the nuclear incineration of Hiroshima and Nagasaki, but Japan was almost entirely embodied by Akio Morita, the purveyor of the Walkman as well as the blonde-wood encased Sony Trinitron (both much coveted in India's still austere early 1990s). No political and intellectual movements animated the East or Asia in my mind as they did India and the West.

It is easy to sneer, in our intricately interdependent world today, at the quasi-orientalist concepts of the 'East' and 'Asia.' Both came into the world conjoined with their domineering twin, the idea of Europe. Denoting the West's barbaric or inferior 'other,' they were originally meant to quicken Western self-consciousness. In the late nineteenth century, however, a range of Chinese, Japanese, and Indian thinkers put 'East' and 'Asia' at *their* service, infusing these categories with particular values and traits such as respect for nature, communitarianism, simple contentment, and spiritual transcendence. This supposedly Asian tradition of anti-materialism was then counterposed to modern Western ideologies of individualism, conquest and economic growth. The idea of Asia became an expression of cultural defensiveness against conceited Westerners who claimed a monopoly on civilization and regarded people without its manifest signs—the nation-state, industrial capitalism and mechanistic science—as inferior.

This proposed cultural unity of Asia acquired a geopolitical edge during early postcolonial struggles for national wealth and power—an endeavour in which Indian, Chinese and Indonesian leaders self-consciously invoked solidarity with each other. Thus, the experience of domination and racial humiliation and the claims to freedom and dignity that once bound Rabindranath Tagore to Liang Qichao and Okakura Tenshin, came to link Jawaharlal Nehru to Mao Zedong and Sukarno. Contemplating the great turmoil and trauma of their societies, artists such as Satyajit Ray and Kurosawa Akira came to share a troubled humanism.

Such imagined communities have now fragmented, both at home and abroad, replaced by pragmatic economic associations such as ASEAN and cross-border networks of manufacture, finance, and trade. Authoritarian-minded leaders still invoke 'Asian Values,' positing Asia's Confucius-sanctioned communal harmony against the West's evidently amoral and fissiparous individualism. They are little more than a rhetorical cover for regimes that enjoy harmonious relationships with local plutocrats while denying political rights to the majority.

The idea of Asia has acquired a different coherence today. What connects geographically disparate experiences—of rural migrants in Jakarta, factory workers in Manesar, tribals in Chhattisgarh, nomads in Tibet as well as the gated-communitarian patrons of Hermès and Jimmy Choo in Hangzhou and Gurgaon—is the late arrival of capitalism.

The great shifts that convulsed nineteenth-century Europe can now be witnessed across Asia: the commodification of life and land, their valuation by supply and demand, the disintegration of communities into aggregates of self-seeking individuals, the scramble for personal wealth and status, the desperation and anxiety of the also-rans, and the resentful resistance and hectic improvisations of those left, or pushed, behind.

What gives Asia its provisional unity today, cutting across boundaries of ethnicity, religion, geography, class, and nationality, is the experience of an often bitterly paradoxical modernity: the promise of self-transformation and growth that is frequently realized through the destruction of familiar landmarks, an atmosphere of agitation and contradiction in which the betrayal and disintegration of old bonds goes necessarily together with renewal.

It took me many years after that awakening to Tibbat's proximity to see familiar fault lines, threats and possibilities in this new Asia—the setting of immense collective and individual strivings, violence, suffering, frustration, despair and optimism. My intellectual blindness was due largely to my intense desire to be a writer in English. To be born in an Anglophone culture was to not only be reflexively West-centric, and to reserve one's profoundest attention for Western literatures and philosophies. It was also to assume that the institutions (parliamentary democracy, nation-state), philosophical principles (secularism, liberalism), economic ideologies (socialism, followed by free-market capitalism) and aesthetic forms (the novel) introduced or adopted during the long decades of British rule belonged to the natural, indeed superior, order of things.

They would, one simply assumed, banish irrational religion, improve governance, expand private freedoms, enlarge our moral imagination, and bring prosperity and contentment to hundreds of millions of our less-privileged compatriots. The national well-being once promised by socialism came to be linked in recent decades with another set of ideas imported from Anglo-America: privatization, deregulation, and minimal governments.

Few people today will argue that events have vindicated these assumptions. The Indian nation state, which began its existence by extending adult franchise to an overwhelmingly poor and diverse population, is one of the world's most audacious experiments in democracy and political pluralism. It can claim some successes, particularly the politicization of long-underprivileged peoples. But this progress is far from being continuous and irreversible; it is accompanied by great losses, and, punctuated by points of stagnation; it generates powerful countervailing forces. It is easier to perceive the state of general crisis: insurgencies by ethnic and religious minorities in border states, which are now accompanied by more militant rebellions by the dispossessed in central Indian states; a slow-motion agrarian calamity signified by the suicides of hundreds of thousands of farmers; a rapidly enlarging urban population exposed to a dehumanized existence; and, finally, a fragmenting polity, presided over by men who, unrepentantly guilty of a staggering venality, seem further than ever from liberalism and secularism.

An increasingly Americanized Indian elite continues to look to its Western counterparts for self-affirmation and support. But the old masters of the universe, struggling with multiple economic crises, rising inequality, and political discontent, have lost sight of their model of universal progress, and lack the confidence to export their cherished values to others. Like everyone else, European and American countries live—or survive—from day to day, sinisterly omniscient with their militaries and surveillance technologies, but no longer a vital source of redemptive moral and political ideas. Even the analytical guidance offered by Europe's long intellectual and philosophical tradition seems less and less reliable in an age of dazzlingly heterogeneous political and cultural forms.

In this context, India's obsession with the West, which radical Chinese and Japanese thinkers in the early twentieth century regarded with appalled fascination and foreboding, seems much more debilitating than before. India doesn't struggle alone with its intensifying conflicts between the demands of politicized masses and the imperatives of transnational capitalism. But we don't know enough, outside of academia, about political and social experiments in other Asian societies: what they consist of, how things seem to be tending, and how they may turn out (and *bien pensant* opinion-mongering about 'containing' or 'matching' China is no substitute). We know even less about how the particular challenges and dilemmas of China and its neighbouring countries have been formulated in modes of governance, technologies, religions, and art.

But then it is not always easy to look beyond the horizon defined by one's upbringing and preoccupations. In late

1995, I travelled to Indonesia on my first trip abroad. I had just published a book about the arrival of neo-capitalist modernity in small-town India. Some of the political and cultural energies noisily unleashed by it, which radically redefined India, were also present in Indonesia, which had embraced the project of private wealth creation much earlier. But it was the ninth-century temples of Prambanan and the stupas of Borobudur that induced the shock of recognition. And Bali, which Nehru had memorably and with uncharacteristically precise lyricism called the 'morning of the world,' made me feel less clueless about the Sanskrit cosmopolis that Mr Sharma had spoken of.

Indeed, Bali, conquered late by the Dutch, and only patchily modernized, seemed to belong enchantingly to the old Hindu world with its household shrines, gamelan music, moss-adorned statues, shadow plays, and rice fields. I had no idea that much of the island's much-revered 'ancient' culture was of recent origin. Unexpectedly, in the northern Balinese city of Singaraja there was an Arab quarter, evidence of the spiritual island's long-standing maritime—and solidly materialist—links with the larger world. But I lingered in a touristic stupor. Java, with its smooth toll roads and skyscrapers, induced a primitive sense of wonder, but no curiosity.

Indonesia was then run by Suharto, a business-friendly despot with stalwart American and European allies; his crony capitalism had generated a small but loyal middle class and a compliant media. Did this axis prefigure the appeal of authoritarian capitalism in our own time? Did it look ahead, through the eras of Deng Xiaoping's China and Thailand's Thaksin Shinawatra, to the age of Narendra Modi? My eyes—unschooled in East Asian histories and the stodgy but revealing facts of political economy—could not see much. Much experience and many re-orientations of perspective were needed before I could return to Indonesia in 2011 with a writing commission.

During this long interregnum, my personal discovery of Asia proceeded through a series of accidents. Many of the intellectual journeys I took led to China. While researching a book on the Buddha, I learned about the transmission of his teachings to East Asia via Kashmir and Tibet, where they mingled with pre-existing belief systems and ethical philosophies such as Confucianism and Daoism. In this indirect way I began slowly to understand how China had been the Greece of Asia, imparting its Confucian cultures to its Korean, Japanese and Vietnamese neighbours. Its empires were at the centre of a trade and diplomatic web extending from Nepal to Java, and the Amur region to Burma. China's economy was central to the region; overseas Chinese merchants and traders were later to become major players in the economies of Southeast Asia.

This history clarified how China, emerging in our own time from decades of economic autarky, had quickly become Asia's pre-eminent country, eclipsing Taiwan, reviving Hong Kong and enriching Mongolia, and forcing an anxious Japan into an atavistic nationalism. Travelling in Malaysia and Indonesia, it became easier to see how their ethnic Chinese, part of the population of overseas Chinese, had become, despite institutionalized discrimination and neglect, the greatest economic power in Southeast Asia. As I read further, it became clear that to understand contemporary Asia as a whole, one had to understand China—now more than ever.

And it was where my compass began to point.

Beginning in 2004, I began a regime of regular travel to China. Personal experience, of course, gives no special access to reality, even though it lends authority and glamour to two overrated figures of Western bourgeois culture: the foreign correspondent and the travel writer. One still has to learn to see, and find the right intermediaries. It was Chinese writers and thinkers who exposed me to the great changes afoot in that country: how progress there, too, proceeded with leaps and bounds, creating new kinds of turbulence, and, often, more victims than beneficiaries.

Much of my early knowledge of China was acquired from the work of Western Cold Warriors and liberal internationalists, who reflexively counterposed its authoritarianism with 'democratic' India. And so it took me a while to see that the ideological dualisms that helped keep American think tanks solvent—free versus unfree worlds, communist totalitarians versus Buddhistic Tibetans—were nearly useless in understanding, say, the rapidly changing situation in Tibet.

There is more religious freedom in Tibet than any time since the Cultural Revolution. It has also recorded higher GDP growth rates than any province in China. Still, economic development has not made for political passivity (as it has elsewhere in China). This is partly because the new economy, heavily favouring urban areas over rural ones, threatens to terminate immemorial peasant and nomadic lifestyles. Following the incursions of modern capitalism everywhere, the 'rationalization' of everyday life has also expedited 'the development of underdevelopment'—the creation of modern poverty and inequality. Furthermore, like predominantly rural ethnic minorities elsewhere, Tibetans are turning out to lack the temperament or training needed for a fervent belief in the utopia of modernity—a consumer lifestyle in urban centres—promised by post-Mao China. Dragged into a comprehensive reorganization of their public and private lives, Tibetans have been forced into sturdier affirmations of their cultural and religious identity—a commonplace phenomenon in Asian countries exposed to Western-style modernizers in the nineteenth century.

The mobile capital, multinationals, and digital communications that create transnational networks of elites also help reconfigure 'medieval' and other apparently anachronistic identities. Indeed, the deepening and mutually reinforcing links between cosmopolitan globalism and the quasi-parochial mutinies by ethnic and religious minorities are deeply characteristic of our age.

Such were the ambiguities and contradictions of modernity, which dissolved expedient ideological oppositions between democracy and authoritarianism. The Tibetans, I began to see, share their plight with farmers and tribal peoples in India, who, though inhabiting the world's largest democracy, confront a murderous axis of politicians, businessmen, and militias.

The following pages describe a packed self-education, particularly in China, conducted through physical journeys but also excursions into politics, history, and literature. I had no institutional compasses, and my early guides, randomly chosen, were numerous, manifold, and mostly erratic. China and its neighbours have hosted many dreamers, from the counter-culturalist Walter Spies in Bali to the easy riders on Rising Asia bandwagons today: they primarily describe their own fantasies of personal power and status, their desire to escape from or enlist in the apparently universalizing and homogenizing history of the West.

Even intellectually resourceful travel writers have been unable to break out of their casually inherited prejudices. Whether writing about yoga, Islam, or the Japanese, both V.S. Naipaul and Arthur Koestler proclaimed, with varying literary power, that the West is best. Self-consciously rejecting all such naïve Westernism, Claude Levi-Strauss still recoiled fastidiously, in *Tristes Tropiques*, from Asia's ostensibly Malthusian fate: a 'vision of our own future which it is already experiencing'; and then succumbed to a simple-minded Japanphilia in his later years. Shrewdly perceptive on Japan, Roland Barthes produced only banalities on China. Rabindranath Tagore, Amitav Ghosh, and Rahul Sankrityayan, who redeem a very weak Indian tradition of writing about East and Southeast Asia, have been much more stimulating. After decades of restriction, and brisk commerce in stale Cold-War stereotypes, foreign journalism in China is enjoying a new golden age. Donald Richie, Ian Buruma, and Pico Iyer have shrewdly decoded Japan's 'otherness.' East and Southeast Asia is also the realm where such giants of modern humanities scholarship as Jonathan Spence, Benedict Anderson, Clifford Geertz, and James C. Scott have roamed. Still, broad overviews or granular histories by outsiders are good only for initial positioning.

It takes a different effort—chance conversations and random reading as well as patterned travel—to sense the inner life of a society. Few things turn out to be more important than eavesdropping on its debates—and quarrels—with itself about politics and culture—those not meant for foreign consumption. The writings of Indonesian thinkers and writers such as Soedjatmoko and Goenawan Mohamad, the Chinese Wang Hui, or the Japanese Takeuichi Yoshimi and Karatani Kojin opened up perspectives unavailable in accounts by outsiders. And in the literature and films of East Asia, a more exhilarating revelation awaited me.

For much of my adult life, I had been trained to see self and the world through a predominantly Western and South Asian canon. To read the novels of Ōe Kenzaburō or watch the films of Hou Hsiao-hsien was to discover fresh correspondences and resemblances. Modernizing early, with much confusion of purpose, Japan's experience of disorientation in the new world set the cultural template for many Asian writers, artists and thinkers. I found that the confusions and dilemmas of R.K. Narayan's deracinated young men and women were prefigured more precisely in Natsume Soseki's *Sanshiro* and *Kokoro* than in anything by Italo Svevo and Thomas Mann; that Naruse Mikio's film *When a Woman Ascends the Stairs* spoke as directly to the dilemmas of lower-middle-class Indian women I knew as Satyajit Ray's *Mahanagar*; and that Calcutta had more in common with semi-colonial Shanghai and Tokyo in the 1920s and 1930s than with Dublin.

This discovery of new relationships of symmetry helped de-familiarize the country I have lived in and primarily written about for most of my life. Exposure to foreign countries tends to estrange us from the everyday; it relativizes what we have held to be unique—political processes, cultural norms—about ourselves. But I was still surprised by how dramatically my travels broadened the frame of reference to which my thinking about India had been long confined. The following pages about some decisive stages in the story of contemporary East Asia are, above all, an attempt at bifocalism: an inquiry about China and its neighbours whose starting and end point is, inevitably, India.

It is why they contain more uncommon juxtapositions and contrasts than colourful description and inventories of exotic facts. *A Great Clamour* also tries to maintain a careful distance from the instrumentalist world views of foreign affairs pundits, security experts and financial analysts. It describes, after all, a world where grand, unilinear visions—according to which better technology, education, entrepreneurship, and productivity are taking us all to convergence with Western-style affluence and stability—look increasingly threadbare. Elections have not produced functional democracy or even political stability, free markets have not led to freedom, or higher literacy and better communications to greater tolerance and human rights. Rather, we have witnessed political chaos, corporate greed, climactic depredation, xenophobic nationalism, and ethnocide on a greater scale. The allegedly universal laws of progress, lately amplified by smooth-tongued Davos Men, have proved yet again to be bogus.

But life goes on, as it always has, beyond the miscarried rationalities of science, market, and the state, and in unexpected ways. This is attested diversely by the Japanese with their 'post-growth' economy, the Tibetans recoiling from 'development' to fresh faith in their reincarnated spiritual leader, or the growing Indonesian preference for 'bottom-up' governance. Any attempt to understand the new Asia must acknowledge such deep structures of difference that exist behind the superficial unity proclaimed by the vendors of nationalism or globalization. Above the collision of inhuman ideologies with ordinary human lives looms the phantom of alternative histories, what has not but could have existed, and modes of living and thinking that may yet have a future. Such at least were the temptations of the East—its fabulously multifarious ways of being human, and the determination of many people to preserve them—as I set out to find my own private Tibbat.

PART 1

DRUMROLL TO
MODERNITY

A SENTIMENTAL EDUCATION
IN SHANGHAI

1.

In April 1924, Rabindranath Tagore arrived in Shanghai for a lecture tour of China. Soon after receiving the Nobel Prize for Literature in 1913, Tagore had become an international literary celebrity, lecturing to packed audiences from Japan to Argentina. His message—that modern civilization, built upon the cult of money and power, was inherently destructive, and needed to be tempered by the spiritual wisdom of the East—had a receptive audience among many people in the West who had been forced by World War I to question their faith in science and progress. But when, travelling in the East, he exhorted Asians not to abandon their traditional culture, he was often heckled and booed.

In Japan in 1916, Tagore's warning against the 'special modern enthusiasm for Western progress and force' was mostly contemptuously dismissed. However, it was in China that Tagore's praise for Asia's spiritual traditions faced the fiercest opposition. The poet Qu Qiubai, who had been a student of Buddhism before embracing communism, summed up the general tone of Tagore's reception in China when he wrote, 'Thank you, Mr. Tagore, but we have already had too many Confuciuses and Menciuses in China.' Repeatedly assaulted with hostile questions, Tagore was forced to cut his tour short.

In the years after World War I, China was one of the largest and one of the weakest countries in the world. In previous decades, Western powers, and a rising Japan, had repeatedly forced unequal treaties and harsh indemnities upon the country. However, like Qu Qiubai, many leading intellectuals such as Chen Duxiu, editor of the radical journal *New Youth* and a founder of the Communist Party of China, called for a total rejection of Chinese tradition. They wished China to become a strong and assertive nation using Western methods, and they admired such visitors as Bertrand Russell and John Dewey, whose belief in science and democracy seemed to lead the way to China's redemption.

This intellectual consensus had formed early in China's modern history. Growing up against a background of national humiliation and shame, the first generation of reform-minded intellectuals, such as Kang Youwei (1858–1927) and Liang Qichao (1873–1929), agreed that China needed to modernize, with or without its Manchu imperial rulers. After the disastrous Boxer Rebellion between 1898 and 1900, when Western powers and Japan crushed a popular uprising against foreign interference in Chinese affairs, even the tottering Manchus attempted Western-style reform. They abolished the traditional examinations for the civil service, established modern schools, and sent Chinese students abroad. Thousands of young Chinese were first introduced to modern sciences, engineering, medicine, law, economics, education, and military skills, and voluntary organizations dedicated to modernizing China sprang up in both China and the Chinese diaspora.

The collapse of Manchu rule in 1911, and the inauguration of the Chinese Republic, may have appeared to be speeding up China's political and economic transformation. But warlords supplanted the Manchu rulers, and plunged much of the country into violence and chaos. Japan continued to press its mostly unreasonable claims upon Chinese territory, and on 4 May 1919, students in Beijing erupted in violent protest after the Allied Powers at the Paris Peace Conference awarded to Japan the territorial rights previously held by Germany.

The protests were the beginning of the 'May Fourth Movement,' the explosion of intellectual energy in China that crystallized a conviction which many Chinese shared and which continues to shape politics and culture in the country even today: that China has to throw off the shackles of tradition and urgently modernize itself in order to be a strong, self-confident nation. For the May Fourth generation the egalitarian ideals of the French and Russian Revolutions, and the scientific spirit underlying Western industrial power, were self-evidently superior to an ossified Chinese culture that exalted tradition over innovation and kept China backward and weak. In 1924, few of them were ready to listen to an apparently otherworldly poet from India holding forth on the problems of modern Western civilization and the virtues of old Asia.

2.

In the 1920s and 1930s, most of the modern Chinese intellectuals and writers were based in Shanghai, the most westernized of Chinese cities, whose bookshops offered magazines such as *Harper's*, *The Dial*, and *Vanity Fair* along with translations of Joyce and Woolf and other modernist writers. Though dominated by foreign businessmen since the mid-nineteenth century, Shanghai's Western-style theatres, dance halls, cafes, racecourses, imported cars, and bookshops appeared to open up many possibilities of self-invention to young Chinese. Returning to China in 1937 after a few years in Europe, the young hero of Qian Zhongshu's classic novel *Fortress Besieged* (1947) caustically observes, 'Shanghai is certainly avant-garde culturally. The phenomenon of high school girls painting and plastering their faces to attract men is rare even abroad.'

Nevertheless, it couldn't have been easy to be a westernized intellectual in a city like Shanghai where Chinese in the so-called International Settlements were forced to use separate elevators, not admitted to foreign clubs except as guests, and prevented from using the most modern hospitals. The large Japanese presence in the city may have been even more tormenting. Many Chinese intellectuals saw Japan as an example of how catching up with the West in industrial growth and military skills could make an Asian nation strong if not unassailable. Most of the Western literature available in Chinese consisted of retranslations from Japanese, and many leading writers and activists such as Lu Xun and Sun Yat-sen had spent much time in Japan. At the same time, Chinese writers were daily confronted with growing evidence of Japan's malevolent intentions towards China.

The Chinese hoping for personal liberation through the West or Japan couldn't avoid reckoning with the political and economic degradation of their country. But as the critic Shu-mei Shih describes it, fiction writers in the 1920s and 1930s tended to avoid dealing with the more humiliating aspects of a foreign presence in China, of which Shanghai, with its racist and exploitative businessmen, opium traffickers, and evangelists, offered the most egregious example. Also, having developed an ambition to be seen as the equals of Westerners, many Chinese intellectuals felt contempt for their resolutely backward and poverty-stricken counterparts. As C.T. Hsia, the first major critic in English of modern Chinese literature, put it:

> Perhaps in their younger days they had been proud of China, but this pride had turned into a frankly masochistic admission of what they saw as inferiority in every department of endeavour. Disgusted with pigtails, bound feet, and opium—palpable symbols of China's backwardness—they were no less ashamed of her art, literature, philosophy, and folkways.

Not surprisingly, faced with such inner conflicts, Lu Xun, a ferocious critic of traditional Chinese culture, became one of the many Chinese writers to embrace Marxism. Others, such as Shao Xunmei, a poet who edited the poems and drawings of Aubrey Beardsley and who became, briefly, the lover of the *New Yorker* writer Emily Hahn, seem to have resolved their ambivalences through a cosmopolitan dandyism.

Many decades later, the question of how China would become modern is far from being settled—despite, or perhaps because of, the long years of China's isolation from the West enforced by Mao Zedong. In depicting Chinese tradition as moribund and comparing China unflatteringly to the modern West, the popular television documentary series *River Elegy* (1988) expressed the sentiments of many educated Chinese. For much of the 1980s and 1990s, Chinese intellectuals, recovering from the excesses of the Cultural Revolution, were united in their faith that swift political and economic westernization could free China from its feudal past—a consensus that was disrupted but not broken by the killings of unarmed protesters near Tiananmen Square in 1989.

In recent years, however, young conservative nationalists have denounced what they see as the indiscriminate Chinese adoption of the decadent Western values of consumerism. Aware of its ideological vacuum, the communist regime tried in the 1990s to resurrect Confucius as the source of values. More recently, writers and academics described as the 'New Left' have highlighted the steep costs—growing social inequality and unrest, environmental damage—of China's long-delayed integration into the modern global economy.

China's romance with the modern world seemed to have gone very sour when Qian Zhongshu wrote in the early 1940s about the ineffectual westernized intellectual in *Fortress Besieged*, a novel widely regarded as one of the masterworks of twentieth-century Chinese literature. The brutal Japanese invasion of China in 1937—the bombing of Shanghai and the Rape of Nanking—and the apparent Western indifference to Chinese suffering had finally muddied the image of China's cultural and political models. Disillusionment with Republican China's fractious rulers—the Nationalist Chiang Kai-shek, the warlords, and the communists—had also grown. The 'New Life Movement,' Chiang Kai-shek's campaign in 1934 to morally regenerate China through mass adherence to four traditional virtues—politeness, integrity, self-respect, and righteousness—seemed no more than empty rhetoric, given the obvious brutality and corruption of the Nationalist regime.

The May Fourth impulse to learn from the West had decayed into empty ritual. As Qian's hero, the twenty-seven-year-old Fang Hung-chien, asserts:

> Studying abroad today is like passing examinations under the old Manchu system. . . . It's not for the broadening of knowledge that one goes abroad but to get rid of that inferiority complex.

Appropriately, Fang exerts himself as little as possible as a student in Europe, and buys a bogus doctorate from a non-existent American university called Carleton in order to please his family. When the novel opens, he is returning to China after some idle years subsidized by his relatives; and for much of the year during which we follow him across China he seems best equipped to observe insincerity and pretentiousness within himself as well as in other westernized Chinese.

Unable to decide what he wants, he manages to alienate the two modern women he courts. Drifting through Shanghai, he meets a Cambridge-educated poet whose heavily annotated modernist poem 'Adulterous

Smorgasbord' contains allusions to works by T.S. Eliot, Leopardi, and Franz Werfel, among others. Fang also meets a self-proclaimed philosopher who writes flattering letters to famous Western thinkers and who claims personal friendship with 'Bertie,' Bertrand Russell:

> 'Do you know Russell well?'
>   'You could call us friends. He respected me enough to ask my help in answering several questions.' Heaven knows Ch'u Shen-ming was not telling a lie. Russell had indeed asked him when he would come to England, what his plans were, how many sugar cubes he took in his tea, and other similar questions that he alone could answer.

A rich comprador businessman who sees Fang as a prospective match for his daughter sprinkles his speech with what he thinks are American expressions while showing off his porcelain collection:

> Worth quite a lot of money, *plenty of dough*. . . . Sometimes I invite foreign *friends* over for dinner and use this big K'ang-hsi 'underglaze-blue-and-colored-ware' plate for a *salad dish*. They all think the ancient colors and odor make the food taste a little *old time*.

The deeper pathos of nouveau-riche aspiration lies in the businessman's daughter's bookcase, where, among copies of the *Reader's Digest* and the screenplay of *Gone with the Wind*, Fang discovers a book titled *How to Gain a Husband and Keep Him*. Another young woman interested in Fang turns out to have plagiarized a poem from a German folk song.

If Shanghai's modern veneer seems counterfeit to Fang, he is an even greater misfit in his native town. Fawned upon by his family, he struggles to ward off their attempt to arrange his marriage:

> All his life he had detested those modern girls from small towns with outdated fashions and a provincial cosmopolitanism. They were just like the first Western suit made by a Chinese tailor with everything copied from a foreigner's old clothes used as a model.

Revered locally for his European education, Fang is invited to deliver a lecture entitled 'A Reevaluation of the Influences of Western Civilization on Chinese History.' His old-fashioned father presses upon him some Chinese books which claim, among other things, that 'the Chinese were square and honest by nature, so they said the sky was square' and 'foreigners were roundabout and cunning and therefore maintained that the earth was round.' Fang seems to express more than a personal sense of irrelevance and failure when he tells his bewildered small-town audience that 'there are only two items from the West which have been lasting in Chinese society as a whole. One is opium, and the other is syphilis.'

The Japanese invasion of Shanghai disrupts Fang's lassitude and forces him to accept a job offer from a university set up in the hinterland. On rickety buses and boats Fang and his companions make what turns out to be an epic journey through provinces full of the chaos of war and refugees. Their struggles with petty officials, prostitutes, and innkeepers inspire some of the best comic set pieces in the novel. Here they are in a typical flophouse, considering whether to eat what looks like cured meat:

> From the wall the waiter took a pitch black, greasy object and offered it for their inspection, repeatedly saying, 'How delicious!' his own mouth watering as he spoke, fearful only that the fat meat would waste away under the greedy stares of the guests. Wriggling and squirming from its greasy slumber, a maggot on the meat awoke. Li saw it and was repulsed by the sight; from a distance his mouth pointed toward it and he exclaimed, 'We can't have it.'
>
> The waiter quickly stuck his finger over the tender, soft, white object and pressing down lightly, drew a shiny, black, oily streak like a freshly poured asphalt road across the filthy surface of the meat. At the same time he said, 'It's nothing!'
>
> Infuriated, Ku asked the waiter, 'You think we're blind?'
>
> 'Outrageous,' they cried.
>
> . . . The commotion brought in the innkeeper. Meanwhile two other maggots in the meat also heard the noise and poked their heads out for a look. . . . The waiter, no longer able 'to do away with the corpse and destroy the evidence,' merely retorted, 'If you won't eat it, then other people will. I'll eat it to show you—'
>
> The innkeeper took the pipe from his mouth and remonstrated, 'Those aren't bugs. They don't hurt anything. Those are "meat sprouts"—"meat sprouts."'

Modern satire usually requires as its backdrop a relatively stable society with clear rules of behaviour. The social comedies of Evelyn Waugh, whom Qian admired, gain their power from the ordered conventions of Edwardian England. But violent disorder defined the China Qian knew, and made his task as a novelist hard.

Born in 1910, a year before the collapse of the Manchu dynasty, Qian was educated at Beijing's prestigious Tsinghua University and then at Oxford. Besides being a gifted scholar of classical Chinese literature, Qian was extremely well read in Greek, Latin, English, German, French, Spanish, and Italian literatures; his erudition may have kept despair at bay during the many difficult times in his life.

Returning to China from Europe in the middle of the war in 1937, he was forced, like his protagonist Fang and indeed like millions of people, to flee coastal territories invaded or occupied by Japan for the deep Chinese hinterland. He taught at an improvised university in Kunming, the capital of the south-western Yunnan province, before returning in 1941 to Shanghai, then run by a pro-Japanese collaborationist regime, where he taught and wrote—much of *Fortress Besieged* among other things—until the end of the war.

Qian holds his characters to a personal aesthetic standard, when all other norms have collapsed. In his characteristically elegant and perceptive foreword to the new edition of *Fortress Besieged*, Jonathan Spence mentions *Sentimental Education* as a likely influence. Certainly, Qian has, underneath his exuberant comedy, something of Flaubert's melancholy sense of life as a series of missed opportunities for happiness.

He also shares Flaubert's keen eye for bourgeois deception and self-deception, and his scorn of platitudes about human progress. As Fang observes:

The uneducated are fooled by others because they're

illiterate. The educated are taken in by printed matter like
your newspaper propaganda and lecture notes on training
cadres because they are literate.

In a semi-literate society that measures intellectual
accomplishments by academic degrees, impostors and
frauds proliferate. Fang discovers that the chairman of his
university department also has a doctorate from the non-
existent Carleton University. This academic also claims in his
curriculum vitae to have contributed articles to the *Saturday
Review of Literature* though, in reality, he has published only
ads in the magazine's personals section. ('Well-educated
Chinese youth wishes to assist Sinologists. Low rates.')

No one, however, has a more assured command of
pompous clichés than the university president, who is
'fluent' in the disciplines of all three colleges and all ten
departments of the school. 'Fluent,' that is, in the sense of
flowing smoothly, as in the 'free flow of trains' or a 'smooth
intestinal flow.'

... [At] the Literary Study Group ... he encouraged the
audience to become India's Tagore, England's Shakespeare,
France's—uh—France's Rousseau (also pronounced '*loso*'),
Germany's Goethe, and America's—American writers
were too numerous. The day after at the Physics Club's
meeting to welcome new members, having no atomic
bomb to talk about yet, he could only call out a few times
to the theory of relativity, making Einstein, all the way on
the other side of the ocean, run a fever in his right ear and
even sneeze. Besides this, he could even say 'Shit' once or
twice during a chat with the military instructor.

Fang resolves to be a 'star professor' after discovering that 'just as getting a degree is a matter of duping one's professors with a thesis, so teaching is a matter of duping the students with the lecture material.' He joins the various academic intrigues at his department, but fails to secure his job. Before leaving for Shanghai, he drifts into an engagement with one of the neurotic modern women he keeps meeting throughout the novel. He doesn't love her, but apparently marriage didn't require a very great love.

> Not detesting each other was already foundation enough
> for marriage. . . . In the dull state he was in now, his
> emotions did not constitute a burden on his mind, which
> was just as well.

This relationship, begun with so little promise, is doomed after it is exposed to the malice of Fang's and his wife's relatives in Shanghai. Fang begins to see marriage as a besieged fortress: those who are outside want to rush in, and those inside want to get out.

Qian's narrative has a Stendhalian briskness, enabling it to move quickly from the humorous to the intellectual and the emotional. We see clearly the stages through which a weak but good man such as Fang loses his convictions and drifts into insincerity and falsehood. Remarkably for a comic, picaresque novel, *Fortress Besieged* contains much psychological drama, particularly in the last pages which contain what Jonathan Spence seems right to call 'one of the finest descriptions of the disintegration of a marriage ever penned in any language.'

Here is Fang, leaving the house after a row with his wife:

His thoughts churned chaotically in his brain like snowflakes whirling about in the north wind. He let his legs carry him where they would. The all-night street lights passed his shadow along from one lamp to the next. Another self inside him seemed to be saying, 'It's all over! All over!' His scattered, random thoughts immediately seemed to come together at one point, and he was beset with anguish. His left cheek suddenly tingled. He found it damp to the touch, and thinking it was blood, was so shocked his heart stood still and his legs went limp. He moved under a lamp post to look, and when he found no traces of blood on his fingers, realized it was only tears.

Nevertheless, readers may be dissatisfied by a long novel whose main character fails to amount to anything. But then, as the Shanghai writer Eileen Chang once wrote, responding to criticism from Fu Lei, an important literary critic of the 1940s, that her fiction failed to realize the nationalistic and politically engaged ideals of the earlier literature of the May Fourth Movement:

> My fiction . . . is populated with equivocal characters. They are not heroes, but they are of the majority who actually bear the weight of the times. As equivocal as they may be, they are also in earnest about their lives. They lack tragedy; all they have is desolation. . . . Although they are merely weak and ordinary people and cannot aspire to heroic feats of strength, it is precisely those ordinary people who can serve more accurately than heroes as a measure of the times.

The shrinking choices, the sense of personal defeat, and the compulsion to compromise that Qian saw in his character's life were partly also his own fate—and those of millions of Chinese. Qian chose to stay on in communist China, and, though he quoted Mao in an anthology of classical Chinese poetry he published in 1958, his critics claimed that he wasn't Marxist enough. During the Cultural Revolution, he and his wife were sent to do labour on a farm. 'Rehabilitated' and allowed to travel abroad by the Deng regime, Qian published scholarly works but did not write another novel. He died in 1998.

Fortress Besieged was reprinted in China in 1980, and became a popular success, leading to a television serialization in 1990. It is not hard to understand the reasons for its continuing success. Pre-communist China, especially the semi-colonial world of Shanghai, has been lavishly commemorated in much contemporary literature and film, including the Chinese TV version of *Fortress Besieged*, which evokes a fantasy of a lost arcadia.

But many Chinese readers of the novel can also identify its characters and themes in China today. As the country, still largely poor, rushes headlong, under a nominally communist regime, to embrace Western-style capitalism and consumerism, it not only imposes many psychological conflicts and tensions on its population; it also creates an unusually large number of Babbitts, plagiarists, and hucksters.

This frenzy among educated Chinese to acquire money and fame may seem pathetic to an outsider. But Qian refused to condemn his characters, and in fact treated them with sympathy. Fang himself leaves the reader with an impression

of moral striving and seriousness. There is something noble
and moving about his eventual failure.

He may seem an early instance of a type familiar to us
from other works of twentieth-century literature. Thomas
Mann, Italo Svevo, and Saul Bellow, among others, described
how the modern Western intellectual, the product of a rich,
bourgeois society, struggled to apply the lessons of his vast
learning to his private life. But Fang's own moral confusion
seems to be caused not so much by his personal inadequacies,
or by an excess of hedonism and materialism, as by the
amorphous nature of his society. In this, he resembles the
aimless, small-town characters of R.K. Narayan's novels or
the bored civil servant of Upamanyu Chatterjee's *English,
August: An Indian Story* (1988) more than he resembles the
tormented heroes of Italo Svevo or Philip Roth.

Far from being private, his dilemmas belong to a wider
world in which large political, economic, and moral questions
have yet to be settled. China's chaotic recent history has
ensured that these questions continue to haunt the country
today. An insightful and entertaining work of fiction in its
own right, *Fortress Besieged* gains resonance from its large and
momentous backdrop of China in transition—a transition
that still seems unfinished and grows more uncertain as
educated Chinese, unmoored finally from tradition, grapple
with the ambiguous promise of the modern world.

THE HUNGRY YEARS

Between 1876 and 1879, in North China, as many as thirteen million people died in what came to be called the Incredible Famine. It was one of many calamities around the world during that decade which were caused by extreme weather. However, according to the British-owned *North China Herald*, an influential mouthpiece of the Western business communities clustered in Shanghai, the famine was proof of the folly of big government—the Qing imperial administration, in this instance. A fatal Chinese indifference to science, to railroads, and, most important, to laissez-faire economics was to blame. The famine and the many deaths in China would not have occurred 'in vain,' the *Herald* editorialized, if they could persuade the Chinese government to cease its paternalistic interfering in the laws of 'private enterprise.'

Never mind that more than twelve million people had died during the Madras Famine of 1877, even though India had been equipped by its British rulers with railroads and a free market in grains, or that Ireland, during the Great Potato Famine, thirty years earlier, had suffered from

Britain's heartlessly enforced ideology of laissez-faire. The *Herald* deplored the 'antiquated learning' of the Chinese, and described the heroic figure who could rescue China from misery: 'The man wanted in China now, as in its early days, is a patriotic engineer,' someone 'single-minded and energetic' and possessing 'commanding energy and resolution.'

In due course, China got just such a big-thinking, single-minded 'patriotic engineer.' His name was Mao Zedong, and his uneducated infatuation with the signs and symbols of modern progress—gigantic projects and economic statistics—caused a famine that dwarfed even the Incredible Famine. The Great Famine of 1958–62 is thought to have taken more than thirty million lives, and perhaps as many as forty-five million. Two new books use fresh evidence to describe the stubborn delusions and cruelties of the man who believed that, among other things, hundreds of millions of Chinese making steel in their backyard furnaces could surpass the industrial production of Western countries. *Tombstone* (2012), by the Chinese journalist Yang Jisheng, is the first major Chinese account of the causes and consequences of that famine. *Mao: The Real Story* (2012), by Alexander V. Pantsov and Steven I. Levine draws on Russian archives to show, more clearly than before, that this apparently unparalleled tale of cruel folly was not without precedent in the twentieth century—the age of ideological excess.

The Soviet Union was the first among many 'underdeveloped' countries in which national leaders with pseudo-scientific visions of socioeconomic engineering exposed their societies to immense suffering. In the early 1920s, the Bolsheviks, emerging from a destructive civil war and an invasion by Western countries, urgently wanted to industrialize their country, as the first step to communism. In the absence of any foreign investment, industrialization depended on generating adequate capital from agricultural surpluses, and the Bolsheviks initially experimented, partly successfully, with free-market agriculture and private ownership. In 1929, however, Stalin decided to speed up the Soviet Union's tryst with industrial power, by forcing peasants into collective farms. Those who resisted—for instance, by slaughtering livestock or by refusing to plant or harvest grain—were ruthlessly crushed. The toll in human suffering was enormous—millions of peasants, many of them in Ukraine, were killed or starved to death. By the mid 1930s, the Stalinists had won. Collective farms became a permanent feature of Soviet life; and the Soviet Union became an industrialized country. Its seemingly limitless ability to produce the military hardware necessary to fight—and win—its ferocious war with Nazi Germany was a testament to its success.

Few people in China in the 1920s and 1930s observed Stalin's brutal but efficacious engineering more closely than Mao Zedong, then a restless young convert to communism. Like many Chinese picking their way through the ruins of the Qing Empire, Mao was convinced that China had to transform itself, as the Soviet Union had done, into a powerful nation state in order to survive the hostility of the capitalist-imperialist West. In this project, the Soviet Union was the indispensable nation, first as fraternal pioneer and then as ideological foil. Pantsov and Levine's examination of

Russian archives reveals that the Chinese Communist Party, from its inception, in 1921, was deeply dependent on Soviet money, expertise, and ideological guidance. It also shows, in absorbing detail, how Mao's catastrophic 'concept of a special Chinese path of development,' as Pantsov and Levine assert, 'could arise only in the post-Stalin environment.'

In 1949, Mao achieved victory in the drawn-out civil war against the nationalists, who were backed by the Americans and led by Chiang Kai-shek, and he began the 'Stalinization' of China soon afterwards. He used the Stalinist toolkit—coercion and propaganda—to build a strong state upheld by a single party, a loyal military, and intrusive micromanagement of the lives of the citizens. Henceforth, the Chinese were told where to live, work, and study, and how many children to have. The Soviets offered models for everything, from urban planning to labour camps and physical fitness drills. And Soviet experts were on hand to supervise, as Mao instituted land reforms, abolished private property, silenced intellectual critics, segregated rural and urban populations, and launched Stalinist-style purges against counter-revolutionaries and rich peasants.

As in the Soviet Union, Chinese leaders had to raise capital through increased agricultural yields before they could start investing in extensive industrialization. However, unlike Stalin, Mao faced relatively little resistance to his programme of collectivization. Furthermore, the first modernizing attempts of the People's Republic of China were strikingly successful. Industrial and agricultural production soared—the annual growth rate in the early 1950s was almost 18 per cent. The Party acquired a popular base in the countryside among peasant beneficiaries of land reforms. (Affection for Mao among the rural population was one reason for the strange lack of public disaffection when the famine came.) The social climate improved, thanks to mass campaigns against prostitution, arranged marriages, and opium use. Expanding literacy and health care gave China an early and enduring lead over other postcolonial countries, including India.

But China's 'patriotic engineer' was not content, telling his personal physician, 'When I say, "Learn from the Soviet Union," we don't have to learn how to shit and piss from the Soviet Union, too, do we?' Mao was intellectually insecure, having risen to power only after long and bitter struggles with better-educated, Soviet-backed Party leaders; he had always resented the unbalanced and yet unavoidable Chinese relationship with the Soviet Union. Stalin's death, in 1953, and Nikita Khrushchev's repudiation of Stalin, in 1956, helped Mao finally break free of his dependency. Socialism in China, as he saw it, was to be 'more, better, faster' than even Stalin could imagine. Using the country's great advantage—cheap and abundant labour—China would make the Great Leap Forward, doubling, even tripling, agricultural and industrial production in a few years.

As Pantsov and Levine point out, 'Mao had no concrete plans for the Great Leap Forward.' All he did was repeat the incantation 'We can catch up with England in fifteen years.' In fact, as Yang Jisheng's *Tombstone* shows, neither experts nor the Central Committee discussed 'Mao's grand plan.' The Chinese president and Mao cultist Liu Shaoqi endorsed it, and a boastful fantasy became, as Yang writes, 'the guiding ideology of the party and the country.'

A hundred absurd schemes, such as close planting of

seeds for better yields, now flowered, as loudspeakers
boomed out the song 'We Will Overtake England and
Catch Up to America.' Mao constantly looked for ways to
productively deploy the world's biggest national population:
farmers were taken out of fields and sent to work building
reservoirs and irrigation channels, digging wells, and
dredging river bottoms. Yang points out that, since these
projects 'were undertaken with an unscientific approach,
many were a waste of manpower and resources.' But
there was no dearth of sycophantic officials ready to run
with Mao's vaguest commands, among them Liu Shaoqi.
Visiting a commune in 1958, Liu swallowed the claims by
local officials that irrigating yam fields with dog-meat broth
increased agricultural output. 'You should start raising dogs,
then,' he told them. 'Dogs are very easy to breed.' Liu also
became an instant expert on close planting, suggesting that
peasants use tweezers for weeding the seedlings.

The disaster that unfolded closely followed the ghastly
precedent set by the Soviet Union. Under the experiment
known as 'people's communes,' the rural population was
deprived of its land, tools, grain, and even cooking utensils,
and was forced to eat at communal kitchens. Yang calls the
system 'the organizational foundation for the Great Famine.'
Mao's plan of herding everyone into collectives not only
destroyed the immemorial bonds of the family; it made
people who traditionally used their private land to grow
food, secure loans, and generate capital helplessly dependent
on an increasingly maladroit and callous state.

Ill-conceived projects such as backyard steel making

took peasants away from the fields, causing a steep decline in agricultural productivity. Led, and often coerced, by overzealous Party officials, the new rural communes reported fake harvests to meet Beijing's demand for record grain output, and the government began to procure grain based on these exaggerated figures. Soon, the government granaries were full—indeed, China was a net exporter of grain throughout the whole period of the famine—but most people in rural areas found themselves with little to eat. Peasants working on irrigation projects fared no better: they were 'treated as slaves,' Yang writes, 'and hunger exacerbated by arduous labor caused many to die.' Those who resisted or were too weak to work were beaten and tortured by Party cadres, often to death.

Yang Jisheng's father was one of the tens of millions who died of starvation. Yang's book is a delayed homage, an enduring 'tombstone in my heart,' from a son whose grief over his father's death did not diminish his loyalty to the Party; Yang even extolled the Great Leap Forward in a newspaper that he edited at school. Studying at Beijing's prestigious Tsinghua University as the Cultural Revolution began, Yang came to know about other casualties of the famine. His political education deepened during thirty-five years as a reporter for the official news agency Xinhua, when he reported covertly—a role often required of senior Chinese journalists—to leaders in Beijing on such sensitive subjects as official corruption and impunity. But, according to Yang, it was not until the killings of unarmed protesters near Tiananmen Square, in 1989, that he was cleansed 'of all the lies I had accepted over the previous decades.'

One of Yang's most compelling case studies is of

Xinyang, a city in Henan province, where a million people out of a population of more than eight million were victims of Maoist experimentation. Here, as in many parts of China, exaggerated reports of harvests and aggressive procurements of grain by the state led to mass starvation. By the spring of 1960, according to one of Yang's witnesses, corpses lay on the roads and in the fields, hardened by the winter cold and bent, often with holes in their buttocks and legs where flesh had been torn off. The survivors blamed dogs for the disfigurement. But the dogs had already been eaten. The truth was that many people that winter and the next survived by preying on the dead, sometimes even on their own family members.

The subject of the famine remains taboo in China; the official, absurdly generous, verdict on Mao's record is that he was '70 percent correct, and 30 percent wrong.' Yang's book, which inverts that anodyne ratio, is unlikely to be published in mainland China. (The Chinese-language edition was published in Hong Kong.) Yang had to investigate the Great Famine undercover, posing as a researcher of the history of China's grain production. He was helped by an assortment of people—journalists with useful contacts, demographers who had taken big risks to keep accurate records, and provincial archivists keen to please an old comrade. Though the English translation is abridged, it is often overwhelming in its detail and analysis. Still, *Tombstone* easily supersedes all previous chronicles of the famine, and is one of the best insider accounts of the Party's inner workings during this period, offering an unrivalled picture of socioeconomic engineering within a rigid ideological framework.

Apprised of the catastrophe in Xinyang, Mao blamed

'counter-revolutionaries' and 'ruthless class retaliation' by Chiang Kai-shek's nationalists (his old rivals, who were by then ensconced in Taiwan). Someone had to be punished, and though Mao balked at the death sentence—'I've never killed a county Party secretary,' he claimed—the officials responsible were imprisoned and persecuted. Yang denounces the outcome as 'manifestly unjust': local operatives were punished while the central government, which formulated and promoted the fatal policies, remained 'correct and glorious.' Mao, much more than China's leaders today, was the beneficiary of a widespread faith in the wisdom and the noble intentions of the central government. In *Tombstone*, Mao emerges as patriotic but megalomaniacal, crudely vindictive, and utterly inept. Yang is clear that Mao presided over a 'totalitarian' system, but he avoids simple-minded Western presentations of Mao as the Oriental Hitler.

Yang is more interested in examining the defects within the political organization that produced the famine. He writes, 'The great famine occurred within a system that produced incentives for local officials to exaggerate production while the state monopoly stifled incentives for increasing production.' Yang quotes the criticisms of many Party members, such as Bo Yibo (the father of Bo Xilai, the recently disgraced Party secretary of the city province of Chongqing). Mao wasn't entirely immune to self-doubt and periodically revealed himself to be a clear-sighted observer of the system's debilities. In an internal Party communiqué in 1959, he admitted, 'Much of the falsehood has been prompted by the upper levels through boasting, pressure, and reward, leaving little alternative to those below.'

Tombstone also presents fascinating instances in which

local officials ignored or reversed orders from the central
government, improvising policies of their own. In early
1961, Zeng Xisheng, the Party chief of Anhui province,
who had condemned thousands to premature death in his
zeal for high procurement targets, boldly overturned Mao's
collectivization project by contracting land to individual
households. This commonsensical solution dawned on him
after he heard of a seventy-three-year-old peasant who, with
his tubercular son and using a single shovel, cultivated a plot
of land in the mountains: after reaping an abundant harvest,
the man sold his surplus grain to the state while also feeding
himself. Mao encouraged Zeng to experiment with the so-
called 'responsibility fields.' 'Give it a try,' he reportedly said.
'If it doesn't work, carry out self-criticism. If it works well
. . . that will be splendid!'

Zeng's experiment, which daringly contradicted Mao's
fantasy of collectivism, proved to be successful, and Anhui
was among the first provinces to recover from the famine,
in 1962. But by then Mao had been made insecure by the
open acknowledgement of the Party's policy errors by Liu
Shaoqi and others. In early 1962, Liu, clearly striving for an
acceptable ratio, described the famine as 'three parts natural
disaster and seven parts man-made disaster.' Later that year,
he had the temerity to inform the Chairman that 'history will
record the role you and I played in the starvation of so many
people, and the cannibalism will also be memorialized!'
Mao, recoiling from such criticism, now wanted to assert his
ideological infallibility and revert to the old method—the
evidently true one of communism.

Zeng ignored him, despite complaints from Maoists that
he was engaged in 'bourgeois restoration.' But, by the end

of 1962, ideological pressures from above had curtailed his innovation. Later, like many Party officials responsible for mass suffering during the famine, Zeng was exposed to the fury of the Cultural Revolution's victims. After brutal interrogation and public humiliation, he was put to death by young Red Guards. But there was another coda to his efforts. In 1978, Yang writes, as Deng Xiaoping ushered China into a market economy, 'Anhui province took the lead in reinstating the responsibility fields, after which the practice spread throughout China.'

Yang's meticulously researched book brings to light many such revealing details; they confirm his description of the Chinese Communist Party as being marked, from the 1950s onward, by a battle between pragmatists and idealists (or, more accurately, ideologues), the latter represented by Mao's faction. For Yang, this rough distinction also provides a useful way of explaining China's post-Mao evolution. 'The pragmatists salvaged the situation after Mao's death,' he writes, 'by pushing China into the road of "re-form and opening."'

Since the Maoist generation of Deng Xiaoping, a new generation of technocrats, almost all with engineering degrees, has come to the fore. Determined to avoid the 'unscientific approach' of their predecessors and greatly influenced by the example of Singapore, these leaders have helped build the gigantic infrastructure—airports, highways, high-speed railroads—underpinning the country's rapid economic growth. The rise of these technocrats and the corresponding eclipse of ideologues complicate the popular

notion that China is a 'totalitarian' state with no alternative
but to transform itself into a democracy. *Tombstone* shows
that, even during a catastrophe caused by a profoundly
undemocratic system and a fanatical ideologue, the Party
accommodated a degree of dissent, improvisation, and
pragmatism. It makes you wonder about the opaque and
little-understood one-party state now run by Mao's heirs.
How has it absorbed the lessons of Mao's disasters? Yang's
account of the Chinese Communist Party (of which he
remains a member) raises even more vital questions: How
has China managed to retain many of the features of
Mao's regime—coercive public security, control of strategic
industries, censorship, and state propaganda mechanisms—
while nonetheless transitioning to a market economy? And
how long can a nominally communist party maintain its
right to rule over a largely capitalist country?

Certainly, the Party seems to have broken with Maoist
mass campaigns and ideological indoctrination. Since
the 1980s, it has sought to rebuild its legitimacy among a
restless Chinese population by promising to bring prosperity
through a market-driven economy. The Communist Party,
once the domain of peasants and factory workers, now
attracts rich businessmen and middle-class professionals, and
it has suffered a corresponding loss of ideological coherence.
Its leaders periodically announce, as they did in 2006, such
grandiose projects as 'building a socialist countryside.' But
such old-fashioned rhetoric sounds hollow in a state where
corrupt 'princelings,' or sons of senior Party leaders, such
as Bo Xilai, enrich themselves with impunity, while protests
by the urban working classes and dispossessed peasants
erupt across the country. The Chinese scholar Minxin Pei,

in *China's Trapped Transition: The Limits of Developmental Autocracy* (2006), summed up the orthodox wisdom, declaring that the technocratic regime now running China can 'no longer build broad-based social coalitions to pursue its policies and defend itself.'

The logical way out of China's impasse seems to be electoral democracy, and Yang, echoing the axioms of modernization theory, is convinced that the country's market economy furnishes a solid basis for a 'democratic political system.' But it is far from clear that either the Chinese beneficiaries of economic growth or its victims (displaced peasants and exploited urban workers) are ready to launch the political movement necessary for a shift to representative government.

The problems and challenges facing the Party, which has just undergone its once-a-decade leadership change, have tended to obscure its remarkable durability. Adapting rapidly to the age of private consumption, the Party no longer seeks to tightly control the personal lives of the Chinese people; it has a staggering eighty-three million members, ranging from hard-line Maoists and patriotic students to Shanghai bankers and critics such as Yang Jisheng. Neither the atrocity near Tiananmen Square and the worldwide collapse of communist regimes in 1989 nor the reportedly tens of thousands of protests since then have much delayed China's economic modernization. As Sebastian Heilmann and Elizabeth J. Perry, two scholars of Chinese politics, write in their introduction to the collection of essays *Mao's Invisible Hand: The Political Foundations of Adaptive Governance in China* (2010), China, unlike the Soviet Union and many other communist states, 'not only survived the 1989 crisis with its party-state system intact'; it also managed, within a single generation, 'to engineer an economic and social transformation of . . . stunning proportions.'

Heilmann and Perry counter-intuitively argue that 'much of the explanation for this singular achievement lies in the creative adaptation of key elements of China's revolutionary heritage.' Apparently, policymaking for the technocrat rulers of today's China is synonymous with endless change, improvisation, and ad-hoc adjustment—'guerrilla-style policy-making,' which is marked by 'secrecy, versatility, speed, and surprise.'

Such pragmatism, which encourages 'decentralized initiative within the framework of centralized political authority,' helps to explain phenomena that otherwise seem contradictory. On the one hand, there is the rise, in the 1980s, of Zhao Ziyang, former general secretary of the Party, and for a time the presumed successor to Deng Xiaoping, who made several conciliatory gestures to the student protesters at Tiananmen Square; on the other, there is the surprisingly long run of Bo Xilai, who built a Maoist cult around himself and was apparently given a free hand to enact a series of 'decentralized initiatives' along populist lines. But Chinese leaders since Mao, many of whom suffered during the anarchy of the Cultural Revolution, also seek to insure themselves against excesses of ideology, personality cults, and populism. Thus, ad-hoc adjustments can include ruthlessly eliminating opponents for the sake of maintaining centralized political authority. Deng Xiaoping finally sent tanks to clear Tiananmen Square, and Zhao Ziyang, brusquely marginalized, spent the rest of his life—fifteen years—under house arrest. A much more severe punishment may await the stridently Maoist—but apparently brashly venal—Bo Xilai.

Other quick improvisations by the Chinese regime seem to include periodic and carefully controlled explosions of a near-xenophobic mass nationalism. Apparently condoned and even facilitated by Beijing, anti-Japanese riots and protests of the kind witnessed recently on Chinese streets act as release valves for politically disaffected masses. Although tainted by corruption scandals and beset by a slowing economy, Chinese leaders—men of uniformly sombre countenance and dyed hair—have not lost more conventional ways of securing their legitimacy among ordinary Chinese. As China watchers obsessively speculate about the fall of Bo Xilai and the rise of Xi Jinping, another princeling, the bigger, if less exciting, story coming out of the country, according to the *Financial Times*, is the apparent success of the 'socialist countryside' campaign, an attempt to improve rural conditions. In 2006, the Chinese government abolished all agricultural levies (overturning two thousand years of precedent), and poured 6 trillion renminbi into infrastructure—nearly the same amount as Barack Obama's stimulus package in 2009. The result is that 95 per cent of Chinese villages now have roads, electricity, running water, natural gas, and phone lines. Nearly all Chinese have basic health insurance, up from just 30 per cent in 2003.

From a Western perspective, the long ubiquity of Bo Xilai before his eventual disgrace indicates a deep rot within the Chinese political system. It is tempting to suppose that, like the despots of the Arab world, the Party's leaders are unlikely to survive the inevitable revolution of rising expectations in a globalized economy. But it is equally possible that our preoccupation with the Party's apparently fractious and corrupt senior leaders and the growing incidence of social unrest obscure the resilience of the Chinese one-party state—just as Western obsession with the poster-bright reforms of Mikhail Gorbachev, in the 1980s, obscured the internal weakness of the Soviet Union. Certainly, the old view that consigns an aberrantly authoritarian China to the anteroom of Western-style democracy is up for re-examination.

Yang Jisheng himself is deeply ambivalent about the prospects for democracy in China. He starts *Tombstone* by confidently declaring that the day of its arrival in China 'will not be long in coming.' Five hundred pages later, he has changed his mind, asserting that 'it will take a very long time.' Yang seems to be echoing the post-Mao Chinese elite's wariness of impatient patriotic engineers in China; he warns that 'the very people who are most radical and hasty in their opposition to autocracy may be the very ones who facilitate the rise of a new autocratic power.'

Yang has in mind the fate of Russia, where Boris Yeltsin, the nemesis of Soviet communism, tried to rush an entire society towards democracy and the free market, only to pave the way for years of general impoverishment and suffering and for the return of authoritarianism under Vladimir Putin. For many Chinese, the former Soviet Union embodies the perils of rash, top-down westernization. And, as European and American leaders struggle to emerge from the free-market dogmas of recent years, the ostensibly communist Chinese regime shuts down a radical Maoist challenger. Such are the ironies of the cautionary tales we tell ourselves about socioeconomic engineering. No doubt there will be more in our intensely ideological age.

NOT A DINNER PARTY: MAO AND
THE MAOISTS

'A revolution is not a dinner party,' Mao Zedong declared. Rather, as he helpfully clarified in 1927, it is 'an insurrection, an act of violence.' He might have warned that nation building is no picnic, either. Mao rose to supremacy within the Chinese Communist Party, through several bloody purges of 'revisionists' and 'rightists.' After long years as a marginal peasant leader, he finally brought his revolution to all of China, forcing his great rival Chiang Kai-shek to flee to Taiwan (then called Formosa). Founding the People's Republic of China in 1949, Mao exulted, 'The Chinese people, comprising one quarter of humanity, have stood up.' He soon knocked them down, overwhelming the gradual processes of China's modernization with the frenzy of permanent revolution.

Modernizing autocrats elsewhere in Asia—Turkey's Atatürk, Iran's Reza Shah Pahlavi, and Taiwan's Chiang Kai-shek—also dragooned their peoples into traumatic social and political experiments. But Mao tormented the Chinese on a far bigger scale, condemning tens of millions to early death with the Great Leap Forward, and then exposing many more to persecution and suffering during the Cultural Revolution.

Just five years after his death, the Chinese Communist Party officially blamed the 'mistaken leadership of Mao Zedong' for the 'serious disaster and turmoil' of the Cultural Revolution, and the garishly consumerist and inegalitarian China of today seems to mock Mao's fantasies of a communist paradise. Nevertheless, China's leaders today continue to invoke 'Mao Zedong Thought.' Taiwan, now rowdily democratic, has begun to dismantle the personality cult of Chiang Kai-shek, removing his statues and erasing his name from major monuments. But Mao still gazes across Tiananmen Square from the large portrait hanging on the Gate of Heavenly Peace. Visitors from the countryside often line up all day for a fleeting glimpse of his embalmed corpse south of the square, and in folk religions throughout China Mao is revered as a god.

This persistence of Mao in official discourse and popular imagination may seem an instance of ideological pathology—the same kind that makes some Russian nationalists get misty-eyed about Stalin. Indeed, the communist state's vast propaganda apparatus first exalted Mao to divine status. But then a non-ideological view of Mao has rarely been available in the West, even as he has gone from being a largely benign revolutionary and Third Worldist icon to, more recently, sadistic monster. This is largely due to China's ever-shifting place in the Western imagination. Three books—Patrick Wright's *Passport to Peking* (2010), Frank Dikötter's *Mao's Great Famine* (2010), and Timothy Cheek's anthology *A Critical Introduction to Mao* (2010)—

attest to the difficulty of definitively fixing Mao's image, a
project that amounts to writing a history of China's present.

Early visitors to Mao's guerrilla base camp in Yan'an in
the 1930s—notably the American writer Edgar Snow—
managed to project onto the revolutionary the ideals of
American progressivism. Snow's popular report 'Red Star
over China' (1937) presented a 'Lincolnesque' leader who
aimed to 'awaken' China's millions to 'a belief in human
rights,' introducing them to 'a new conception of the state,
society, and the individual.' More perceptively, Theodore
White, then a reporter for *Time*, who visited Yan'an in 1944,
concluded that the communists were 'masters of brutality'
but had won peasants over to their side. Other 'China
Hands'—an assortment of journalists, American Foreign
Service officials, and soldiers who succeeded in meeting
the communists—preferred Mao to Chiang Kai-shek, who,
though corrupt and unpopular, was receiving enormous
amounts of military aid from the United States. 'The trouble
in China is simple,' Joseph Stilwell, the commander of US
Forces in China–India–Burma, told White. 'We are allied to
an ignorant, illiterate, superstitious, peasant son of a bitch.'
But, as the Cold War intensified, the China Hands found
themselves ignored in the United States. Following Chiang
Kai-shek's defeat and flight to Taiwan in 1949, the Republican
Party angrily accused the Truman Administration of having
'lost' China to communism. Then they berated it for
hindering Chiang Kai-shek's reconquest of the mainland.
The China Hands in particular came under sustained fire
from early and zealous Cold Warriors for their supposed

sympathy with the Chinese agents of Soviet expansionism. Henry Luce, who saw the Christian convert Chiang Kai-shek as a vital facilitator of the 'American Century,' fired White from *Time*.

The Korean War, which China entered on the side of North Korea, fixed Mao's image in the United States as another unappeasable communist. The Eisenhower administration now vigorously backed Chiang Kai-shek, signing a mutual defence treaty with him in 1954, and threatening China with a nuclear strike the following year. The State Department imposed a full trade embargo on China and prohibited travel there. Sinologists were reduced to speculating from afar whether Mao was more nationalist than Marxist.

The god of communism had failed for many admirers of the Russian Revolution by the time Mao reunified mainland China, in the early 1950s. Still, many Western intellectuals, recoiling from the excesses of McCarthyism, and hampered by lack of first-hand information, gave the benefit of the doubt to Mao in the decade that followed. Travelling to China in 1955, Simone de Beauvoir drew a sympathetic picture of a new nation overcoming the after-effects of foreign invasions, internecine warfare, natural disasters, and economic collapse. Neither Paradise nor Hell, China was another peasant country where people were trying to break out of 'the agonizingly hopeless circle of an animal existence.'

The British visitors to China described in Patrick Wright's entertaining *Passport to Peking* tried to maintain a similarly open mind. Then, as now, plenty of liberal as well as left-wing Brits resented their government's reflexive adherence to Washington's foreign policy. When Zhou Enlai, China's urbane foreign minister, made his first public appearance in Europe, many were persuaded that China was more than a clone of Soviet totalitarianism, and that 'peaceful coexistence' was a real possibility. 'Come and see,' Zhou said, and a motley bunch of politicians, artists, and scientists took up his invitation in 1954. Among them were a few fellow travellers, most notably the artist Paul Hogarth. Some, like members of the Labour Party delegation headed by former prime minister Clement Attlee, were seasoned anti-communists. Others were simply self-absorbed tourists, routinely stumbling into comic misunderstandings. The British artist Stanley Spencer first accosted Zhou Enlai with a rapturous account of his native village of Cookham, and then went on about the delights of a little island in the Thames called Formosa, not realizing the name was shared by his hosts' fiercest international adversary.

The Chinese, who, Wright says, 'had learned a lot from Moscow about the art of seducing foreign visitors,' laid on extravagant banquets for the British. (The headline in the *Daily Mail* was 'SOCIALISTS DINE ON SHARK'S FINS.') The mammoth Chinese construction of factories, canals, schools, hospitals, and public housing awed these visitors from a straitened country that American loans and the Marshall Plan had saved from financial ruin. They were impressed, too, by the new marriage laws that considerably improved the position of Chinese women, by the ostensible abolition of prostitution, and by the public health campaigns.

Yet no 'useful idiots' of the kind who had made the Soviet Union under Stalin appear the saviour of humanity emerged from the trip. The parade held in Beijing to mark the fifth anniversary of the People's Republic reminded the philosopher A.J. Ayer of the Nuremberg Rallies. Though impressed by the 'dedicated and dignified' Mao, the trade unionist Sam Watson was dismayed by Chinese talk of the masses as 'another brick, another paving stone.' Mao asked Attlee to help reverse the American policy of encircling his country through defence treaties with Southeast Asian countries and the rearming of Japan. Attlee firmly informed Mao that 'two-way traffic was needed' for peace, and asked Mao to help persuade the Soviet Union to free its satellite states in Eastern Europe.

Other European visitors to China were relative pushovers. François Mitterrand, who visited China at the height of the devastating famine in 1961, denied the existence of starvation in the country. André Malraux hailed Mao as an 'emperor of bronze.' Richard Nixon, who consulted Malraux before 'opening up' China to the United States in 1972, and Henry Kissinger were no less awed by Mao's raw power and historical mystique. Two decades after Nixon himself denounced China as Stalin's puppet state in the East, the country seemed to the United States a likely counterweight to the Soviet Union. Accordingly, American attitudes to China in the 1970s were marked by what the Yale historian Jonathan Spence characterized as 'reawakened curiosity' and 'guileless fascination,' followed soon by 'renewed skepticism' as travel and research in China became progressively easier.

In the 1970s and 1980s, American scholars and journalists could finally experience the realities they had only guessed at, and they began compiling a grim record of China under Mao—a task that was speeded up by Deng Xiaoping's repudiation of the Cultural Revolution after Mao's death, in 1976. More Chinese also began to travel outside their country. Some, safely settled in the West, published memoirs of the Cultural Revolution. This fast-growing genre, which flourished particularly after the brutal suppression of the protests in Tiananmen Square, in June 1989, described the violence and chaos suffered by ordinary Chinese during Mao's quest for ideological and moral renewal. One émigré Chinese writer, who had previously been Mao's private doctor, published the first intimate account of the Chinese leader, *The Private Life of Chairman Mao* (1994). It depicted a luxury-loving narcissist who was at once autocratic, whimsical, and calculating. Jung Chang and Jon Halliday's best-selling biography *Mao: The Unknown Story* (2005) went much further, describing a man who was unstintingly vile from early youth to old age. Far from Edgar Snow's champion of human rights, this particular Mao was working towards 'a completely arid society, devoid of civilization, deprived of representation of human feelings, inhabited by a herd with no sensibility.' In Chang and Halliday's account, Mao killed more than seventy million people in peacetime, and was in some ways a more diabolical villain than even Hitler or Stalin. The authors claimed—among other comparisons they made to twentieth-century atrocities—that the victims of the famine caused by the Great Leap Forward (1958–62) were worse off than the slave labourers at Auschwitz.

In *Mao's Great Famine*, Frank Dikötter, a professor of modern Chinese history at the University of Hong Kong, deepens this trend in Mao studies. Boldly and engagingly revisionist in his previous books—which stressed the benefits of opium smoking to the Chinese and judged China under

Chiang Kai-shek to be vibrantly cosmopolitan—Dikötter hopes that his new book will help make the famine 'as well known as the two other man-made catastrophes of the twentieth century, the Holocaust and the Gulag.' Drawing on fresh research and a new tally, Dikötter revises upward the commonly accepted estimate of thirty million deaths in these four years, exceeding the thirty-eight million proposed by Chang and Halliday. His conclusion: out of a total population of 650 million, 'at least 45 million people died unnecessarily between 1958 and 1962.' This is still a conservative estimate, he judges, and by the end of the book Dikötter speculates that the body count could be as high as sixty million. Not only that: Mao also precipitated the biggest demolition of real estate, the most extensive destruction of the environment, and the biggest waste of manpower in history.

How did this come about? Dikötter is not much interested in a wide-ranging account that would necessarily include China's internal political and economic situation in the 1950s, the shifting hierarchy of the Communist Party, or the Chinese sense of siege following the Korean War and the sharpening of Cold War divisions in Asia. He describes in some detail Mao's personal competitiveness with Khrushchev—made keener by China's abject dependence on the Soviet Union for loans and expert guidance—and his obsession with developing a uniquely Chinese model of socialist modernity. Hence the Great Leap Forward, which Mao designed to boost China's industrial and agricultural output and move the country ahead of the Soviet Union as well as Britain in double-quick time. An urban myth in the West held that millions of Chinese had only to jump simultaneously in order to shake the world and throw it off its axis. Mao actually believed that collective action was sufficient to propel an agrarian society into industrial modernity. According to his master plan, surpluses generated by vigorously productive labour in the countryside would support industry and subsidize food in the cities. Acting as though he were still the wartime mobilizer of the Chinese masses, Mao expropriated personal property and housing, replacing them with People's Communes, and centralized the distribution of food.

Organized in very short chapters, Dikötter's book takes its reader through a brisk tour of the follies, inefficiencies, and deceptions of Mao's commandeered economy: impossible targets, exaggerated claims, maladroit innovation, lack of incentive, corruption, and waste. Ordered to go forth and make steel, Chinese flung anything they could find—pots, pans, cutlery, doorknobs, floorboards, and even farming tools—into primitive furnaces. Meanwhile, fields were abandoned as farmers fed furnaces in giant cooperatives, worked in similarly wasteful irrigation schemes, or migrated to urban factories in their millions.

Having mobilized the masses, Mao continually searched for things for them to do. At one point, he declared war on four common pests: flies, mosquitoes, rats, and sparrows. The Chinese were exhorted to bang drums, pots, pans, and gongs in order to keep sparrows flying until, exhausted, they fell to earth. Provincial record keepers chalked up impressive body counts: Shanghai alone accounted for 48,695.49 kilograms of flies, 930,486 rats, 1213.05 kilograms of cockroaches, and 1,367,440 sparrows. Mao's Marx-tinted Faustianism demonized nature as man's adversary. But,

Dikötter points out, 'Mao lost his war against nature. The campaign backfired by breaking the delicate balance between humans and the environment.' Liberated from their usual nemeses, locusts and grasshoppers devoured millions of tons of food even as people starved to death.

While food shortages deepened, the Chinese regime continued to insist on huge grain procurements from the countryside. The aim was not only to maintain outstanding export commitments but also to protect China's image in the world. According to Dikötter, Mao ordered the Party to procure more grain than ever before, declaring that 'when there is not enough to eat, people starve to death. It is better to let half of the people die so that the other half can eat their fill.' In 1960, the worst year of the famine, which was exacerbated by drought as well as flash floods, grain was sent, often gratis, to Albania, Cuba, Vietnam, Indonesia, and Poland.

Not all Chinese died of starvation or of the diseases that accompany malnutrition. 'Coercion, terror, and systematic violence were the foundation of the Great Leap Forward,' Dikötter writes, estimating that at least two and a half million were worked, tortured, or beaten to death or simply executed by Party officials, and between one and three million people committed suicide. Some of those who survived did so by selling or abandoning their children or by digging up and devouring the dead.

Dikötter closes his vivid catalogue of horrors with the 'turning point' of the Party meeting in early 1962, where Mao's colleague and head of state Liu Shaoqi admitted that a 'man-made disaster' had occurred in China. Dikötter evokes Mao's fear that Liu Shaoqi could discredit him just as completely as Khrushchev had damaged Stalin's reputation. The book ends with a chilling foretaste of the next catastrophe to overwhelm China: 'Mao was biding his time, but the patient groundwork for launching a Cultural Revolution that would tear the party and the country apart had already begun.'

This narrative line is plausible: exhorting young Chinese to assault the allegedly expanding bourgeoisie within the Party, Mao hoped to preserve his power and revolutionary legacy from bureaucratic 'revisionists' like Liu Shaoqi, who was among the leaders who died at the hands of the Red Guard. Yet Dikötter's account of Mao's inner life scants some crucial details that would give a richer picture of his motivations and his constant manoeuvring within the Party, while also undercutting the image of him as an indefatigable megalomaniac; for instance, the fact that Mao, after resigning as head of state in 1959, was unhappy with his diminished role in day-to-day decision-making, or that he had already called for a major change of course in November 1960, and criticized himself at the Party Conference in 1962.

Dikötter is, indeed, generally dismissive of facts that could blunt his story's sharp edge. Explaining Mao's well-known defence of farmers' evading grain procurers in 1959 and his advocacy of 'right opportunism,' Dikötter writes, 'Mao took on the pose of a benevolent sage-king protective of the welfare of his subjects,' but, he says, historians have erred in seeing this period as 'one of "retreat" or "cooling off."' This would be persuasively contrarian if Dikötter hadn't mentioned four pages previously that while Mao was pretending to be a 'benign leader,' from November 1958 to June 1959, 'the pressure temporarily abated.'

Focusing relentlessly on Mao's character and motivations, Dikötter confirms the man's reputation as sadistic, cowardly, callous, and vindictive. Yet his bold portrait bleaches out much of the period's historical and geopolitical backdrop (the uprising in Tibet in 1959, anti-American riots in Taiwan, border clashes with India, the Sino-Soviet rift), and he misses, too, the abusive relationship between Mao and the Chinese people: how sincerely and deeply, for instance, they trusted and revered their leader before being betrayed by him.

Dikötter's explanation of the Great Leap Forward omits the fact that—despite the damaging effects of the Korean War and the American trade embargo—China had, by 1956, made remarkable progress in securing social stability, achieving economic growth, and improving living conditions. According to Roderick MacFarquhar, a leading historian of Mao's China, 'what Mao accomplished between 1949 and 1956 was in fact the fastest, most extensive, and least damaging socialist revolution carried out in any communist state.' The distinguished expatriate writer Liu Binyan recalled the early 1950s as a time when 'everyone felt good . . . and looked to the future with optimism'; most were eager to do their bit for their country.

Little did these enthusiasts know that they were about to be kicked in the teeth. Dikötter doesn't make the imaginative move into ordinary people's lives, their longings for stability and dignity, which Mao's utopianism so cruelly trampled. The manifold victims in *Mao's Great Famine*, keenly computed but cursorily described, remain a blur. And Dikötter's comparison of the famine to the great evils of the

Holocaust and the Gulag does not, finally, persuade. A great many premature deaths also occurred in newly independent nations not ruled by erratic tyrants. Amartya Sen has argued that 'despite the gigantic size of excess mortality in the Chinese famine, the extra mortality in India from regular deprivation in normal times vastly overshadows the former.' Describing China's early lead over India in health care, literacy, and life expectancy, Sen wrote that 'India seems to manage to fill its cupboard with more skeletons every eight years than China put there in its years of shame.'

The discrepancy between democratic India and authoritarian China is due to a complex interplay of political, geographical, and economic factors. Certainly, it cannot be explained through the fantasies and delusions of an Oriental despot. Mao's individual pathology goes only so far in explaining China today, and it is pretty much useless in figuring out the Chairman's enduring, even growing, influence outside China. What, for instance, is one to make of the irruptions of Maoism in the age of globalization? The Maoists of Nepal, who overthrew the monarchy in 2006 and won nationwide elections in 2008, remain a formidable political force. The Indian Maoists, whom India's prime minister, Manmohan Singh, describes as the country's gravest internal security threat, are ranged against mining corporations and security forces in a vast swath of central India. Consisting largely of forest-dwelling peoples and landless peasants, these insurgent groups mouth a Mao-inspired rhetoric against foreign imperialists and local 'compradors.' But, like Che Guevara and the Vietcong, they also adopt Mao's tactic of marshalling rural populations against the cities, establishing, in addition to a cohesive party and militia, their own administrative structures and organizations.

This model of mass mobilization was Mao's singular contribution to the making of the modern Chinese nation state, though it also nearly unmade China after 1949. The most stimulating chapters in the academic collection *A Critical Introduction to Mao* (2010), edited by Timothy Cheek, discuss Mao's 'Sinification' of a European tradition of revolution. Mao belonged to a Chinese generation of activists and thinkers who developed a fierce political awareness at the end of a long century of internal decay, humiliations by Western powers and by Japan, and failed imperial reforms. Whatever their ideological inclinations, they all believed in a version of Social Darwinism—the survival of the fittest applied to international relations. They worried about the social and political passivity of ordinary Chinese, and were electrified by the possibility that a strong, centralized nation state would protect them from the depredations of foreign imperialists and domestic warlords. As Sun Yat-sen, China's first modern revolutionary, explained in a speech shortly before his death, in 1925, 'If we are to resist foreign oppression in the future, we must overcome individual freedom and join together as a firm unit, just as one adds water and cement to loose gravel to produce something as solid as a rock.'

Others took on the arduous task of welding a defunct empire into a nation state, most prominently Chiang Kai-shek, whose urban-based Nationalist Party first brought a semblance of political unity to post-imperial China. But it was Mao who, helped by a savage Japanese invasion and Chiang Kai-shek's ineptitude, came up with an ideologically like-minded and disciplined organization capable of enlisting the loyalty and passions of the majority of the Chinese population in the countryside. More enduringly, Mao provided a battered and proud people with a compelling national narrative of decline and redemption. As he stressed shortly before the founding of the People's Republic, 'The Chinese have always been a great, courageous and industrious nation; it is only in modern times that they have fallen behind. And that was due entirely to oppression and exploitation by foreign imperialism and domestic reactionary governments.' This would change: 'Ours will no longer be a nation subject to insult and humiliation. . . . We will have not only a powerful army but also a powerful air force and a powerful navy.' Unlike India and Nepal, China contains very few active Maoists today, but strains of Mao's anti-imperialist rhetoric grow more potent every year. As Timothy Cheek, a historian at the University of British Columbia, explains, 'Most people in China appear to accept the assumptions in this story about China's national identity, about the role of imperialism in China's history and present, and about the value of maintaining and improving this thing called China. Increasingly, moreover, China's middle classes accept the additional story in Maoism—the story of rising China: China was great, China was put down, China is rising again.'

Though better informed about Mao's calamitous blunders, Chinese intellectuals today are far from united in their assessment of him. Attacked for his despotism by liberal-minded scholars, Mao is admired by New Left intellectuals for his assault on communist bureaucracies and advocacy of 'extensive democracy' during the Cultural Revolution. Summing up the diverse and contested meanings of Mao in China, Xiao Yanzhong, a professor at People's University in Beijing, describes Mao scholarship as 'a bellwether that can indicate changes in China's politics, economy, and society, as well as the states of mind of the Chinese people.'

Certainly, the Party, which remains as opposed to free elections as ever, has no choice but to derive its legitimacy from Mao Zedong even as it drifts further away from his ideals. Shortly after the sixtieth anniversary of the People's Republic last year, the Chinese premier, Wen Jiabao, visited the tomb of Mao Anying, Mao's favourite son, who died in the Korean War. Laying a wreath, Wen abruptly addressed a stone statue of the dead soldier. 'Comrade Anying,' he said, 'I have come to see you on behalf of the people of the motherland. Our country is strong now and its people enjoy good fortune. You may rest in peace.'

Comrade Wen surely realizes that, absent Mao's exploits, the Chinese people would have started to enjoy their present good fortune three decades earlier. But would China have found a strong political basis for its prosperity without Mao? This is the harder counterfactual question. Asked for his views on the French Revolution, Zhou Enlai replied that it was too early to say; and he must have hoped for a similarly delayed verdict on the Chinese Revolution, the human costs of which truly did make the Reign of Terror look like a dinner party. Zhou, in pleading for the long view, was not being entirely shifty (nor is George W. Bush, who, after unleashing violent revolution in Iraq, has also entrusted his scoresheet to future historians).

We have surely made up our minds about Mao. But the Chinese judgement on Mao's revolution has been complicated and deferred by the longevity of the communist regime and the country's extraordinary economic successes. Another revolution, such as the one that has occurred in Taiwan, could bring, along with political freedoms, a new self-image to China, which would likely disown Mao. But it is also possible that the Chinese nation will continue in the decades ahead to acknowledge Mao as its father—disgraced, discredited, and irreplaceable.

IN TIANANMEN'S WAKE

It is still not clear how many unarmed civilians the People's Liberation Army (PLA) killed in Beijing on the night of 3 June 1989, as it sought to expel protesters from Tiananmen Square. The names of the victims, who were officially denounced as 'counter-revolutionaries,' were never published. Their relatives are forbidden from mourning them in public. On every anniversary of the massacre, policemen proliferate in the square, quick to extinguish any attempt at honouring the dead and wounded. The massacre cannot even be mentioned in the Chinese media.

This attempt to engineer collective amnesia seems to have worked: some students at Beijing University recently failed to identify the iconic Tiananmen photograph of the young man with the plastic bags confronting tanks. Once famous student leaders—Chai Ling, Li Lu, Wang Dan, Shen Tong, Wu'er Kaixi—went into exile, and several transformed themselves into venture capitalists and hedge funders. To the Chinese, who have been released with miraculous swiftness from the deprivations and traumas of the Mao years into hectic consumerism, struggles for democracy waged in the late 1970s and 1980s seem increasingly remote. As Dai Wei, the comatose but mordantly alert narrator of *Beijing Coma* (2008), the novel by Ma Jian, observes, 'No one talks about the Tiananmen protests any more.'

Ma Jian, a former resident of Beijing who was at the Tiananmen protests, now lives in self-imposed exile in London. His narrator, who lingers in a coma for years after being shot in the neck by a stray bullet during the PLA's crackdown, gives a remarkably detailed, and often only thinly fictionalized, account of the events and their brisk disappearance from Chinese memory. 'The struggle of man against power,' Milan Kundera once wrote against a similar backdrop of communist indoctrination, 'is the struggle of memory against forgetting'; and, at nearly six hundred closely printed pages, *Beijing Coma* seems determined to enshrine the strivings of 'the Tiananmen Generation.'

Ma Jian writes about China with the obsessiveness of a writer in exile who cares about only one society. There is no doubting his passion and sense of urgency. 'We've been crushed and silenced,' says a colleague of Dai Wei's whose legs are trampled under a PLA tank. 'If we don't take a stand now, we will be erased from the history books.' Dai Wei, whose inner life is periodically stimulated by visitors to his sickbed, notes each new diversion—cell phones, email, video disks, anti-Western nationalism, New Age religion, the Olympics—that beguiles his countrymen away from the idealism of 1989. 'As society changes, new words and terms keep popping up, such as: sauna, private car ownership, property developer, mortgage and personal instalment loan,' he notes. He watches helplessly as his own decaying body is commodified, his urine used in quack therapy, and his still responsive penis employed by seekers of kinky sex. His hapless mother resorts to selling one of his kidneys to pay for his treatment. Finally, a real estate developer from Hong Kong demolishes his cramped home during Beijing's pre-Olympic prettification. In the novel's Wagnerian finale, the bulldozers of the hustling new China and the tanks of the PLA combine in a frenzy of violence and destruction.

Philip Roth once contrasted, slightly enviously, the American writer, who can say anything he wishes but is usually ignored, with his Eastern Bloc counterpart, who, since nothing is permitted to him, receives respectful attention for everything he writes. China—garishly capitalist but still officially communist—seems to impose its own peculiar ordeal on writers; they risk the state's malevolence without exercising any great moral or political influence in their easily distracted society. *Beijing Coma* is unlikely to be published on the Chinese mainland (though editions printed in Hong Kong and Taiwan will probably be pirated there), and will be read mostly by readers outside China.

Some of its more pungent criticisms are likely to be lost on the non-Chinese reader. To Westerners, the students at Tiananmen may have given an impression of a solid and energetic consensus against dictatorship and for democracy, but they were an egotistical and fractious lot, riven by disagreements over tactics and money. These schisms widened during the years of exile as leaders blamed each other for the failure of the protests. Ma Jian retraces these recriminations over hundreds of pages, closely (and controversially) approximating actual events and real-life personalities. Nailing down the differences between the respective stances of the Hunger Strike Headquarters, the Beijing Students' Federation, and the Provincial Students' Federation is as important to him as evoking the scent of Dai Wei's girlfriends.

The novel's style feels more familiar when, following much dissident literature from the former Soviet Union and Eastern Europe, it mixes gritty realism with absurdist satire. In one memorable scene, Dai Wei is fellated by a horny visitor while the new nationalists of Beijing lustily celebrate Hong Kong's return to the Chinese motherland. Writers in communist countries inevitably focus on what Ivan Klíma once called the 'intriguing plots offered by the totalitarian system'—'the humiliation of man, life based on lies and pretenses'—and state repression and terror also tend to distil the writer's art, giving it a metaphysical rather than a material heft, a poetic rather than a literalist cast. While most of *Beijing Coma* renders the protests against communist rule with the doggedness and precision of ordinary social realism, shorter sections of the novel, describing Dai Wei's regrets and desires with ironic nostalgia, recall the ambitious collages in which Kundera and Klíma frictionlessly juxtaposed political commentary, erotic memories, and philosophical reflections. Readers of Kundera and Josef Škvorecký would recognize the novel's frequent invocation of sexual love as an antidote to totalitarian control, and Ma Jian shares an affinity for the artistically gifted and the emotionally vulnerable, and for social outcasts. Immersed in his memories, Dai Wei brings to mind the protagonist of Klíma's *Love and Garbage*, a banned writer 'hemmed in by prohibition' who wants to escape into a 'private region of bliss.'

Born in 1953, Ma Jian is one of the Chinese artists and intellectuals who came of age in the last years of the Cultural Revolution. Exempt from personal participation in the worst excesses of Maoism, this generation, which includes China's best-known film-makers, Chen Kaige and Zhang Yimou, as well as the artist Ai Weiwei, was the first to dare embrace the possibilities of artistic manoeuvre in China's unruly transition from the 'struggle session' to the free market. As the Communist Party, adopting a market economy, shed some of its ideological orthodoxy, anything seemed possible—at least, until the next crackdown.

Ma Jian seems to have hovered on the raffish end of the new countercultural spectrum—what the Sinologist John Minford termed the 'culture of the *liumang* (an untranslatable term loosely meaning loafer, hoodlum, hobo, bum, punk).' Divorced from his first wife and abandoned by his girlfriend, Ma Jian feigned illness at work and hung out with other misfits, drinking beer and discussing *Waiting for Godot*. Accused of 'spiritual pollution' by the authorities, he left Beijing in late 1983 and, travelling with a camera, a notebook, and Whitman's *Leaves of Grass*, wandered around China for three years, subsisting on odd jobs and the kindness of friends and strangers. The commissars caught up with him in 1987, when, having just moved to Hong Kong, he published a story based on his travels in Tibet. The story, describing the degradation of China's most religious minority, apparently spurned socialist realism's demand for cheerful uplift, and it earned Ma Jian a blanket ban on publication in China.

On his travels across China in the mid 1980s, which he later described in *Red Dust* (2002), the book that made him known in the West, Ma Jian repeatedly chafed at official brutality and philistinism. Speaking to a small-town book club, he proclaimed, 'I will not let a political party tell me how to live, when to die or what to believe in.' Reciting Allen Ginsberg's 'Howl' to a fellow writer, he mocked Ginsberg's angry rejection of America. 'He implies his country is not fit for humans to live in. Well, he should live in China for a month, then see what he thinks. Everyone here dreams of the day we can sing out of our windows in despair.'

Tiananmen Square in early 1989 attracted many dreamers like Ma Jian, who returned from Hong Kong to a one-room shack in Beijing in order to join the student protests. The protests initially seemed like a political consummation of the previous decade of cautious economic freedom. China in the mid 1980s had been, as Ma Jian put it, 'starting to shake, like a kettle coming to the boil.' *Red Dust* remains the most vivid description of the Chinese people freshly liberated from Maoism, picking their way through a transformed moral landscape in which extreme poverty and repression coexist with alluring new possibilities of self-invention. Selling chiffon scarves in a traffic jam in Xuelin or painting cartoons in Chengdu, Ma Jian not only seems to have relished his own improvised life; he also appears to have embraced some of his country's entrepreneurial exuberance. In one of the book's many bracingly unexpected scenes, he finds himself exhorting the residents of an isolated village, 'This country is changing, opening up. You can't just stay here like vegetables. You should travel, broaden your minds. Haven't you heard about Shenzhen Economic Zone?'

Beijing Coma bathes in the poignant glow of youthful hope and excitement. It was this optimism, more than any coherent political demand or principle, that drove the protests of 1989, even inspiring ordinary workers to organize demonstrations. (Far more numerous than the students, Beijing's protesting civilians prevented the military from reaching Tiananmen Square for days on end; they also formed a large proportion of the casualties on the night of 3 June.) As Dai Wei puts it, 'China had emerged from the catastrophe of the Cultural Revolution, and we were eager to build our country up again. We were fired by a sense of mission.' At its best, *Beijing Coma* movingly evokes the bliss many Chinese felt at that dawn to be alive, especially the young for whom the occupation of the square 'was like a huge party,' with plenty of opportunities for drinking, flirtation, and sex.

The massacre at Tiananmen Square, and the additional shock of its erasure from Chinese memory, seem to have been almost as harshly clarifying for Ma Jian and his peers as the failure of the 1848 revolution in France was for Flaubert and his contemporaries. Not surprisingly, *Beijing Coma* analyses the protests almost as fiercely as it condemns the suppressors; the student leaders, like the 1848 revolutionaries in Flaubert's *Sentimental Education*, come across as governed by self-interest and vanity. 'What was wrong with our generation?' Dai Wei says. 'When the guns were pointing at our heads, we were still wasting time squabbling among ourselves.' One of the protesters tells a student leader, 'You're supposed to be fighting dictatorship, but deep down you all want to be little emperors.' Dai Wei's girlfriend, who is one of the most passionate demonstrators, believes that the leaders 'all want to run away to graduate school in America, they have no ideals.'

Ma Jian's political anguish gives *Beijing Coma* a sour tang. Much of its prose transcends its utilitarian purpose only when, while evoking Dai Wei's loves and his austere childhood, Ma Jian summons up some of the offhand lyricism of *Red Dust*: 'I picture the dusty string of garlic hanging from a peg on the kitchen door; my father squatting down beside a washbowl, rubbing his bare legs with a wet cloth; a swathe of fallen bicycles sparkling in the sun like a field of wheat.'

The novel's bitterness apparently derives not only from the futility of the Tiananmen protests and the abominations of the Cultural Revolution—Ma Jian uses research that raises the possibility of cannibalism among Red Guards in Guangxi—but also from what he sees as an older Chinese tendency towards autocratic cruelty, submission, and conformity. In 1997, Ai Weiwei, who is now one of China's most famous artists, published an image of Tiananmen Square with his upraised middle finger in the foreground. In an accompanying essay, he asserted that 'the history of modern China is a history of negation, a denial of the value of humanity, a murder of individuality. It is a history without a soul.' Ma Jian seems to concur. 'What a gruesome history China has,' a foreign visitor to the Forbidden City remarks in *Beijing Coma*. 'That's why we've occupied the square,' Dai Wei's girlfriend replies. 'We want to put an end to millennia of autocratic rule.'

Reflecting on the murderous suppression of the protests, Dai Wei concludes that 'we were courageous but inexperienced, and had little understanding of Chinese history.' As the bulldozers move closer to his home, and his friends and relatives abandon him, a sparrow—the humble bird once marked for extermination by Mao Zedong—becomes his constant companion. His slow decay, attended by the depredations of post-Tiananmen China, turns out to be the most accomplished part of *Beijing Coma*; the eerie fascination of an active mind inside an inert body easily compensates for the conventional consolations of plot and drama. Still, some of Ma Jian's images and metaphors—Dai Wei's coma, for instance, symbolizes the moral torpor of contemporary China—seem to require a more carefully rationed narrative for their fullest effect; their poetic intensity is muffled in a novel so long and crowded. As it turns out, the many students squabbling about tactics and logistics, to whom *Beijing Coma* is largely devoted, remain a blur. It is as though, having chosen a historically and emotionally resonant setting, Ma Jian felt exempted from the task of individualizing and animating his characters on the page.

The commemorative urge, in literature as in architecture, risks petrifying into the blandly monumental. Towards the end, even Dai Wei's hyperactive consciousness feels a bit overchoreographed, his formulations ('The world I used to live in has been transformed') as explicit as the documentary realism of the rest of the novel. What comes through most strongly and often repetitively is Ma Jian's own alienation from his country, and while there is much to agree with in his dire prognosis for China, its very comprehensiveness feels too limiting for a novelist. A dissident writer's pessimism, you suspect, can be as relentless and simplistic as a socialist realist's optimism. After all, many benign impulses surely flourish under the frantic and gaudy surface of modernizing China—as the outpouring of compassion and material help for the victims of the earthquake in Sichuan shows.

In any case, China's metamorphosis, bigger and swifter than that of nineteenth-century Europe and America, furnishes material of unsurpassed richness to its artists and writers. Ma Jian himself mined some of this in *Red Dust*, which seethes with the fraught humanity of a people lurching between credulousness and opportunism, deprivation and semi-bourgeois respectability. His new novel, however, reads like a prolonged and unhappy farewell to an irrevocably corrupted China. 'If I do wake up,' Dai Wei says, 'I'd probably want to forget about politics and concentrate on living a happy life.' Like many a work produced in exile, *Beijing Coma* upholds spiritual self-sufficiency against the sentimental illusions of mass politics. It also suggests that by turning away from China's complex struggles Ma Jian will deny himself the moral passion that is the truest wellspring of his art.

PART 2

A DIN OF QUESTIONS

NEW SHANGHAI AND THE SHAPE
OF THINGS TO COME

The ruins of Shanghai always come as a surprise in a city so defiantly modern. Communist party officials and real estate speculators who power much of China's economic boom have sentenced to death almost every old house and district; demolished low-rise houses lie exposed in the downtown district, next to gated American-style luxury condominiums with names such as 'Rich Gate,' the wreckage surreally reflected in the glass facades of tall office buildings. In Dongjiadu, Shanghai's oldest quarter, where I went walking one evening in the spring of 2005, bulldozers were expected within the fortnight; and the old Chinese women squatting silently in the cramped alleys seemed helpless before them. The storm of progress, whose devastation Walter Benjamin saw in early twentieth-century Europe, is now blowing through China, propelling the angel of history into the future even as a pile of debris grows at his feet.

But you can't get too sentimental about a place like Shanghai, which was built in the nineteenth century by something as unsentimental as the opium trade: the poppies harvested in India and then imported into China by foreign and comprador businessmen and soldiers.

To be an Indian in Shanghai is to know a sensation of familiarity, if tinged with unease. It is also to be inevitably reminded of Bombay, the city most complicit with Shanghai in nineteenth-century inequity. Both port cities began to flourish after the British bullied China into opening up its markets to India-grown opium. The political and economic networks of British imperialism created a native class of comprador traders in the two cities, attracted to them a cosmopolitan cast of businessmen and adventurers, and set them apart from their vast, steadily impoverished hinterlands. Jews from Baghdad, such as the Sassoons, who opened the city's famous Cathay Hotel (renamed the Peace Hotel in 1956), and the Kadoories, founders of the Hong Kong-based Peninsula Hotels, as well as Sikhs from India, who worked as policemen in the city's exclusive International Settlement. The Japanese built up the city's industrial infrastructure; they were followed by other foreign businessmen. Moneymaking took precedence over political and racial hierarchies and made the city one of the freest in the world.

Fleeing the Russian Revolution across Siberia, thousands of White Russians eventually settled in Shanghai. Turned away almost everywhere in the world, Jewish refugees from Nazi Germany found a hospitable home in the city between 1938 and 1941—Ehud Olmert, the former Israeli prime minister, was born to a family of Chinese Jews. In the 1920s and 1930s, when one of its currencies was Mexican (due to old trading links with the Philippines), its policemen Sikh, and its prostitutes Russian, Shanghai was one of the great

global cities in the world—even more so than London or
New York. These years before World War II were a time of
celebration. In the Chinese quarter of the city, mafia dons
may have been fighting turf wars and the nationalists, led by
Chiang Kai-shek, conducting brutal purges of communists.
But little of this violence and chaos touched the International
Settlement. Jazz bands played foxtrots and jitterbugs at the
Tudor-style bar in the Cathay Hotel (where Noël Coward
wrote *Private Lives*). Even the Japanese invasion of China,
which began in the early 1930s, didn't break the mood in the
International Settlement. (The Japanese moved to intern
Europeans and Americans in the city only after their attack
on Pearl Harbor in December 1941.)

During one of my early visits to Shanghai I often found
myself gazing upon the Bund from a stylish new hotel in the
Pudong. The architecture before me was more eclectic than
that in colonial Bombay. It was also more pompous. But then
the British abroad were always prone to self-aggrandizement
in stone and their European rivals, trying hard to keep up,
conjured even greater fantasies of grandeur.

The imposing solidity was once meant to awe the natives
into obsequiousness. But things had changed dramatically in
the last half-century. The natives now not only 'swarmed,' as
the European traveller might have said, in the buildings on
the Bund, they had also erected their own grand monuments
on the once-desolate mudflats of the Pudong. Still, as in
Bombay, it was hard to appreciate the architecture, colonial
as well as postcolonial, for its own sake. I couldn't rid myself
of the feeling that what I saw was a facade and that behind

it lay another country and a history that still shaped, in
significant ways, the present.

In 1921, Gandhi claimed that Bombay's big buildings hid
'squalid poverty and dirt.' He was referring to the dubious
sources of the city's wealth. But it wasn't just the trade in
contraband goods but a kind of institutionalized brutality
and callousness that underpinned daily life in both cities. As
Shanghai's great chronicler Lynn Pann describes it, in 1935
alone, the municipal corporation in Shanghai collected more
than 5000 corpses of poor people from the pavements of
the International Settlement.

The British claim to represent civilized Western values
in India somewhat limited the potential for exploitation
in Bombay and the deaths by starvation. But no such
commitment to civilization was deemed necessary in
Shanghai, where modern capitalism assumed its most
rapacious forms, and where an axis of gangsters, politicians,
and foreign businessmen effectively ruled the city until the
communist takeover in 1949. Bombay had its sadistic police
officers but there were more of them in Shanghai, where
Sikh policemen imported from India were always ready to
fire upon unruly Chinese.

Unrestrained greed and brutality largely defined the
foreign presence in Shanghai. But those decades of semi-
colonial occupation, when Shanghai came to be known
as the 'The Whore of Asia,' glow with an old-fashioned
glamour in such films as Zhang Yimou's *Shanghai Triad*
(1995), Chen Kaige's *Temptress Moon* (1996) and Merchant–
Ivory's *The White Countess* (2005). And it is possible for
expatriates today to retreat entirely from the flashy present
into the sepia-tinted Shanghai of the pre-communist era—

in the style commemorated by the designers of Shanghai Tang, probably Asia's most famous fashion brand. At the Old China Hand Reading Room, a bookshop-café on one of the elegantly shaded streets in the French Concession, coffee addicts linger late into the night amid the Ming-dynasty-style decor. Until recently, a jazz band plays in the Peace Hotel's Tudor bar, ageing Chinese saxophonists blowing out 'These Foolish Things.' Borscht soup, the culinary legacy of the White Russians, can still be found on Shanghai menus.

The truly destitute are invisible in Shanghai, though you can easily spot the visitors from the impoverished countryside in their faded blue Mao jackets and dusty shoes gazing awestruck at the super-malls on Nanjing Lu and the luridly throbbing neon lights of Pudong, the ultra-modern extension of Shanghai, which make the 'peaceful rise' of China appear, apart from everything else, an occasion for lovers of kitsch. One day on the Bund I found a beggar—the only one I saw in several walks around the city—and he was so melodramatically seedy that I half-wondered if he had been put there by the tourist board as a reminder of the city's sordid imperial past.

Sitting in the lobby of my hotel in one of the kitsch towers of Pudong, the famous Shanghai novelist Wang Anyi said, 'There is no culture here!' But culture doesn't seem required yet in this sleek new part of the city which, built in less than a decade on the once desolate mudflats across the river from the Bund, is designed to project the wealth and power of globalizing China.

Skyscrapers of a postmodern snootiness dwarf the Bund's pseudo-colonial domes and clock towers, which were once a reassuring sight to the taipan or straw-hatted tourist arriving from Europe. Gleaming new industrial parks—with landscaped gardens to soften the harshness of working conditions—sprawl across the suburbs. After what seems to have been a brief communist interlude, Shanghai has regained its role as the engine of the Chinese economy and the premier Asian city of capitalism.

The fruits of China's export-driven economy are only partly apparent to most Chinese. More than 150 million Chinese still survive on a dollar a day; about 200 million of the rural population is crowding many of the world's most polluted cities in search of livelihood; and millions of Chinese participate in the astonishing tens of thousands of protests recorded each year. But among the vast showrooms of Armani and Ferrari, where a new elite works hard to prove that, as Deng famously declared, 'to get rich is glorious,' the China where local party officials impose arbitrary fees and taxes on taxes, and where public health and primary education systems deteriorate due to lack of state investment, seems remote.

Business and management books and biographies of American CEOs dominate the massive bookshops on Fujian Road, where in the 1920s and 1930s many Chinese intellectuals read Marx and Lenin and dreamed of revolution. BlackBerried American and European businessmen crowd hotel lobbies and expatriate cafés and bars—slicker versions of the old taipans, they can still be heard complaining of high local wages and the shortage of skilled labour. Nightclubs once again heave with griffins, or single young white men, often escorted by more than one Chinese woman. And demand for amahs dominates the classified pages of local newspapers.

After the communist takeover in 1949, the Paris of the East sank into drabness and austerity, and it was not until China's economic reforms, which began in the early 1980s, that the expats returned. The more liberal economic and social climate encouraged thousands of Australians, Americans, and Europeans to move to Shanghai, following a huge influx of Taiwanese. In the late 1980s, Shanghai had yet to emerge from decades of communism and still struck foreigners as an alien city. Many early expatriates didn't venture out much, living or socializing at the Portman Hotel on Nanjing Road, the first high-end hotel in Shanghai, and working at the adjacent Shanghai Centre. In the mid 1990s, they began to spread across the city. Shanghai now attracts some of the best talents from the large Chinese diaspora spread across Southeast Asia. The new bars and restaurants on the Bund are still obliged by local authorities to fly the Chinese flag. But even the bright red cloth emblazoned with stars seems to add to the general impression of capitalist gaiety.

The old historic heart of the city has been razed to meet the ramifying needs and desires of this new elite. Everywhere in the city luxury villas have sprung up to accommodate expatriate businessmen, senior Communist Party officials, and nouveau riche Chinese. Shortly after I left Shanghai I read that the central government in Beijing, presumably acting on its own report that up to 90 per cent of land acquisition in the cities was illegal, had banned the allocation of land for these villas. But many of them already stand, often alongside demolished housing for the poor, and in their bewilderingly mixed facades—American colonial-style decking, neoclassical columns, baroque plasterwork, Tudor beams—they symbolize a city under fresh occupation by the transnational elite.

Most other people make do with what they have—and in a society as unequal as China's they have the consolation of knowing that it is superior to what others possess. One afternoon soon after arriving in Shanghai I found myself on one of the elevated expressways that, moving swiftly away from downtown, lead to the clusters of high-rise housing estates built for Chinese expelled from their downtown neighbourhoods of *longtang* alleys and lanes.

Rust and grime already tainted these buildings; and it wasn't hard to imagine the cramped rooms, the lack of water pressure, the malfunctioning lift, and the Chinese residents with plastic buckets trudging up and down the gloomy stairs. But the inhabitants of this premature decay still seemed privileged, compared to other cast-offs of Shanghai, residents of the remoter suburbs, who were crammed in subdivided houses with enclosed balconies, with a view of oil-blackened dust lanes and exposed drains.

I was travelling that day to meet Professor Zhu Xueqin, the most famous among the Chinese intellectuals claiming to be 'liberal.' In 1998, Zhu, often openly critical of the communist regime, had introduced a popular and controversial book, *Pitfalls of Modernization*, that the Chinese authorities had subsequently banned; and I expected to meet someone living in somewhat straitened circumstances.

Zhu's home, however, turned out to be in a gated residential complex called California Gardens—the exuberant and oddly placeless architectural styles of the houses with private garages and small front gardens lived up to their name. Visitors to such oases are expected to maintain their Western-style order and cleanliness. I took off my shoes at the front door to Zhu's house and encased my feet in what looked like two plastic shower caps. The open-plan living room in which Zhu, a genial, gracious man, seated us had a gleaming faux-marble floor, a staircase leading to bedrooms upstairs, and a marble fireplace that Shanghai's mild winters seemed to have left unused. A half-finished bottle of Chinese wine—wine, too, is one of the many realms in which China is trying to catch up with the West—stood on the dining table on one corner.

The house suggested growing cosmopolitan ease and comfort, a life of regular travel to and communications with the West, one of the many increasingly available to Chinese intellectuals. But the journey to it had been hard and long for Zhu.

He had just completed elementary school in Shanghai when the Cultural Revolution began. In line with Mao's desire to expose intellectuals to the conditions of the working class and peasants, Zhu voluntarily spent four years in one of the poorest regions in Henan province with a group of idealistic students who wished to combine a life of manual labour with self-directed study. In 1972, he moved with them to a factory and spent ten years there, working through the day and reading at night, before eventually resuming his formal education in 1982, just as Deng Xiaoping began to marketize large parts of China's state-controlled economy.

Zhu did not linger over those ten years of factory labour; and he described his experience of the Cultural Revolution without self-regard or rancour: how his reverence for Mao gave way to a distrust of not just the Chairman but also of the idea of revolution, and mass political movements as they had existed in the modern world since the late eighteenth century.

It turned out that Zhu had spent his long exile more profitably than most, reading whatever he could find, including books on the French Revolution and Rousseau, on which he eventually wrote a PhD thesis. Among his luckier discoveries in a bookshop frequented by senior party leaders had been an account of Gandhi in a book by Chester Bowles, reluctant Cold Warrior and American ambassador to India in the 1950s and 1960s.

Mao, Zhu told me, had denounced Gandhi as a counter-revolutionary, and that had settled the matter for many Chinese. But, reading Bowles's book, he began to think that Gandhi, who had inspired a democratic revolution without violence or coercion, was greater than Mao.

He still had the book, and he now fetched it from his bedroom upstairs. Handling the tattered volume, its pages giving off a sharp smell of mildew and seeming oddly ancient in that sparkling new suburban home, I felt Zhu's gaze upon my face. 'Even Nehru was greater than Mao,' he said.

Zhu's own allegiance is not to Gandhi or Nehru, to either the former's critique of modern industrial civilization or the latter's Fabian socialism. He is among the majority of Chinese intellectuals who since the 1980s have advocated for China's rapid modernization along Western lines.

Zhu is too independent minded to revere Milton Friedman and Friedrich Hayek, godfathers of Reaganomics and Thatcherism, who became popular in China in the

1980s. He has no time for the neo-Confucianist and the neo-authoritarian intellectuals who periodically offer to fill the ideological vacuum of the post-Mao Chinese state. And he carefully qualifies his support for the influential attempt, launched by an expatriate Chinese academic, to implicate writers and intellectuals of China's May Fourth Movement (1919) in the disasters of Maoism.

His writings on culture and politics invoke an old-fashioned humanism, and though he fears that the latter's possibilities in China may be stifled by a commodified mass culture, he believes that what the country needs is a truly free-market economy, which guarantees all other kinds of freedoms, and is inseparable, at least in its ideal form, from democracy.

This is also the broad consensus among other Chinese liberals, who support market reforms but accuse the communist regime of not modernizing China in the way it matters most: by granting legal and constitutional rights to the people. Many of these 'dissidents,' such as Liu Xiaobo, Liu Junning, or the Christian Yu Jie, feature prominently in the American media's coverage of intellectuals in China—a coverage which often seems underpinned by the post-Cold War assumption that free markets guarantee democracy, and which oscillates between describing the excesses of the authoritarian communist government and the ripening fruits of the free capitalist economy.

But liberalism in China is an ideology under perpetual siege; and it wasn't clear to me if Zhu realized the historical reasons for this, or understood that he, too, partook of a Whiggish narrative of progress, which describes the universalization of liberal democracy and underpins most newspaper editorials, political commentary, and speeches in the West.

The specific socio-economic conditions in which both liberalism and democracy became possible, such as the Reformation's stress on individual responsibility or industrial capitalism, were particular to Western Europe and America. They couldn't be recreated elsewhere easily, especially among countries trying to catch up with the West. Japan, the first non-Western country to try to become modern, became an economic and military power without enshrining liberal concerns for individual rights.

Before Japan, there was Germany, another society that embarked on industrialization relatively late compared to Western Europe, and was modernized by a strong centralized state. Neither Germany nor Japan embraced the traditions of Anglo-American liberalism, which encouraged individualism, laissez-faire economics, and a fundamental distrust of state power. Individual rights were subordinated to the economic and military imperatives of countries lurching late into the modern world.

Few Japanese wished to criticize their government as their country rapidly modernized in the late nineteenth century under the not-so-benign gaze of Britain, Russia, and the United States. Even during the politically favourable conditions of Taisho Japan or Weimar Germany, liberals wanted the state to devise and implement social welfare policies for the benefit of the working poor. Reacting against modern capitalism's built-in inequalities, they trusted in bureaucratic management of the economy (preceding, in some ways, the liberal New Dealers of the United States).

Many Indian liberals, too, stressed state initiative in many areas of public life. India's first prime minister Jawaharlal Nehru was a democrat who ensured that individual consent, periodically sought through elections, would legitimize the great power of the Indian state. But his liberalism had a communitarian and paternalistic bent. The state was to hold great prescriptive powers in the realm of the economy. The Indian constitution held that free speech, too, could be circumscribed in favour of the public good. Alas, a straight line runs from this pragmatic acknowledgement of a diverse society to the present, when just about anyone—a small-town mullah as well as a thuggish politician—can claim to be attacking artists and writers on behalf of the public good. Liberal democracy in India has never seemed more feeble.

But it is China that poses the bigger challenge to the Anglo-American faith in the onward march of liberalism and democracy. It has achieved spectacular growth without embracing electoral democracy. Moreover, the state controls the commanding heights of the globalized economy. And, notwithstanding Zhu's beliefs, there is no sign that this will change any time soon.

China's experience as a late developer is crucial in understanding its peculiar trajectory. Liberals, always a minority among the country's leaders and thinkers, had little chance of flourishing against a backdrop of civil war and foreign invasions. China's biggest challenge, for much of the twentieth century, was survival and self-strengthening. Chinese leaders had to first establish, in double quick time, a centralized national state that could provide security and stability in a dog-eat-eat world of international relations.

Unlike the Japanese, who developed an indigenous *kokutai* family conception of the state, the Chinese had to systematically overhaul the body politic in order to command loyalty from its citizens. Having discarded their imperial system, Chinese leaders—Chiang Kai-shek as well as Mao Zedong—had to inculcate a sense of nationalism and national identity from scratch through mass education and propaganda.

Individual challenges to the state's arbitrary power were ruthlessly crushed. The heirs of Mao finally recognized the blunders of investing too much economic initiative with the state. But even Deng Xiaoping, while liberalizing the economy, did not break with older imperatives: of mobilizing China's resources to make it truly autonomous and secure, and postponing the expansion of individual freedoms.

'Development is the only hard truth,' Deng claimed. 'If we do not develop then we will be bullied.' Speaking of the 'China Dream,' the new Chinese leader Xi Jinping upholds the same imperatives of national unity, strength, and pride against the need for democratic reform. And he may be right to think he has a receptive audience. Soothsayers have been predicting the collapse of the Chinese regime for decades. In recent years, they have now transferred their hopes on to the main beneficiaries of China's economic growth: the middle classes. The leadership transition in late 2012 generated much wild talk about imminent revolution.

But China's middle classes seem too fragmented to mount an effective political movement, let alone spark revolution. And to many Chinese left behind by economic growth, the remote apparatchiks in Beijing may appear more committed to their welfare than an affluent minority devoted to further self-enrichment.

And it is not Chinese liberals who have articulated the intellectual suspicion of, and political resistance to, the claims of globalization—especially the dominant neo-liberal ideology that offers no deeper solution for poverty and inequality than the vague promise that the rising tide of private wealth would eventually lift all boats. It is some of the Chinese writers, academics, and activists, known collectively as the 'New Left,' who have emerged in the last decade as the most prominent critics of China's supposed 'economic miracle' and its increasingly visible social, cultural, and environmental costs: the dismantling of the welfare state, extreme inequality and corruption, rising unemployment, and an air and water pollution so widespread that a thick pall of grey permanently lies over, and rivers literally run black across, large parts of the country.

Many Chinese I met credited writings by New Left thinkers in the mid to late 1990s for starting an intellectual debate over China's modernization, which the country's near double-digit economic growth seemed to have rendered moot. Even the New Left's critics—and they are legion among the 'neo-liberals,' 'post-modernists,' 'nationalists,' and 'old-guard Maoists' that flourish in the new Chinese marketplace of ideas—acknowledge their growing influence among even official circles.

But Zhu was sceptical of the New Left, especially of its advocacy of social movements among workers and peasants. China, he told me, needed more, not less, of market-oriented reforms, and he blamed growing inequality and injustice on excessive state interference in free-market mechanisms—the 'visible foot' stamping on the 'invisible hand.'

China, he said, also needed more openness to the West. He had little time for nationalism, which the New Left saw as a potentially positive resource. Chinese nationalism, he claimed, was a form of anti-Japan and anti-West xenophobia, stoked by the communist regime in order to give itself legitimacy. As the Cultural Revolution had proved, mass political movements were most likely to create chaos and strengthen totalitarian tendencies rather than promote democracy.

These were conservative rather than liberal views, of a recognizable Western cast. But few people seemed more entitled to them than Zhu, who had lived through the frenzies of Maoism. At one point, his son, a tall youth with a long ponytail, joined us. I asked him what he did, and he replied with a grin, in English that for a moment seemed perfect, 'I am a muckraker.' He went on to explain that he was a journalist with one of the bold new Chinese magazines, permitted, if only up to a point, to expose official corruption and incompetence, and the exploitation of workers and peasants.

Based in Beijing, he had been travelling the previous fortnight in Jiangsu province. Investigating a 'model village' held up by party officials as evidence of the success of China's market reforms, he had uncovered a familiar story of cronyism and bloated statistics. He interrupted my conversation with Zhu frequently; and his questions were intelligent and sharp. His confidence couldn't have been possible in the times that Zhu had lived through; it belonged to contemporary China, to a climate of diverse tastes and opinion shaped as much by Chinese editions of MTV and *Vogue* as by *People's Daily*. And the smile on Zhu's face whenever his son asked me for a clarification seemed to speak not only of a paternalist pride but of a conviction that, after the human waste and failure of the Maoist years, China had begun to find its way, and individuals such as him, previously subsumed by collectively defined needs and identity, could now make a small claim upon the world, and even be regarded as a moderate success.

Yet, returning to downtown Shanghai that evening, through the sprawling evidence of plunder and dispossession, I wondered whether Zhu, recoiling from the disorder of the Cultural Revolution, was like those middle-class people in poor countries who after having fought their way to a private stability and security couldn't bear to see them undermined: people who sensed, often correctly, the demand for social and economic justice as a personal threat and unconsciously hoped to size democracy down to legal and constitutional formalism, which inevitably empowered the well-educated and affluent minority more than the underprivileged majority.

Gandhi and Nehru were greater than Mao, Zhu said, and I had briefly wondered then if this was a special gesture to me, his first Indian visitor. But then such comparisons had once been part of everyday conversation for many Chinese and Indians.

In recent years India and China have increasingly starred in a triumphalist historical narrative—a history, essentially, of how Western capitalist modernity has shown the right way of progress and development to non-Western peoples. Yet for many Indians and Chinese their national experience and identity was primarily shaped by the struggle for freedom from Western military and economic domination.

India and China, emerging as sovereign nations in the late 1940s, and committed to a vision of socialist modernization, kept a curious and wary eye on each other. The two countries became particularly close in their first decade of independence, trying to resist American pressures to join the Cold War, and to define a neutralist foreign policy for young postcolonial nations. At the historic summit meeting of new Asian and African nations in Bandung in 1955, Mao and Zhou Enlai appeared to be Nehru's natural comrades, engaged in an equally momentous task of lifting hundreds of millions out of poverty and destitution.

Abruptly, then, India and China went to war in 1962 over a disputed border, one of the many arbitrarily drawn by the British during their domination of South Asia. The Indian army initiated hostilities by constructing 'forward posts' inside Chinese territory; but the Chinese PLA counter-attacked successfully, expelling Indian soldiers from China before declaring a ceasefire and withdrawing to their previous positions. The humiliating Indian defeat broke an ageing Nehru's spirit and appears to have hastened his death. Mao and Zhou Enlai now appeared in the Indian imagination as treacherous; and many Indians, increasingly dependent on American sources for information on China, came to see the country through the fears and prejudices of Western Cold Warriors.

There was much tragic misunderstanding here: though

a personal friend of Zhou Enlai, Nehru had trapped himself into a nationalist corner and eventually military action by insisting on the sacredness of borders created by British imperialists. In a memoir by a former general of the PLA published in China, Zhou Enlai is quoted as being embarrassed at having to fight a fraternal Asian country. Nevertheless, the war inaugurated a long period of mutual hostility and indifference, which was broken only in the late 1980s, as ruling classes in both countries began to liberalize national economies, rendering their border dispute increasingly irrelevant.

Indian politicians and businessmen and their supporters in the English-language media watched with envy the flow of capital into China—ten times greater than the foreign investment in India—and the rapid transformation of its coastal cities. These new Indian elites, impatient with Nehru's vision of economic equality and social justice, pointed to Deng Xiaoping's reforms as a model of how the creation of wealth must precede the planned eradication of poverty, disease, and illiteracy.

Many Chinese intellectuals, as I discovered, had watched closely how democracy in their neighbouring country—the unique experiment of granting universal suffrage at one stroke to all citizens—had ensured a much greater degree of public accountability in India than in China. But many privileged Indians themselves increasingly saw representative politics as a nuisance—one of the reasons, they said, why India had not received as much foreign investment as China. Far from taking pride in its press freedoms or expanding its constitutional liberties, many in the small middle class created by the country's early investments in higher

education were exasperated with manifestations of mass
democracy—especially the flexing of electoral muscle by
low-caste groups in the 1980s, which caused a middle-class
exodus to the upper-caste Hindu nationalists. Chafing at
India's protectionist policies, these Indians regarded the
Singaporean strongman Lee Kuan Yew as their hero and his
squeaky-clean authoritarian state a more suitable political
model for India than Westminster democracy.

Ironically, it was post-Mao China that, in the late 1970s,
embraced the Singapore model: technocrat-supervised
national development by a one-party state. The country's
world-class infrastructure—airports, highways, high-speed
railroads—would have been inconceivable without an
efficient state that ruthlessly appropriated land from peasants
while providing financial assistance and the best scientific
and technical expertise.

For many Indians what China proved (though this was
left unsaid) was how an authoritarian system helped rather
than hindered economic growth on the neo-liberal model,
ensuring that labour laws, trade unions, the legislature or
the judiciary, and the fear of environmental destruction did
not much get in the way of the privatization of state assets,
dispossession of agricultural land, subsidies and tax cuts for
rich businessmen, and the concentration of wealth in fewer
hands than before.

There are still more poor people in India and China
than in all of Africa. Nevertheless, elites in both countries,
having promised to usher their billions into a Western-
style consumer society, now make claims upon the world's
richness as assuredly as their American counterparts.
Striking oil deals in Lagos, Tehran, and Caracas, they scour

the world for iron ore, steel, copper, and timber. China and India also increasingly rank among the world's largest spewers of carbon emissions.

Both countries, encumbered with dynastic elites and crony capitalists, are also struggling to persuasively reaffirm their founding commitments to mass welfare. Protests against corruption and widening inequality rage across their vast territories, while their economies slow dramatically.

If anything, public anger against India's political class appears more intense, and disaffection there assumes more militant forms, as in the civil war in the centre of the country, where indigenous Maoist militants in commodities-rich forests are battling security forces. India, where political dynasties have been the rule for decades, also has many more 'princelings' than China—nearly 30 per cent of the members of parliament come from political families.

The two countries produce, too, a similarity of aspirations and outlook among the newly enriched sections of its population. How easy it was to recognize the rich farmer's house that I visited in a tea-growing village in Zhejiang province: the marble floor, the 26-inch television set, the big poster of the white girl with the inexplicable tear in her eye, the thickly and garishly upholstered sofa, the WC with the shower cubicle and open-hole toilet, and the kitchen with the brand new microwave and other underused mod cons.

To be an Indian in Chinese cities is to find familiar not only the vast crowds, the vivacious life of the streets, the open-fronted shops and food stalls but also the malls with the luxury brand names, the shiny new Mercedes and BMWs marooned in the intransigent traffic, the billboards for *American Idol*-like TV shows, and the blogs and websites mixing sexual exhibitionism with jingoistic nationalism.

Attracting millions of hopeful immigrants from the hinterland, Chinese cities are expanding uncontrollably. Life is mean and desolate for most of the new arrivals, such as the young foot masseuse in Suzhou who, after telling me a moving story of migrant helplessness (sudden death of father, long uncertain journey to the East from Sichuan), tentatively placed a hand on my crotch.

Living and working in extreme squalor, the lowly producers of cheap exports for the West offer the grimmest images of industrial capitalism since the nineteenth century. Nevertheless, there is enough money in private hands in such cities as Shanghai, Beijing, Hangzhou, Nanjing, Qingdao to give their downtowns the gloss of post-industrial Western prosperity and consumerism. And, in any case, it is the urban rich who are the poster people of neo-liberal ideologues, proof of the magical efficacy of free markets, potentially millions of educated and self-confident people who have long induced among Western business and political elites the wet 'China Dream' (one billion new customers for Western goods and values).

Periodically, this dream is replaced by paranoid nightmares about the 'China Peril' (one billion new rivals for the world's resources). Nevertheless, it is hard not to wonder about the political outlook of the affluent Chinese class, and their present inability to articulate it through elections does not make any less urgent the question of what kind of role they are likely to play within China as well as the world at large.

For, given the chance to vote, many newly privileged Indians have failed to prove the thesis that free markets and regular elections leads to an enlightened and harmonious society. Like the Bush-voting Americans, India's new middle class tends to be conservative, if not reactionary, consistently and overwhelmingly electing the Hindu nationalists as their representatives, despite the latter's repeated assaults on Muslims and equally murderous indifference to the rural poor—the hundreds of millions of Indians who are trapped in the cycle of crippling poverty and debt, some of them vulnerable to militant communist movements that draw, ironically, their inspiration from Mao.

In India, big industrialists such as the Tatas and Ambanis, together with the emerging middle class, grow fonder of such business-friendly politicians as Narendra Modi, whose complicity in the murder of over 2000 Muslims in 2002 didn't prevent his landslide re-election—or dampen his ambition to become prime minister. In expropriating public resources for private industrial and infrastructural projects and suppressing his critics, Modi is the primary Indian exponent of capitalism with Chinese characteristics.

In China, too, it could seem that the loss of the old national purpose has resulted in a fragmented and divided society, many of whose most empowered members sought little more from politics than the protection of their own interests. This indifference to politics—conspicuous, too, among privileged youth in India—cannot be blamed entirely on censorship or fear. Many young people I spoke to—those born after the death of Mao Zedong in 1976—expressed a brisk nationalistic paranoia about Japan and America, but otherwise seemed too busy trying to make—and spend—money to be interested in discussing how China, once one of the most equal countries in the world, became one of the most unequal.

It is also true that many Chinese people increasingly follow diverse occupations and live very differently from each other, and the resulting social fragmentation cannot but lead to either apathy or political parochialism. The melting of Tibetan glaciers, the desertification of northern China—and the related deforestation of Borneo—came as news to the celebrity designer I met in Shanghai. Even the intrepid blogger in Beijing, much celebrated in the American press, saw democracy as little more than free speech. It is as though Deng Xiaoping's gamble with the economy has worked; and the prospect of personal enrichment and new forms of consumption has more than compensated for the lack of political freedom and vision.

The loss of moral and ideological moorings can also seem part of China's normalization, its integration into the prevailing global order—what the literary critic Chen Xiaoming calls the state of 'postpolitics.' And it has of course been always easy to conclude that Chinese politics is a simple matter of a totalitarian state holding down a population longing for Western-style freedom and democracy.

Yet there are reminders throughout the country, often far from the glittering downtowns, of a complex Chinese relation with their revolutionary past and counter-revolutionary present. This is evident not only in the commemoration of Mao in T-shirts and posters, or in the reverence with which villagers hoping for justice outside central government headquarters in Beijing speak of their departed leader. The signs are also there in the still widely prevalent 'culture of the masses,' reflected in the middle-aged and elderly dancing unselfconsciously in public parks and on pavements and the groups of old Chinese singing revolutionary songs at memorial museums everywhere.

The presence of this revolutionary past in China is not easy to grasp for even someone like myself, who grew up in a somewhat similar climate of postcolonial and socialistic idealism in India, and then witnessed its rejection by hectically globalizing elites. For India, which escaped the kind of Japanese militarism and civil wars that ravaged much of China during the 1930s and 1940s, had a largely bourgeois revolution. Since many of the feudal and bureaucratic elites retained, or even enhanced, their power in the postcolonial state, India knew greater stability and continuity, and regular elections, however inadequate, saved it from the autocratic arbitrariness that resulted in such disasters and tragedies as the Great Leap Forward and the Cultural Revolution. This also meant, however, that land reforms were never fully carried out and old feudal social and economic structures survived in large parts of the country, often overlaid by fresh inequalities.

In China, the Communist Party strengthened its primary base among peasants by destroying old feudal elites. Much more than Nehru, Mao saw an egalitarian national culture and ideology as indispensable to the new Chinese nation, and deemed the creation of a new Chinese subjectivity even more valuable than economic development. Few elites, feudal or communist, survived his persistent and often brutal campaigns to level hierarchies, and to inculcate a revolutionary culture and self-awareness in the Chinese masses.

It explains why the caste and class consciousness that

marks social and political relations deeply in India today still appears to be new in China. It also explains why, despite the natural appeal of a neo-liberal world view in which economic inequality appears to be a natural, even desirable, stage in the transition to a widely accessible utopia of consumerism, many among the urban intelligentsia in China continue to see egalitarianism as a moral value, and to fear the dissolution of old bonds of class, community, and region and the general sense of anomie and alienation caused by raw forms of capitalism.

Such an apparently old-fashioned concern for the moral and spiritual health of society at large is evident in the work of even the young 'Sixth Generation' film-maker Jia Zhangke, who was born in 1970, too late to know either the idealism or disenchantment of the Cultural Revolution, or to share the Chinese euphoria over Deng's economic reforms in the early 1980s.

Much of post-Mao Chinese cinema that first reached the West in the 1980s and 1990s—the work, in particular, of Zhang Yimou and Chen Kaige—had an inadvertently epic quality, partly because it tried to capture a historical experience of suffering and survival that had not been seen before on film. These films made it possible for many Chinese to reckon, at least partly, with their recent past; their work also satisfied Western critics with a taste for national allegories in non-Western literature and cinema. But now as Zhang and Chen join a transnational artistic elite and pander to a blandly global taste for exotica, the epicness of their films verges on self-parody, just as magic realism in Third World literature often now seems no more than a set of formulaic gestures.

Jia's films mostly describe individuals in contemporary China unmoored from old collectivities, and exposed to unsettling new possibilities of personal fulfilment. *Xiao Wu* (1997) portrays the fate of a pickpocket left behind by the new and sophisticated forms of criminality in China. *Platform* (2000) follows a cultural troupe in the late 1980s coming to terms with new commercialized forms of mass entertainment, and *The World* (2004) depicts the small-town immigrant workers living among a kitsch fantasy of the West at a theme park in Beijing.

Jia himself, the son of a professor who was exiled to the countryside during the Cultural Revolution, grew up in a small town in Shanxi, one of the poorest Chinese provinces. And as in this very long scene in *Xiao Wu*, in which the pickpocket, shunned by his semi-respectable friends, sits silently with a karaoke bar girl on a bed in a small room facing a highway, his films are eloquent with all the dismal poetry of left-behind lives in globalizing China—the peeling paint in dark rooms, the hollow television echoes from the next-door shack, the plaintive horns of passing trucks on the highway, and the deepening sense of a life that is now happening elsewhere, or not at all.

Using neo-realist narratives to describe the losers, drifters, and slackers of the New China, Jia resembles many older post-Mao intellectuals and artists who have turned to exploring the most recent ordeals history has imposed on ordinary Chinese people. Exhausted by the propaganda demands of the Cultural Revolution, and wishing to move away from political representation, these writers and artists initially borrowed heavily from Western postmodern and avant-garde sources. But, in a China changing fast under the pressure of Deng's market reforms, they soon redefined their aesthetic.

Yu Hua, one of China's best-known literary novelists, told me that he had started out as a formally experimental writer in the 1980s, looking up to Jorge Luis Borges and Gabriel García Márquez in conscious reaction to the official norm of socialist realism. But as the 1980s wore on he felt less and less the need to challenge state propaganda, and instead chose to portray experiences of ordinary rural and small-town people in such straightforward narratives as *To Live* (1992) and *Chronicle of a Blood Merchant* (1995).

When I met Yu in Shanghai he appeared to be enjoying the success of his novel *Brothers* (2006). The novel describes how two siblings orphaned during the violence of the Cultural Revolution fare in the aggressively materialistic China of the 1980s and 1990s. The younger brother sets up a beauty pageant for virgins, while the elder surgically enlarges one of his breasts in order to peddle a line of breast enlargement gels in the countryside. With its explicit, and often exaggerated, violence and sex, the novel certainly must have tested the censors in China. But Yu insisted that he had only described a commonplace reality in China. 'Things were bad during the Cultural Revolution,' he said, 'but what we are seeing now is total moral breakdown.'

It was a version of what I heard often: from celebrity writers and artists such as Wang Anyi and Yu Hua as well as ordinary people who attested to a daily life that is relatively free of state control but, deprived of the support networks of community and social security, and exposed to rampant venality, is increasingly unstable and anxious.

Deng's and his successors' obsession with GDP growth

has failed to offer the Chinese a collective and individual vision more inspiring than the idea that to get rich is glorious (with the somewhat deflating proviso that, as Deng added, it was important to 'let some get rich first'). And it could seem, watching the films of the Sixth Generation, reading contemporary Chinese fiction, or hearing the countless stories about selfishness, corruption, police brutality, and callousness, that China, apparently rising and increasingly prosperous, was in the midst of a deep crisis that was as much moral and intellectual as political.

But what appears to the outsider as crisis is considered an opportunity by the New Left intellectuals. Cui Zhiyuan, a professor at Tsinghua University who collaborated with the Brazilian economist Roberto Unger in a series of cautionary articles on Russia's post-communist experiments with a market economy, told me, 'We are still in a phase of development where we can innovate, build new institutions designed for Chinese conditions, whereas things are fixed in Europe and America, and all even left-wing politicians do is some minor tinkering.'

In 1993, Cui, then an economist at the Massachusetts Institute of Technology, published an article titled 'A Second Emancipation' in the Hong Kong journal *Twenty-First Century*, arguing that after emancipating themselves from orthodox Marxism, Chinese intellectuals should liberate themselves from blind faith in Western-style capitalism. 'Those were the days of neo-liberal orthodoxy,' Cui said, 'everything from the West was wonderful, so I became notorious; people shunned me.'

Since then Cui and his New Left colleagues have emerged as some of the most eloquent and influential critics of Chinese neo-liberalism. Arguing that China needs an 'alternative modernity,' they do not seem conventionally left wing: among the inspirations of Wang Hui, the prominent New Left author of a four-volume history of modern Chinese thought, is Zhang Taiyan (1868–1936), a linguist and classicist attracted to Buddhism. And the intellectuals draw upon a broad range of thinkers on political economy and globalization—John Stuart Mill, Fernand Braudel, Karl Polanyi, Immanuel Wallerstein, and Joseph Stiglitz—in their critique of the globalized neo-liberal model of economic growth.

Wang told me that he could not agree with Zhu Xueqin's view of the free market and the state as mutually opposed entities. The commonplace Chinese nexus between local party officials, bankers, and real estate speculators was proof that apparently free markets depend more often than not on brute state power. Nevertheless, New Left intellectuals neither see the Chinese state as homogenous nor wish to overthrow or diminish it; rather, they hope to make the state more responsive to the plight of workers and peasants through what they call 'institutional innovation' and the pressure from grassroots social movements of workers and peasants. They praise, too, the state's role in formulating and implementing policies in the earlier phase of economic reform, which they believe are to be credited more than the 'invisible hand' for China's ability to withstand such crises of global capitalism as the ones that overwhelmed East Asian and Latin American societies in the previous decade. Seeking to check the power of such transnational institutions as the World Trade Organization and the International Monetary Fund, they advocate, much like Western critics of globalization, greater openness and transparency in both domestic and international economic arrangements.

In recent years, Cui's articles in *Dushu* (Reading), a monthly journal of ideas co-edited by Wang Hui, influenced a significant debate over property rights in the communist-run legislature, the National People's Congress. His writings against high tax cuts and subsidies for Chinese and foreign exporters also attracted much official attention. Wang Hui has written extensively about the illegal privatizing of, and subsequent labour unrest in, a highly profitable factory in his hometown Yangzhou. He subsequently helped the factory workers to pursue a lawsuit against the local government responsible for the sale of the factory to a real estate speculator.

Wang told me that intellectuals on both the left and the right had been too obsessed with the state and the market, thus neglecting the growing number of social movements for labour and immigrant rights and environmental protection that have the best chance of expanding democratic rights in China today. 'After all,' he said, 'workers and African-Americans and feminists and other minorities in America, too, had to fight for these rights in a long struggle against entrenched elites; they weren't all guaranteed by the framers of the American constitution.'

Speaking to me of market reforms in China, Wang distinguished between two forms of 'marketization.' 'The first kind is market economy developed from local social relations, small goods, and low-profit production and the other in which state-owned property is illegally acquired.'

Wang blames corruption, large-scale unemployment, and the disintegration of social security in contemporary China on this second kind of 'marketization.' 'It is,' he says, 'a process of reform dominated by the state, but in the form of state withdrawal.' He is also alert to, and fears, the other paradoxical possibility of neo-liberalism in China: how, as in Russia, the anarchy unleashed by an unfettered market could make the authoritarian state appear not only necessary but also attractive.

When I met Wang in Beijing, almost four months after his article on the Yangzhou factory first appeared, I was initially surprised to see it still freely circulating on the Internet, even though the Chinese authorities, presently in a repressive mood, had temporarily closed down *Bing Dian* (Freezing Point), a weekly supplement to the popular *China Youth Daily*, in February, ostensibly for carrying an article critical of Chinese Marxist historiography.

Wang was eventually ushered out of *Dushu*, an apparent victim of ideological struggles and intellectual conflicts within the Communist Party. But the relative immunity of Wang and his colleagues from state persecution not only hints at the increasingly arbitrary rather than systematic nature of political repression in China. It also points to ideological dilemmas within the post-Deng Chinese state—what the New Left itself sees not as a monolith but as a system of extremely intricate relations of interests at both central and local levels.

To get rich may have proved glorious for millions of Chinese, but post-Mao Chinese regimes find themselves unable to shed the legacy of the Chinese Revolution. For the cyber-nationalism of a newly enriched urban minority, stoked occasionally by the communist regime against Japan and America, has not, and perhaps cannot, replace the old promise of equality and justice—what still legitimates the regime in the eyes of millions of Chinese, preserves the Chinese state's traditionally high authority, and makes China less likely to suffer a Soviet Union-style disintegration.

The Chinese Communist Party's public invocations of socialism may be no more than an attempt, neglected during the Deng era, to build national cohesion around quasi-socialist values and ideas, especially as social unrest grows across China. Nevertheless, the choice of words reveals how potent the word 'socialist,' barely mentioned in official circles in the West today, remains in China. It shows, too, how the communist party with its rhetoric of social welfare still monopolizes the ideological sources of mass political legitimacy in a poor country.

It now draws upon an indigenous discourse, such as neo-Confucianism, in upholding the values of discipline, hierarchy, and harmony. It also remains capable of channelling political consciousness among the middle classes into nationalism. In any case, the growing availability in China of some private freedoms—primarily to consume and travel—has defused at least some of the urge for political change. It is why Chinese liberals like Zhu, who insist on the sanctity of individual rights, seem as powerless and isolated as their counterparts in 1920s and 1930s Japan.

Ignoring their plight, many commentators see in China's ability to survive and adapt proof of an 'alternative' model: a developmental state that, presided over by a technocratic elite, is stronger than society, and places the national community above the individual. But these inverted Sinophiles, or Asianized Whigs, make the same mistake as the ideologues of liberal democracy: China's 'model' is not for universal export either. For it is a product of its peculiar history.

The question before us is: is the model sustainable, and what implications would its failure have for China and the larger world? The late modernization of Japan and Germany, though largely successful, did not lead to peace in Europe and Asia. Rather, economic crises and growing social unrest led to greater authoritarianism at home and jingoistic expansionism abroad. Certainly, China's assertive posture with its neighbours and increasing severity against internal dissidents does not bode well. China may turn out to be another cautionary lesson in the dangers of a country arriving too late in the modern world, its elites determined to regard liberal democracy as an unaffordable luxury

'Alternative modernity' and 'institutional innovation' may sound like mere slogans. But their appeal derives from the fact that the post-Mao reversals of ideology and politics—based on simple moral oppositions between socialism and capitalism, the free market and the state, private and public property—are beginning to lose their force as, blowing through China, the storm of progress continues to scatter debris everywhere. And it seems clear, too, that regardless of what the dreamers of the China Dream desire, China follows, even while ceaselessly propelled into an unknown future, a trajectory defined by the country's own unique history—a path likely to be rendered increasingly tortuous by China's deepening contradictions.

A LEFTIST'S CRITIQUE OF CHINA

I first met Wang Hui at the Thinker's Café near Tsinghua University in Beijing, where he teaches. A small, compact man with streaks of grey in his short hair and a pleasant face that always seems ready to break into a smile, he arrived, as he would to all our subsequent meetings, on an old-fashioned bicycle, dressed in dark corduroys, a suede jacket, and a black turtleneck that would not be amiss on an American campus.

Then co-editor of China's leading intellectual journal, *Dushu*, and the author of a four-volume history of Chinese thought, Wang, still in his mid forties, emerged in the 1990s as a central figure among a group of writers and academics known collectively as the New Left. New Left intellectuals advocate a 'Chinese alternative' to the neo-liberal market economy, one that will guarantee the welfare of the country's 800 million peasants left behind by recent reforms. And unlike much of China's dissident class, which grew out of the protests in Tiananmen Square in 1989 and consists largely of human rights and pro-democracy activists, Wang and the New Left view the communist leadership as a likely force for change. Recent events—the purge of party leaders on anti-corruption charges and continuing efforts to relieve hardships in the countryside—suggest that this view is neither utopian nor paradoxical.

In the last decade and a half, Wang has reflected eloquently and often on what outsiders see as the central paradox of contemporary China: an authoritarian state fostering a free-market economy while espousing socialism. On this first afternoon, he barely paused for small talk before embarking on an analysis of the country's problems. He described how the Communist Party, though officially dedicated to egalitarianism, had opened its membership to rich businessmen. Many of its local officials, he said, used their arbitrary power to become successful entrepreneurs at the expense of the rural populations they were meant to serve and joined up with real estate speculators to seize collectively owned land from peasants. (According to Chinese officials, 60 per cent of land acquisitions are illegal.) The result has been an alliance of elite political and commercial interests, Wang said, that recalls similar alliances in the United States and many East Asian countries.

As he spoke about how market reforms have widened the gap between rich and poor, between rural and urban areas, smartly dressed students browsed through a highbrow collection (Leo Strauss, Jürgen Habermas), checked their email, and sipped their mochas. At the privately owned Thinker's Café and the adjoining All Sages bookshop, Wang seemed to be famous. Students greeted him reverentially; the staff was extra attentive. Yet Wang still belongs to a minority. Recoiling from the excesses of Maoism and the failures of the old planned economy, most Chinese intellectuals, even those with no connection to the state, see the market economy as indispensable to China's modernization and revival. They want more, not fewer, market reforms. For them, China's present instability is caused not by economic forces but by a politically repressive regime that has prevented the emergence of a representative democracy and a constitutional government.

Wang readily acknowledges that China's efforts at economic reform have not been without great benefits. He applauds the first phase, which lasted from 1978 to 1985, for improving agricultural output and the rural standard of living. It is the central government's more recent obsession with creating wealth in urban areas—and its decision to hand over political authority to local party bosses, who often explicitly disregard central government directives—that has led, he said, to deep inequalities within China. The embrace of a neo-liberal market economy has meant the dismantling of welfare systems, a widening income gap between rich and poor, and deepening environmental crises not only in China but in the United States and other developed countries. For Wang, it is the task of intellectuals to remind the state of its old, unfulfilled obligations to peasants and workers.

Despite his invocation of socialist principles, Wang was quick to tell me that he dislikes the New Left label, even though he has used it himself. 'Intellectuals reacted against "leftism" in the eighties, blaming it for all of China's problems,' he said, 'and right-wing radicals use the words "New Left" to discredit us, make us look like remnants from the Maoist days.' Wang also doesn't care to be identified with the radical intellectuals of the 1960s in America and Europe, to whom the term New Left was originally applied. Many of them, he said, had passion and slogans but very little practical politics and, not surprisingly, more than a few ended up with the neoconservatives, supporting 'fantasy projects' like democracy in Iraq.

Wang prefers the term 'critical intellectual' for himself and like-minded colleagues, some of whom are also part of China's nascent activist movement in the countryside, working to alleviate rural poverty and environmental damage. Though broadly left wing, *Dushu* published writing from across the ideological spectrum. Wang's own work draws on a broad range of Western thinkers, from the French historian Fernand Braudel to the globalization theorist Immanuel Wallerstein. 'Intellectual quality is important to me,' Wang said. 'I don't want to run just any left-wing garbage.' The magazine carried abstract debates on postcolonial theory as well as, he claims, some of the most interesting analyses in China of how the government's urban-oriented reforms have damaged rural society. There were restrictions on what *Dushu* could publish, of course, and Wang was frank about them. As with all intellectual journals in mainland China, authors and editors at *Dushu* have to exercise a degree of self-censorship. Articles cannot directly criticize the leadership or deviate much from the official line on subjects that the Chinese government considers most sensitive—Taiwan or restive Muslim and Buddhist minorities in Xinjiang and Tibet.

'I get asked in Western countries, "How do you define your position?"' Wang said. '"Are you a dissident?" I say no. What is a dissident? It is a Cold War category. And it has no meaning now. Many of the Chinese dissidents in America can return to China. But they don't want to. They are doing well in the US. To people who ask me if we are dissidents, I say, we are critical intellectuals. Some government policies we support. Others, we oppose. It really depends on the content of the policy.'

Born in Yangzhou in the south-east province of Jiangsu, Wang was just seven and entering primary school when the Cultural Revolution began in 1966. The decade-long chaos, which traumatized older generations, seems to have left benign memories for Wang. He remembers being taken by his school to work in the villages for a week or two during the school year. 'My generation of urban intellectuals,' he said, with a hint of pride, 'is the last to have first-hand experience of conditions in the countryside.'

He counts the twenty months he spent working in factories around Yangzhou after middle school as a valuable experience. In 1977, he took the first university entrance exams to be held after the Cultural Revolution, during which many universities were either shut or would admit only peasants, workers, and soldiers. 'Thousands of aspiring students,' he reminisced, 'were competing for a single place.'

When he moved from Yangzhou to Beijing to begin his doctoral studies in the mid 1980s, Wang found himself part of an even more privileged class. 'Intellectuals,' he said, 'had been targeted during Mao's time; now, post-Mao, they were the elite again.' And by then, Wang said, they all agreed on what needed to be done: China had to abandon its 'feudal' and socialist traditions and catch up with the capitalist West. Scarred by the Cultural Revolution, intellectuals saw socialism in China as a failure. Consequently, they had,

Wang argues, no real debate on whether a Western-style consumerist society could be successfully recreated or was environmentally sustainable in China. The West, especially the United States, was idealized.

Wang first began to develop his own views on contemporary China while working on a dissertation about one of the most admired of modern Chinese writers, Lu Xun (1881–1936). Lu Xun, Wang explained to me, was a writer of the left, but he was very critical of left-wing writers and activists. He criticized Chinese tradition, but was also an excellent classical scholar. He welcomed the Western idea of progress, but was also sceptical of it. The paradoxes in Lu Xun helped Wang to see that Chinese modernity could not be a simple matter of abandoning the old and embracing the new—as it had been for both Maoists and free-market capitalists.

For Wang, the problems associated with China's uneven development were first identified by the demonstrators in Tiananmen Square in 1989. Wang himself was one of the last protesters to leave the square on the morning of 4 June 1989, as the tanks of the PLA closed in. Normally rather brisk and matter-of-fact, he grew animated as he described in fluent, if occasionally idiosyncratic, English how a 'broad social movement' began to grow out of the distress caused by the shock therapy of market reforms. The students demanding freedom of speech and assembly were certainly the most visible. But there were, he said, many more Chinese in the cities—workers, government officials, and small businessmen—demanding that the government control corruption and inflation, which had shot up to 30 per cent after price controls on basic commodities were lifted.

In the spring of 1989, Wang was a fellow at the prestigious

Chinese Academy of Social Sciences. Wang told me that he saw 'democratic potential' in the protests and felt obliged to participate even though he had reservations about the students' lack of 'theoretical or methodological coherence.' For Wang, the student leaders recalled the Chinese intellectuals of the early twentieth century, who were never more united than when they radically rejected everything in the past. Nevertheless, after the government sought to crush dissent by declaring martial law on 20 May 1989, Wang was drawn deeper into the movement. On the night of 3 June, when the tanks and armoured cars charged through Beijing, killing hundreds of unarmed resisters and injuring thousands more, Wang was among those assembled in the centre of Tiananmen Square. He could hear the gunfire, but some of the more radical among the students still refused to leave.

Wang decided to stay and to try to persuade the students not to sacrifice their lives. 'I knew,' he said, 'that if the result was violence, it would be disastrous for the whole country.' Wang said that his fears were proved right: violence shrank the space for political debate, and the Chinese government used the period of intellectual silence that followed to begin dismantling more aspects of the welfare state, like the state-owned enterprises, that had long offered cradle-to-grave benefits to workers.

Eventually, the students advocating peaceful retreat prevailed and persuaded the PLA to give them safe passage in the south-east corner of the square. Just before dawn, hundreds of students left the square through a narrow corridor, jostled and taunted by hostile soldiers. Within minutes, the students dispersed. Some of them were arrested and sentenced to long prison spells; others fled to Hong

Kong and eventually to the West; many others, like Wang, disappeared for a few weeks.

When Wang returned to Beijing in late 1989, the authorities were waiting for him. 'That was the most difficult time for me,' he said. He was asked repeatedly: 'What was your organization? Who were your associates?' After interrogations lasting for many months, he was sent to the north-western province of Shaanxi, where dozens of other young scholars from Beijing were already undergoing—in the uniquely Chinese way—'re-education' by exposure to rural conditions.

In Wang's case, punishment by pedagogy seems to have been more successful than Chinese authorities could have anticipated. He dates his 'real education' to the time he spent in Shaanxi, one of the poorest regions of China. He was shocked by the obvious disparity between the coastal cities, then enjoying the first fruits of economic reform, and the provinces. He was shocked, too, by his own ignorance and that of his colleagues in the 1989 social movement. 'We had no idea that the old order in much of rural China was in deep crisis,' he said.

The commune system in Shaanxi was dismantled as part of Deng Xiaoping's reforms, and land was redistributed. But the area produced nothing of much value, not even enough food. Deepening poverty led to a sharp increase in crime and social problems; violent conflicts broke out over land; men took to gambling, beating up, even selling, their wives and daughters. Wang lived in a low-lying village where his dormitory was frequently flooded while he slept. Much of his daily work consisted of writing didactic pamphlets warning peasants against gambling and crime; he also worked on the reconstruction of a primary school that had been destroyed by floodwaters. 'It was during that year,' Wang said, 'that I realized how important a welfare system and cooperative network remained for many people in China. This is not a socialist idea. Even the imperial dynasties that ruled China kept a balance between rich and poor areas through taxes and almsgiving.

'People confine China's experience to the communist dictatorship and failures of the planned economy and think that the market will now do everything. They don't see how many things in the past worked and were popular with ordinary people, like cooperative medical insurance in rural areas, where people organized themselves to help each other. That might be useful today, since the state doesn't invest in health care in rural areas any more.'

Many poor people Wang met during his year in Shaanxi saw him as the educated man from Beijing who would tell the mandarins of the central government to send them some help. 'I felt burdened by this role,' Wang said. 'I couldn't tell them that I was in no position to do anything.' Wang returned, he told me, from his ten-month exile with a keen sense of the gap between the worlds of intellectuals and ordinary people.

During his time in Shaanxi, the influential *Journal of Literary Review* denounced his research on Lu Xun as an example of 'bourgeois liberalization.' Nevertheless, Wang had no trouble returning to academic life.

Wang doesn't like to talk much about 1989. He complains about the 'stereotype' of China in the Western media conjured by Tiananmen. Nonetheless, our conversation about Tiananmen was unusual. While travelling through

Chinese cities, I had found it hard to get people to talk about it. When Deng Xiaoping sought to bury the ghosts of Tiananmen for good by calling for speedy market reforms in 1992, he may well have calculated that the prospect of personal wealth—and access to Western brand-name goods—would compensate many newly enriched people for the lack of political democracy. If so, he seems to have been proved right. The largest public disturbance in China since Tiananmen occurred in August 1992, when hundreds of thousands of Chinese tried to buy shares in the newly opened stock exchange of Shenzen.

The effort to create wealth in urban areas through export-oriented industries—part of the 'let some get rich first' policy announced by Deng Xiaoping and affirmed by his successors—has given the Chinese economy an average growth rate of 10 per cent in the previous decade. Yet China remains one of the world's poorest countries. More than 150 million people survive on a dollar a day. About 200 million of the rural population are crowding the cities and towns in search of low-paying jobs. Millions of Chinese participate in tens of thousands of protests recorded each year, and these statistics may not fully convey the rage and discontent of Chinese living with one of the world's highest income inequalities and deteriorating health and education systems, as well as the arbitrary fees and taxes imposed by local party officials. Much of this, Wang said, could be laid at the feet of the 'right-wing radicals' or neo-liberal economists who cite Milton Friedman and Friedrich Hayek (advocates of unregulated markets who inspired Ronald

Reagan and Margaret Thatcher in the 1980s) and who argue for China's integration into the global economy without taking into account the social price of mass privatization. And it is they, Wang added, who have held favour with the ruling elite and have dominated the state-run media.

Only in the last decade, Wang said, have intellectuals of the New Left begun to challenge the notion that a market economy leads inevitably to democracy and prosperity. Wang, who helped found an academic journal called *Xueren* (The Scholar) after returning from exile in 1991, was well placed to observe those intellectuals. As they came into greater contact with Western academics and scholars, they became more aware of problems not just in European and American societies but also in post-communist countries that were trying to bring their planned economies closer to neo-liberal models. China's intention to join the World Trade Organization (which it did in 2001) provoked unexpectedly sharp debates among scholars. As Wang described it, the terms of the debate had changed: 'Many people knew by then that globalization is not a neutral word describing a natural process. It is part of the growth of Western capitalism, from the days of colonialism and imperialism.' Which is not to say that the New Left embraced an easy anti-globalist position; it has been critical of recent anti-Japanese and anti-American outbursts among urban, middle-class Chinese—of what Wang dubbed 'consumer nationalism.' That, Wang said, was the same kind of globalization that America advocates: 'It is really a form of hypernationalism, which is why you hear talk of tariffs and penalties on China when American economic interests are hurt.'

Wang paused and then added: 'Many people also learned

that the reason the Chinese economy did not collapse like the Asian tiger economies in 1997 was that the national state was able to protect it. Now, of course, China with its export-dominated economy is more dependent on the Western world order, especially the American economy, than India.'

In January 2006, Wang published a long investigative article exposing the plight of workers in a factory in his hometown, Yangzhou, a city of about one million. According to Wang, in 2004 the local government sold the profitable state-owned textile factory to a real estate developer from the southern city of Shenzen. Worker-equity shares were bought for 30 per cent of their actual value, and then more than a thousand workers were laid off after mismanagement of the factory led to losses. In July 2004, the workers went on strike. In what Wang calls an agitation without precedent in the history of Yangzhou, the workers obstructed a major highway, halted bus traffic, and attacked the gates of local government buildings.

Wang told me that he was helping the workers to sue the local government. He had spent time working in a nearby factory before college and this, he said, made him feel a particular connection to them. He remembered that his pay had been low—less than 2 dollars a month by current exchange rates—but, he said, what was crucial was that the workers he knew then felt secure in their jobs. 'People claim,' he said, 'that the market will automatically force the state to become more democratic. But this is baseless. We only have to think about the alliance of elites formed in the process of privatization. The state will change only when it is under pressure from a large social force, like the workers and peasants.'

Wang's story about Yangzhou is not unique. There are many accounts of how local government officials controlling public property have amassed fortunes by privatizing state assets. According to a report by the Nobel-winning activist Liu Xiaobo, who was subsequently jailed on spurious charges, more than 90 per cent of the 20,000 richest people in China are related to senior government or Communist Party officials.

For Wang, democracy is not just a simple matter of expanding political freedom for the middle class or creating legal and constitutional rights for a minority already substantially empowered by market reforms. Democracy in China, he said, has to be based upon the active consent and mobilization of the majority of its population, and be able to ensure social and economic justice for them.

Yet for some New Left intellectuals, like Cui Zhiyuan, a close friend and collaborator of Wang's who teaches political science at Tsinghua University, there is opportunity in the collision of capitalism and socialism. 'There is more space here for new ideas,' Cui told me as he described why he had returned to China after many years in the United States. 'The capitalist system is fixed in the West, but things are still in flux in places like China and India. We have a historic opportunity to build a better, more just society than the West.' For Cui, it is important to clarify the concepts first. 'It is not helpful,' he said, 'to see socialism and capitalism as opposed and separate. Both have travelled together in the twentieth century. Not just European welfare states, even American capitalism has a socialist component, which was arrived at after compromise with the trade unions.'

In recent years, Cui has found a receptive and powerful

audience on an issue that lies at the very foundation of the Chinese socialist state: the collective ownership of property. Liberal Chinese economists argue that private property is sacred and inviolable in a market economy, a radical idea in the Chinese context. In an article he published in *Dushu* in 2004, Cui challenged this notion, emphasizing the essentially communal nature of property ownership. He cited Thomas Jefferson's decision to reword John Locke's principles of life, liberty, and property with life, liberty, and happiness in the Declaration of Independence.

'Jefferson recognized,' he said, 'that property rights emanate from society, not from nature. That's why there was no specific article on property rights in the US Constitution and it had to be brought in later through the Fifth Amendment.' Cui went on to relate with something close to glee that his article had circulated widely among legislators in the National People's Congress, China's parliament, in 2004. It had helped, he said, to provoke a debate that led the Congress to adopt a compromise amendment to the constitution, similar in wording to the Fifth Amendment to the US Constitution, which simply states that no person 'be deprived of life, liberty or property without due process of law.'

The New Left's advocacy of a welfare state is being increasingly echoed within the communist leadership, which is fearful of social instability and is keen to consolidate its power and legitimacy. In March 2006, a few weeks before I met with Wang, the National People's Congress convened in Beijing and unexpectedly became a forum for the first open ideological debate within the party for years. Legislators accused government officials of selling out China's interests to market forces. Such was the anti-market mood that a bill to defend private property and grant land titles to farmers—one that both foreign investors in China and Chinese businessmen had been lobbying for—was not even discussed. Describing major new investments in rural areas, the Chinese premier, Wen Jiabao, emphasized that 'building a socialist countryside' was a 'major historic task' before the Communist Party. He also outlined steps to balance economic growth with environmental protection.

A German journalist told me that it was the most left-wing speech he had heard from a senior Chinese leader during his eight years in Beijing: 'Even American and European politicians don't talk about achieving a Green GDP.' Wang agreed. He said that he was also pleased to see President Hu Jintao and Premier Wen Jiabao focusing on relations with Asian countries. 'We were too obsessed with the United States during Jiang Zemin's time,' he said. 'We really need to improve our relations with Japan and India. We belong to such old and distinguished civilizations, and we cannot just be simple followers and imitators of America.'

'It is a huge achievement,' he added, a smile on his face, 'that the premier should openly admit that health care and education is a failure. It has never happened before.' Wang said he thought that the government was sincere about eradicating rural poverty. But he was still cautious. 'There has been so much decentralization in China,' he said, 'that it is not easy to translate central government policy into action.' In September 2006, in the first purge of a high-ranking party member since 1995, the central leadership removed the Shanghai party chief on corruption charges, leading to speculation that there would be a reconfiguring of relations between the central government and provincial leaders and perhaps a shift in policy towards shoring up social-welfare systems and stemming pollution. Wang remained sceptical. 'The Shanghai case is encouraging at least,' Wang said in an email message. 'I think there will be some political results from it, but they are results rather than reasons.'

The dangers of failing to improve conditions for the majority are clear to Wang: 'If we don't improve the situation, there will be more authoritarianism. We have already seen in Russia how people prefer a strong ruler like Putin because they are fed up with corruption, political chaos, and economic stagnation. When radical marketization makes people lose their sense of security, the demand for order and intervention from above is inevitable.'

In attacking corrupt local governments, the New Left often seems to want to institute a Big Brotherly government of the kind authoritarian politicians like. Certainly the growing accord between the central government's socialist rhetoric and New Left ideas makes many uneasy. Lung Yingtai, a well-known Taiwanese writer and democracy advocate, told me that she was wary of the New Left intellectuals, who, she said, appear too close ideologically to the communist regime. Taking this view one step further, Liu Junning, a popular liberal political theorist who left China in 1999 after being blacklisted by the Chinese government but has since returned, claimed that the New Left was another name for the nationalistic old guard of the Communist Party, which was inspired by hatred of the West.

While this seems an exaggeration, Wen Tiejun, a former

government official who runs rural reconstruction projects and is identified as New Left, had attended what he called 'brainstorming sessions' with Hu Jintao and Wen Jiabao. Typically, intellectuals in communist countries (Vaclav Havel or Adam Michnik, for example) have gained moral authority by assuming a critical stance towards the all-powerful state. How do New Left thinkers in China calibrate their relationship with a state that has imprisoned many of their colleagues and generally shown little tolerance for criticism of the party?

When I posed this question to Cui, he momentarily lost his exuberant manner. 'It is a very important question,' he said. 'How to deal with the government, both morally and intellectually. This is a big challenge for us.'

Cui does not regard the communist regime as a 'totality.' There were, he said, many different aspects of it, at both the local and central levels. 'Almost every day,' Cui said, 'the *New York Times* carries reports of peasants agitating against the communist government, but if you listen to what the peasants are saying, they are telling the central government that the local government has violated their rights. So even the peasants can see the different aspects of the state, who supports them and who doesn't.'

Wang Xiaoming, professor of cultural studies at Shanghai University, positions himself to the right of Wang Hui but says that he sympathizes with the New Left's pragmatic attitude towards the communist regime. 'Civil society is very weak in China,' he said, 'and since the government is the most active agent of change, we have to push the government to do what it should do besides pushing the government to give up some of its powers.'

When I met with Wang Hui for the last time, he dismissed any claims about increased New Left influence over the regime. 'What we have tried to do is create an intellectual situation in which new policies can be explored,' he said. 'I know that many leaders read Wen Tiejun's article; they also read Cui's article on property rights. There have been other articles in *Dushu* that have been equally influential, and I am pleased about this. But we have no other connection with the regime.'

Wang also seems to have no anxiety that ideological convergence with the regime will turn New Left intellectuals into pro-government policy wonks and hacks, part of an old Chinese tradition of intellectuals advising the state. 'We look at things from a Chinese perspective naturally, but we also try to think beyond the framework of the nation state,' he said. 'People ask in the West, how could China develop capitalism with an authoritarian state? But that's ignoring how modern capitalism grew in the West, without much democracy and with the help of imperialism and colonialism. You have to ask whether this unique economic model of the West can be globalized without great wars and destruction of the environment. This is not an abstract issue. China has stopped felling its forests, most of which have disappeared, but some country still has to produce wood for Chinese consumption.'

At our last meeting, Wang also spoke more about a subject Cui had brought up with me: how the rise of China and India throws up new challenges and possibilities with profound implications for the world at large. 'Western societies have been on top for the last two centuries and shaped the world with the decisions they made,' he said. 'China and India will now play equally crucial roles in the new century. But what will they be? I think it is very important for Chinese and Indian intellectuals not just to imitate the West. They have to explore alternatives to the Western model of modernity. Otherwise, the "consumer nationalists" are already saying, "America was on top; now we are on top."'

Wang laughed, and added, 'This is not interesting.'

THE POET

In 2007 in Beijing I met Woeser, a Tibetan poet and essayist (she uses only one name). Unusual among Tibetans in China, who tend to avoid talking to foreigners, she spoke frankly about Chinese rule over Tibet. Denouncing the recently built railroad to Lhasa as a 'colonial imposition,' she said that the communist leaders in Beijing hoped to use the 4 billion dollar project to speed up Han Chinese emigration to Tibet and to plunder the province's abundant mineral resources.

Views such as these, which have made Woeser famous among Tibetans both in China and in exile, have got her into trouble with the Chinese authorities. In 2003, they banned Woeser's most popular book, *Notes on Tibet*; they also fired her from her government job in Lhasa as editor of the magazine *Tibetan Literature* and forbade her to leave China.

Ordered to undergo 're-education' by writing articles praising the railroad to Lhasa, Woeser left Tibet, and now lives in Beijing with her husband, Wang Lixiong, a writer of Han Chinese ethnicity who specializes in Tibet and Tibetans and in China's other ethnic minorities. Both Woeser and

Wang depend for a living on the Chinese-language press in Hong Kong and Taiwan, and, occasionally, the relatively independent periodicals published in southern China. She also posts articles and poems on blogs, which the Chinese authorities keep shutting down. Policemen constantly monitor the apartment she shares with Wang and his mother in suburban Beijing.

For a Tibetan dissenter, Woeser has an unusual background. Her half-Tibetan father was part of the advance guard of China's PLA that 'peacefully liberated' Tibet in 1951, establishing communist rule over a mostly Buddhist population and eventually forcing its erstwhile ruler, the Dalai Lama, along with thousands of Tibetans, to flee to India. Born in 1966, Woeser grew up in an army family, learning to read and write Mandarin rather than Tibetan, and she never questioned the Chinese presence in Tibet until, in her mid twenties, she came across a book by the American journalist John Avedon about the modern history of Tibet and its devastation by the Chinese.

In 2000, she met Wang Lixiong, who encouraged her to publicly criticize Chinese rule over Tibet. In 2005 a team of translators in India and Europe rendered some of Woeser's and Wang's essays into English. Privately published in Switzerland, and impelled more by political urgency than literary ambition, the translations are scarred by solecisms, typos, and misspellings. A large part of the book consists of Wang's theories about likely constitutional arrangements in the future between a democratic Beijing and ethnic minorities. Nevertheless, the book—especially Woeser's personal essays and Wang's critique of Chinese policies—is important for what it reveals of Tibet today:

how the province's modernization under Chinese auspices has acquired its own momentum.

The violence suffered by Tibet during the Cultural Revolution (between 1966 and 1976), when Red Guards hunting for 'capitalist-roaders' and 'feudal rightists' killed Buddhist monks and destroyed temples and monasteries, appears to belong to the past. Helped by more than a million tourists and generous subsidies from Beijing, the economy of the Tibet Autonomous Region is registering faster growth rates than China's national average. Its wide boulevards lined with glittering shopping malls, office buildings, nightclubs, hairdressing salons, and massage parlours (which are often poorly disguised brothels), Lhasa retains few traces of its medieval origins that were visible to visitors only several years ago. Billboards with Deng Xiaoping's gnomic statement 'Development is the only rationale,' a common sight in Chinese cities, loom everywhere, underlining that Lhasa, too, has been enlisted into the swiftest and biggest urbanization in history.

Woeser, however, is not impressed. In an article on the commercializing of the Potala Palace, the seat of the Dalai Lama, she writes:

Under the dizzying Lhasa sunlight, the material desires of Tibetans have never been fueled by such excitement; but, after all, how many average Tibetans can actually afford those luxurious cars and restaurants that stretch along the two wings of the Potala Palace walls and spread around the square; they all look like clones of large or small cities in inland China. Together with the 'modern' buildings covered in porcelain tiles, with windows framed in aluminum inlaid with dark blue glass, they are the culture of 'contractor troops' made up of peasant-turned-construction-workers from the inland.

Judging China's modernization from the vantage point of an older, subtler civilization, Woeser finds it wanting in both tact and taste. She exhorts Tibetans to choose their ancestral ways in language, architecture, and dress. Careful to say that tradition must be rescued from 'ignorance and conservatism,' she upholds it as a form of resistance against the more vulgar forms of modern Chinese culture:

> Even if we are powerless to resist railway construction, mining, and all kinds of development carried out by the Chinese government, at least we can restrain ourselves from building Chinese-style hotels, restaurants, and shops, or attracting customers and tourists to the business of gambling, karaoke, and Han and Tibetan prostitutes.

Much of this may sound like the anti-modern rhetoric of contemporary Islamist movements. Woeser told me that she wasn't against modernization per se. She said that Tibetans ought to be able to choose their own form of modernization, one suitable to their physical landscape, religion, and culture. China's connections with its rural past and traditions were broken by the successive disasters and tragedies of the communist revolution; it had, and has, little choice but to rush headlong into an urban and purely materialist future. But Tibetans, who have preserved their culture against great odds, neither desire nor deserve the fate of the Chinese.

Woeser told me about the American novelist and travel

writer Paul Theroux, who in the 1980s travelled to the then
rail terminus of Golmud in Qinghai province, which borders
Tibet. In the book he subsequently published, *Riding the
Iron Rooster: By Train Through China* (1988), he wrote that
the impassable Kunlun mountain range, which begins near
Golmud and forms a natural northern boundary of the
Tibetan plateau, 'is a guarantee that the railway will never
get to Lhasa.'

Woeser said that almost all the reports in the Chinese
press celebrating the rail link to Tibet had quoted this line,
crowing that the extension of the tracks beyond Golmud
proved the American writer wrong. She then added excitedly,
'The reports don't quote his next sentences: "That is probably
a good thing. I thought I liked railways until I saw Tibet, and
then I realized that I liked wilderness much more."'

Lhasa was still far from being made over in the Chinese
image when Paul Theroux visited it in 1986. The Chinese
rather than the Tibetan quarter is now expanding rapidly,
towards the new railway station to the south of the ethnically
segregated city. Luxury hotels are being built in expectation
of visitors from China and abroad. Tibet's high altitude
and remoteness still deter many foreign tourists. But jaded
Chinese with money to spend are discovering what they
take to be the spiritual ways of Tibetan culture, and there
is a growing fascination with the province. Almost every
major Chinese city has shops selling Tibetan knick-knacks.
The streets of Lhasa are full of Chinese youth claiming to be
'artists' and 'seekers'; and groups of nouveau-riche tourists
from the prosperous coastal cities of China throng the

monasteries and temples rebuilt by the Chinese government.

The Chinese regime in Beijing is keen to make Tibetan culture profitable rather than defunct, as was the case during Mao's time. The Chinese authorities are increasingly assisted by a local elite of Tibetan officials and businessmen, who can be seen cruising down Lhasa's boulevards in big cars or dining at expensive restaurants, and whose children—the beau monde of Lhasa—fill the nightclubs around Potala Palace, bantering among themselves in a Chinese full of English words rather than the Tibetan that most of their less-well-to-do compatriots speak.

Many of the Tibetans are investors in the nascent industry of tourism. In an essay, 'A Killing Trip,' Woeser describes travelling to a hot spring with four young Tibetan entrepreneurs. Born in the 1970s, educated in China, these men have resigned from government jobs to become hoteliers. As Woeser describes these members of the small Tibetan business elite, they:

> come from well-to-do families, their parents mostly being
> born to families of "liberated serfs". They love the Party,
> the Party treats them well and generously, so in the being
> of their children is an air of superiority.

Armed with rifles, these brash young men shoot at every animal in sight. They feel no compunction about forcing out some nuns from their convent near the hot spring and turning it into a hotel. Intoxicated by a sense of power, one of them tells an appalled Woeser: 'You like to write about Tibet, you should write about young Tibetans like us. We are masters of Tibet's future.'

This sounds like bragging. Tibetans capable of exploiting the connections between Chinese Party officials and businessmen belong to a tiny minority among the Tibetan population of seven million. Indeed, the biggest Tibetan fear is of being overwhelmed by Han Chinese. In recent years, Tibet absorbed some of the floating Chinese population, estimated to be as big as 100 million, of migrant workers, criminals, carpetbaggers, and prostitutes. These Chinese drifters conspicuously dominate native Tibetans, at least in the main cities of Lhasa, Gyantse, and Shigatse, where they own most of the shops and businesses, including the brothels disguised as massage parlours and hairdressing salons. Tibetan activist groups in the West expect a significant increase in Han Chinese migration to Lhasa in the next few years.

The railroad in Tibet seems to be doing what it has accomplished in recent years in other minority regions. In Xinjiang, Urumqi, the capital, is already a predominantly Han city, and Kashgar's Han population increased by 30 per cent in 2001, the year after the railway there was completed. Ordinary Tibetans told me that rents have gone up steeply in Lhasa since the arrival of the first train. Remarkably, no one among the Tibetans I spoke to expects their lives to be improved by the railway. They all saw it as something devised by, and for, the Han Chinese majority.

In Beijing Woeser told me about a tale that had spread among Tibetans as the railroad crossed into the Tibetan grasslands to the north of Lhasa. Construction workers, it was said, had dug up a frog from the earth. The frog had been badly injured; but as the story moved from teahouse to teahouse he became bigger in each retelling, to the point where, in one story, he had to be hauled off in a truck.

Woeser said that the story would make sense if you knew of the high status of animals as guardian spirits in Tibetan culture. She explained that the frog injured by Chinese workers represented the Tibetan sense of defeat and frustration over the railway.

Certainly a sense of siege lay heavy over the Tibetans who risked police scrutiny in order to speak to me. Listening to them, I often remembered the gloomy prediction of Jamyang Norbu, the Tibetan novelist in exile, who believes that the Chinese are turning the Tibetans into a 'sort of broken third-rate people,' who some years from now will be reduced to 'begging from tourists.'

However, Chinese claims about Tibet present a very different picture; and after allowing for some inflation in official statistics, they have to be taken into account, partly to understand the extreme Chinese distrust of the Dalai Lama. Woeser is right to claim that not many Tibetans can enter the utopia of 'development' promised by the Chinese—a consumer lifestyle in urban centres. Most Tibetans living in rural areas have seen few benefits of economic growth. But the Chinese have announced plans to improve facilities for education, health care, sanitation, and transport in large parts of rural Tibet. Both the ongoing extension of the railroad to the southern city of Shigatse and an even more ambitious highway construction plan are expected to integrate the remotest regions of Tibet into the national economy.

To allay fears that the railroad would worsen Tibet's already very serious environmental crisis, the Chinese government has announced many measures, including systems to store garbage and waste water and treat them in designated facilities. The official Chinese documentary on the railroad offers a touching story about Chinese construction workers nursing orphaned baby antelopes, and claims that thirty-three 'animal underpasses' have been put in place under the tracks.

State-imposed modernization tends to incite more resentment than gratitude among the supposedly backward people it aims to uplift. Still, in view of the hectic Chinese efforts to appease it, the Tibetan mood struck me as extremely sullen. 'Virtually all Tibetans,' Wang Lixiong claimed in an article in 2002, 'have the Dalai in their hearts.' More than a decade later, the Tibetans remain defiantly loyal to their long-exiled spiritual leader. That the Chinese have brought, in the meantime, many more roads, bridges, schools, electricity, regular jobs, and salaries to Tibet has not changed their allegiance to him.

In 2006, the Dalai Lama's disparaging remarks about fur-wearing Tibetans sparked bonfires of animal skins and fur-trimmed clothes across Tibet. Mass protests erupted in 2007 in the town of Lithang after police arrested a Tibetan nomad who climbed on a stage erected for Chinese officials at an annual horse festival and, seizing a mic, pleaded for the return of the Dalai Lama to Tibet. Then, after monks celebrated the awarding of the US Congress's highest civilian honour to the Dalai Lama, the Chinese police sealed off the biggest monastery in Lhasa.

In 2008, the Tibetan monastery of Kirti was a focal point for the anti-Chinese protests that consumed dozens of lives and led to the imprisonment of innumerable Tibetans. In March 2011—the third anniversary of the protests—a young

Tibetan from the monastery doused his body with kerosene and set it on fire. Dozens of young Tibetan men and women have immolated themselves since then.

Self-immolation is a radical form of protest for Tibetan monks, a violation of Buddhism's basic tenets of respect for all sentient lives. 'Desperation' was the response from Kyabje Kirti Rinpoche, the seventy-year-old exiled abbot of Kirti monastery, when I asked him to explain the recent spate of self-immolations. He described the repressive measures of local Chinese authorities: indiscriminate arrests; checkpoints on the roads; police camps inside monasteries; and the ideological re-education campaign in which the 2,500 monks at Kirti, confined to their cells, are forced to repeat such statements as 'I oppose the Dalai clique' and 'I love the Communist Party.'

Wang Lixiong has described how the Communist Party's oversized bureaucratic machines in Tibet, which reflexively respond to mass disaffection with heavy-handed measures, impair the central government's ability to provide an imaginative solution to the Tibetan crisis. And Tibet seems, on first glance, an instance of an unremittingly authoritarian and secular regime pressing down on a docile religious population. But it is also true that, as a path-breaking study of the 2008 protests by the Beijing-based NGO Gongmeng law research centre (subsequently shut down by the Chinese authorities) points out, 'there is now a new frame of reference for measuring reality' in Tibet. The report asserts that it is no longer 'a self-sustaining Tibet protected by the natural environment, but a realm which, whether actively or passively, is intimately connected to all of China and the rest of the world.'

For some years now, Tibet has been part of the world's fast-growing and globalizing economy. Many Han Chinese may reasonably wonder why Tibetans, apparently showered with government largesse, are so ungrateful. But as the Gongmeng report points out, 'the assistance and "development" brought by the Han is often accompanied by forced change and conflicts.' The logic of development, for instance, forces Tibetan nomads off their grasslands and brings Han Chinese migrants into Tibet's cities. The unavailability of jobs together with the undermining of Tibetan language has led to a general feeling of disempowerment among the population. And rural–urban inequality has rapidly grown.

Of course, much of the Chinese population also suffers from the humiliation of being left behind by a few lucky rich. But as Wang Hui writes, the gaps of income and opportunity in minority areas are 'closely connected with the difference in traditions, customs, language, and the position in the economic market that exists between ethnic groups.' The radical dissimilarity of *Weltanschauung* (world view) is crucial here. One Tibetan interviewed by the Gongmeng researchers clarifies that 'a Tibetan's prosperity is more about freedoms such as religious belief, a respect for people, a respect for life, the kind of prosperity you get from extending charity to others.' Chinese-style modernization has imposed alien values on Tibetans, forcing them to accept 'development' and 'consumption' as the last word.

The authors of the Gongmeng report sum it up: 'When the land you're accustomed to living in, and the land of the culture you identify with, when the lifestyle and religiosity is suddenly changed into a "modern city" that you no longer recognise; when you can no longer find work in your own land, and feel the unfairness of lack of opportunity, and when you realise that your core value systems are under attack, then the Tibetan people's panic and sense of crisis is not difficult to understand.'

In this sense, Tibetans are akin to other uprooted and bewildered victims of globalization and modernization, such as the Indian villagers protesting against nuclear plants on their lands or the indigenous forest-dwelling peoples in central India resisting their dispossession by a nexus of mining corporations and governments.

The usual simple-minded oppositions between authoritarianism and democracy deployed in discussions of India and China are not of much use here. What these conflicts, cutting across differences in political systems, illustrate is a deeper clash: a powerful and aggressive ideology that upholds social and economic individualism against a traditionally grounded respect for collective welfare and the environment.

But what specific conditions triggered these recent protests in Tibet? The sociologist Béatrice Hibou offers a persuasive answer in her new book, *The Force of Obedience*, which, ostensibly about Tunisia, is also insightful about the psychologies of many other semi-globalized and unequal societies. Hibou describes how it wasn't so much top-down coercion by a one-party state as the promise and practices of inclusion into global modernity—the visible bonanza of GDP growth, the creation and co-optation of local elites, and the myth of an ever-imminent 'economic miracle' that would lift all boats—that had generated a kind of 'obedience' among the majority of the population.

For a long time, things seemed appealingly 'stable' to foreign governments and investors. Tunisia had achieved a satisfactory macroeconomic equilibrium. It was slowly integrating into the world market. The widely advertised possibility that anyone could join the conspicuously consuming new middle class seemed to be defusing political anger among the disenfranchised. And then a poor vegetable vendor called Mohamed Bouazizi broke the spell, burning himself to death and igniting mini-revolutions across West Asia and North Africa.

Writing to Martin Luther King about the dozens of Buddhist monks who immolated themselves in Vietnam in the 1960s, the Vietnamese monk Thich Nhat Hanh clarified that they 'did not aim at the death of the oppressors, but only at a change in their policy.' Events in the Arab world following Bouazizi's death have confirmed the political efficacy of this extreme act of self-negation.

Still, Tibetan self-immolations cause more embarrassment than anxiety among Chinese authorities. As China increasingly appears as a saviour of many struggling economies, the world's conscience looks likely to be as little troubled in the future by Tibet as it is by Kashmir. Most people may also be too distracted by the destruction of their own fantasies of easy wealth and consumption to notice a greater tragedy: that, as Philip Larkin wrote in his poem 'Nothing to be Said,' 'For nations vague as weed/ For nomads among stones . . . Life is slow dying.'

Far from losing his aura during his long exile, the Dalai Lama has come to symbolize more urgently than ever to Tibetans their cherished and threatened identity. Not surprisingly, Chinese authorities are trying hard, if often clumsily, to undermine the Dalai Lama's authority. In 1995, Chinese authorities kidnapped the boy—called Gendun Choekyi Nyima—whom the Dalai Lama had identified as the eleventh Panchen Lama, and installed their own child candidate in this important position in Tibetan Buddhism. (The whereabouts of the kidnapped boy remain unknown.) In an attempt to forestall the Chinese regime from usurping his position, the Dalai Lama announced that he would be reincarnated outside Tibet, guaranteeing that his successor would be born among the Tibetan community in exile. In August 2007, the officially atheist Chinese regime passed legislation effectively banning Buddhist monks in Tibet from reincarnating without government permission. According to a statement issued by the State Administration for Religious Affairs, the law, which stipulates the procedures for rebirth, is 'an important move to institutionalize management of reincarnation.'

Wang Lixiong, who is one of the very few Chinese intellectuals to have met the Dalai Lama, told me that Tibetans have no faith in the Chinese-appointed Panchen Lama, whom they refer to as 'that little brat.' He thinks that the Chinese missed an opportunity in suppressing Gendun Choekyi Nyima, the Dalai Lama's candidate for the seat of the Panchen Lama. Traditionally, Panchen Lamas have had a crucial part in choosing the Dalai Lama, and had the Chinese respected the choice of Nyima and educated him carefully, they would have had a good chance of legitimizing their choice of the next Dalai Lama. As things stand now, few Tibetans are likely to accept the decisions of China's substitute.

Remarking on the missteps the Chinese have made in Tibet, Wang said that market reforms have weakened Beijing's authority. Communications between central and provincial governments have broken down, leading to arbitrary and thoughtless decisions such as the expulsion of Woeser from Lhasa, which has led to her acquiring bolder views and a higher profile in Beijing. Communist Party officials correctly feel themselves most vulnerable in regions like Tibet and Xinjiang, where Han Chinese are a minority; the oppressive atmosphere of the Cultural Revolution still lingers in Tibet, where villagers are required to fly the communist flag and display a picture of a laughing President Hu Jintao flanked by Tibetans in colourful ethnic costumes. Tibetans talking to foreigners invite the attention of the police. By contrast, small spaces for dissent have opened up almost imperceptibly in Beijing and the coastal cities, escaping the scrutiny of officials who are busy either pursuing private fortunes or grappling with corruption, social breakdown, and environmental disasters.

For instance, I found that I could talk to Woeser without fear of police harassment. I met her a few times in my hotel room and once in an Indian restaurant. On two occasions she was accompanied by Wang Lixiong, who was born in 1953 and is thirteen years older than Woeser; his calmly cerebral and courtly presence contrasts attractively with her ebullient manner. Woeser told me that she first heard of him through his outspoken writings on Tibet; Wang was, she said, the first Han Chinese writer to have written honestly about Tibet. They emailed each other for a year before finally meeting in 2000 when Wang visited Lhasa to research an article.

Wang said that Woeser had helped him shed his

condescending Han Chinese perspective on Tibet as an integral part of China and on Tibetans as a backward people. He said, 'It is widespread in China. I still have to be on my guard against it.'

Shortly after corresponding, Woeser sent Wang some revealing photos taken during the Cultural Revolution by her father, an officer with the PLA in the late 1960s, when Red Guards rampaged across Tibet. Wang, who had himself been a Red Guard, encouraged her to interview the people in the photographs, which show scenes of mob fury and individual humiliation, and to write a text to accompany the photographs.

The book was subsequently published in Taiwan. Chinese authorities tend to be very sensitive to anything related to Taiwan and Tibet. But Wang spoke equably of the double hazards for a China-based writer on Tibet publishing in Taiwan. Certainly he now takes risks that would have struck his parents as near suicidal.

Like Woeser, Wang, too, had been born into China's ruling elite. His father, an early member of the Communist Party, received his education at a Moscow polytechnic at the same time as Jiang Zemin, China's former president. Then, in 1968, at the height of Mao Zedong's Cultural Revolution, his father, denounced as a 'capitalist-roader' and 'Soviet-revisionist spy,' committed suicide after months of detention in a cowshed, and his mother, an editor at a film studio, was sentenced to hard labour in the countryside.

Wang spoke with remarkable detachment about the destruction of his parents' lives. As a Red Guard, he said, he had even wondered if his parents were suffering for a noble ideal. He told me that he first became interested in Tibet in the mid 1980s, when, after giving up a conventional career as an engineer, he built a raft out of the rubber inner tubes of truck tires and floated down the entire great length of the Yellow River.

In 1991, he published a novel titled *Yellow Peril*, which became a bestseller before being banned by the Chinese authorities. In 1999, while researching a book about Xinjiang, he was arrested and detained for forty days in the Uighur-majority province. Undaunted, Wang travelled to the United States in 2001, and published an account of his meetings there with the Dalai Lama.

Wang is a member of a 'lost generation' of Chinese youth that was unmoored by the chaos created by Mao in his last years. He struck me as someone who had become fearless while improvising his life. He told me that ethnic minorities like the Tibetans and the Uighurs desperately needed courageous public intellectuals. Tibetans were lucky to have Woeser, who could articulate, both at home and abroad, their wishes and aspirations. He added that it would be a mistake for foreigners to see her simply as protesting human rights violations, for she represented something new: a Tibetan who had come through the Sinicized education and literary system, and who now used her fluency in Chinese to bypass the system of state patronage and participate in the transnational free market in culture that had opened up for Chinese writers in recent years.

On my last afternoon with Woeser and Wang I asked them if I could visit the apartment they share with Wang's elderly mother. Woeser had earlier told me that this was not a good idea since it risked provoking suspicions by the policemen monitoring her home. Now it was Wang who looked doubtful. He said that I could go but that he was very likely to be followed and would rather not accompany us.

Woeser's apartment looked far from downtown on the city map. But the taxi took a freeway running across Beijing's six ring roads, and brought us very quickly to what looked like the edge of the city. Her apartment house seemed new but, like most new construction in China, already touched by decay. I glimpsed uniformed men in the guardroom watching us, and was reassured to see Woeser indifferently walking past them to the elevator.

Wang's mother opened the door. A small, grey-haired, gentle-looking woman, she smiled faintly at us and then abruptly left the apartment—in order to give us, Woeser explained later, more privacy. I remembered what Wang had told me of his father's suicide and his mother's three-year imprisonment in a cowshed during the Cultural Revolution, followed by four years of hard labour in the countryside. I couldn't help staring at her, half-expecting her face to hold some trace of her ordeals. But she looked serene, like many of the old Chinese of her generation I often saw sitting in public parks, on whose faces a cruel history had finally bestowed a kind of grace.

Carefully organized, the apartment looked bigger than its two small bedrooms and kitchenette leading off the living room. Woeser busied herself with tea. I walked over to her desk in one of the bedrooms. The shelf beside her desk held Chinese translations of books by Susan Sontag, V.S. Naipaul, Edward Said, and Orhan Pamuk, among other writers.

Woeser had been dismissive about the few Chinese

writers I mentioned. Wang had explained, 'None of them really say what they feel about China today, so it is hard for us to respect them.' The books on her shelf revealed something of how Woeser, who has never left Chinese territory, had formed her sensibility; how she had arrived at the aesthetic and political judgements that depend on a deep acquaintance with the experiences of other societies.

From where I stood I saw the view from the window: Beijing sprawling to the west, light wintry mist blurring a harsh landscape of new anonymous city blocks, freeways, factory chimneys, construction cranes, and planes hanging low in the sky, waiting to land at the airport to the north. Wang had told me that he saw the communist system in China in serious peril. The Party could not control China any more; it had allowed no other political institutions to grow and when it collapsed the whole oppressive structure was bound to crumble. But looking out of Woeser's window— the planes circling in the sky, as if in homage to the feverishly blooming city—the power and wealth of China could seem unassailable, and Tibet a forgotten, perhaps lost, cause.

Returning to the living room I noticed pictures of the Dalai Lama hanging from one recessed corner; DVD recordings of his teachings were stacked below them. The casual display of the prohibited image in a Beijing apartment, a few hundred feet from a policeman below, startled me. Woeser saw me examining the DVDs on her shelf. She said, 'Tibetan friends of mine often get together to watch them. We dim the lights and project the films on a big screen. It feels wonderful, even though the evenings usually end with all of us in tears.'

Woeser had not spoken to me of her religious beliefs.

I wasn't even sure if she, a writer in the modern secular mode, had any. More likely, images of the Dalai Lama keep alive an idea of Tibet as much for Woeser and her friends in their suburban exile as for the devout farmers in the Tibetan vastness, and the monks and nuns willing to immolate themselves. Such desperate affirmations of Tibetan identity, or Woeser's and Wang's testing of the limits of intellectual freedom in China, may not accomplish much at present. Nevertheless, they show how the great consolidation of Chinese power today obscures many collective and individual gestures of dissent and defiance in Tibet—gestures that may yet cohere into a movement, not so distant perhaps, of political change.

THE IMPORTANCE OF BEING
THE DALAI LAMA

In November 2007, a couple of weeks after the Dalai Lama received a Congressional Gold Medal from President Bush, his old Land Rover went on sale on eBay. Sharon Stone, who once introduced the Tibetan leader at a fundraiser as 'Mr Please, Please, Please Let Me Back Into China!' (she meant Tibet), announced the auction on YouTube, promising the prospective winner of the 1966 station wagon, 'You'll just laugh the whole time that you're in it!' The bidding closed at more than 80,000 dollars. The Dalai Lama, whom Larry King, on CNN, once referred to as a Muslim, has also received the Lifetime Achievement award of Hadassah, the Women's Zionist Organization of America. He is the only Nobel laureate to appear in an advertisement for Apple and guest-edit French *Vogue*. Martin Scorsese and Brad Pitt have helped commemorate his Lhasa childhood on film. He gave a lecture at the annual meeting of the Society for Neuroscience, in Washington, DC, in 2005. In spring 2008, in Germany, he spoke on human rights and globalization. For someone who claims to be 'a simple Buddhist monk,' the Dalai Lama has a large carbon footprint and often seems as ubiquitous as Psy.

As Pico Iyer writes in his book, *The Open Road: The Global Journey of the Fourteenth Dalai Lama* (2008), it is easy to imagine that the Dalai Lama is 'the plaything of movie stars and millionaires.' Certainly, like all those who stress the importance of love, compassion, gentle persuasion, and other unimpeachably good things, the Dalai Lama can appear a bit dull. Precepts such as 'violence breeds violence' or 'the quality of means determine ends' may be ethically sound, but they don't seem to possess the intellectual complexity that would make them engaging as ideas. Since the Dalai Lama speaks English badly, and frequently collapses into prolonged fits of giggling, he can also give the impression that he is, as Iyer reports a journalist saying, 'not the brightest bulb in the room.'

His simple Buddhist monk persona invites scepticism, even scorn. 'I have heard cynics who say he's a very political old monk shuffling around in Gucci shoes,' Rupert Murdoch has said. Christopher Hitchens accused the Dalai Lama of claiming to be a 'hereditary king appointed by heaven itself' and of enforcing 'one-man rule' in Dharamsala, the town in the Indian Himalaya that serves as a capital for the more than 150,000 Tibetans in exile. The Chinese government routinely denounces him as a 'splittist,' who is plotting to return Tibet to the corrupt feudal and monastic rule from which Chinese communists liberated it, in 1951. Many Tibetans in exile grumble that he is too attached to non-violence, and too much in the grip of Western event coordinators, to prevent the Chinese from colonizing Tibet.

But the ongoing protests in Tibet are a reminder of the

fervour he inspires among the six million ethnic Tibetans. It was a protest on the forty-ninth anniversary of his exile that led to the current civil unrest in Tibet; the initial peaceful demonstrations met with a predictably harsh response from the Chinese authorities. As the prominent Chinese intellectual Wang Lixiong acknowledges, 'Virtually all Tibetans have the Dalai in their hearts.' And the more their economic prospects and traditional culture are undermined by Han Chinese immigration, the more this long-distance reverence is likely to grow.

Iyer writes that 'the heart and soul, quite literally, of the Dalai Lama's life existed precisely in parts that most of us couldn't see.' His arduous daily regimen begins at 3.30 a.m., after which he proceeds, as he told Iyer, to 'meditation, prostration, reciting special mantras, then more meditation and more prostrations, followed by reading Tibetan philosophy or other texts; then reading and studying and, in the evening, "some meditation—evening meditation—for about an hour. Then, at eight-thirty, sleep."'

This sounds like a lot of meditation and reading for a monk in his seventies—especially someone who, beginning at the age of six, underwent a gruelling education for nearly two decades in Buddhist metaphysics, Tibetan art and culture, logic, Sanskrit, and traditional medicine, and eventually secured a *geshe* degree (roughly equivalent to a doctorate in Buddhist philosophy). But Buddhist spiritual practice is relentlessly exacting. 'Strive on diligently' were the Buddha's last words, and even the Dalai Lama can't presume to have reached a summit of wisdom and serenity. It is his fairy-tale childhood that exalts him above most mortals. Born in 1935 to a family of farmers in the outer reaches of the Tibetan cultural domain, he was a two-year-old toddler when a search party of monks from Lhasa identified him as the potential reincarnation of the recently deceased Thirteenth Dalai Lama. Rainbows arcing across the north-eastern skies of Lhasa were among the colourful portents that alerted the monks to his presence. In 1939, the child was brought ceremonially from his mud-and-stone house to Lhasa, and given the run of the marvellously labyrinthine Potala Palace.

The Dalai Lama learned calligraphy by copying out his predecessor's will—which, in its prophetic cast, is one of the spookiest documents in Tibetan history. It was written in 1932, when Tibet, after centuries of uneasy coexistence with its big neighbour in the East, enjoyed a degree of political autonomy. Mao Zedong's communists were still far from winning their civil war with Chiang Kai-shek's nationalists. Nevertheless, the Thirteenth Dalai Lama sensed that Tibet's isolation would soon be shattered by 'barbaric red Communists':

> Our spiritual and cultural traditions will be completely eradicated. Even the names of the Dalai and Panchen Lamas will be erased. . . . The Monasteries will be looted and destroyed, and the monks and nuns killed or chased away. . . . We will become like slaves to our conquerors . . . and the days and nights will pass slowly and with great suffering and terror.

Even if the Dalai Lama shared his predecessor's forebodings, he couldn't do much about them. In the Potala Palace, he lived perilously close to the dark intrigues and conspiracies that had undermined his predecessors, and exposed Tibet's weakness to its overbearing neighbours. The Ninth, Tenth, Eleventh, and Twelfth Dalai Lamas died young, some rumoured to have been poisoned. The Thirteenth Dalai Lama, who barely escaped an assassination attempt allegedly by his own regent, recognized his insular country's vulnerability to the highly organized empires and nation states of the modern world. But his plans for upgrading the Tibetan administration and army were thwarted by a monastic elite that lived off the labour and taxes of peasants and fought brutally to preserve the status quo. In 1934, shortly after the Thirteenth Dalai Lama's death, the reformist politician Lungshar was punished by an ancient Tibetan method of blinding: the knucklebones of a yak were pressed on both of his temples to make his eyeballs pop out.

In 1947, the Dalai Lama, then eleven years old, watched from the Potala Palace through a telescope as monks shot at the Tibetan Army. The weeks-long battle had been sparked by the arrest of his former regent, and it killed dozens. Finally, in 1950, he assumed full political authority as the Dalai Lama. But he had no time to heed his predecessor's warnings against Tibetan apathy. The Chinese communist People's Liberation Army had invaded eastern Tibet and was standing poised to overrun the rest of the country. A decade later, the Dalai Lama and tens of thousands of Tibetans were forced into exile.

The story that the Dalai Lama himself emphasizes to his Western audience is that of his initiation into the modern world—both its vicious ideologies and its redemptive

knowledge of science and democratic governance. This
intellectual journey is what principally interests Iyer, a
novelist, travel writer, and contributor to *Time*, who has
written incisively on the dawning of our present moment
in history 'in which almost every culture could access
every other.' He presents the Dalai Lama as a heartening
product of the same encounters between the old and the
new, the East and the West, that have stung many other
tradition-minded people around the world into a reactionary
fundamentalism.

'In Tibet, the Dalai Lama was an embodiment of an old
culture that, cut off from the world, spoke for an ancient,
even lost traditionalism,' Iyer writes. 'Now, in exile, he is
an avatar of the new, as if having travelled eight centuries
in just five decades, he is increasingly, with characteristic
directness, leaning in, toward tomorrow.' Iyer marshals a
variety of evidence for the Dalai Lama's forward-looking
programme. The Tibetan leader cast doubt on his divine
ancestry, pointing to his premature endorsement of the
founder of the Aum Shinrikyo group, which released sarin
gas in Tokyo subways, as an indication that he is not a 'living
Buddha.' The most famous Buddhist in the world, he advises
his Western followers not to embrace Buddhism. He seeks
out famous scientists with geekish zeal, asserting that certain
Buddhist scriptures disproved by modern science should be
abandoned.

In his public appearances before English-speaking
audiences, he prefers to speak of 'global ethics' rather than
of the abstruse Buddhist concept of Nirvana. Doubtless
he doesn't want to put off the largely secular middle-class
Americans in weekend casuals who crowd Central Park to

listen to him, but, as Iyer points out, this is also a reaffirmation of a Buddhist philosophical vision in which all existence is deeply interconnected. Indeed, this notion may be why the Dalai Lama was early to grasp the existential and political challenges of globalized human existence, decades before they were underlined by the disasters of climate change.

'For the first time in history,' Hannah Arendt wrote in 1957, 'all peoples on earth have a common present. . . . Every country has become the almost immediate neighbor of every other country, and every man feels the shock of events which take place at the other end of the globe.' Arendt feared that this new 'unity of the world' would be a largely negative phenomenon if it wasn't accompanied by the 'renunciation, not of one's own tradition and national past, but of the binding authority and universal validity which tradition and past have always claimed.'

As the spiritual leader of six million people, the Dalai Lama can be credited with a significant renunciation of the authority of tradition—of the conventional politics of national self-interest as well as of religion. Such is his influence that a curt decree from him could trigger a massive, probably uncontrollable, uprising in Tibet. Yet he continues to reject violence as unethical and counterproductive, even threatening to resign from his position as head of the government-in-exile, in Dharamsala, if Tibetan violence against the Chinese persisted. Increasingly, he has been forced to walk a difficult rhetorical line, accusing China of 'cultural genocide' while still supporting its stewardship of the Olympic Games. He has consistently disapproved of even relatively modest attempts to influence the Chinese government, including hunger strikes and economic boycotts. In his view, Tibet needs good neighbourly relations with China: 'One nation's problems can no longer be satisfactorily solved by itself alone,' he has said. He bravely promotes 'universal responsibility' to people who want to be citizens of their own country before they start thinking about the universe.

He speaks remorsefully about Tibet's retrograde and self-serving ruling elite in the pre-communist period, and the country's fatal lack of preparation for the twentieth century. For the Tibetan community in exile, he has introduced a democratic constitution and legislative elections. Recently, he offered his most radical idea yet, one that overturns nearly half a millennium of tradition: that the next Dalai Lama be chosen by popular vote.

The Dalai Lama's awareness, deepening over decades of exile, of the high costs of Tibetan isolationism has helped turn Dharamsala into an exemplary cosmopolitan community, where young Israelis coming off compulsory military duty mingle with freshly arrived refugees from Tibet. Still, it seems remarkable today that the boy who once perched upon a golden throne in a thousand-room palace has become an icon of 'globalism'—the word Iyer uses, occasionally a bit broadly, to denote the decidedly mixed blessings of speedy communications and easeful travel. After all, the Dalai Lama's only consistent lifeline to the metropolitan West when growing up had been the magazine *Life*. (He moved on to *Time* and to the BBC.) Regular exposure to Henry Luce's periodicals did not, however, inoculate the Dalai Lama against Maoism. Visiting China in 1954, during a period of uneasy collaboration with Beijing, the Dalai Lama declared himself to be impressed by the Chinese Revolution. Charmed by Mao's unassuming demeanour, he was startled when the Great Helmsman announced on their last meeting that 'religion is a poison'—the belief that, over the next two decades, helped the Chinese justify killing thousands of Tibet's monks and destroying most of its monasteries.

Arriving in India in 1959, the Dalai Lama was still, Iyer points out, 'an innocent in the ways of the modern world.' He did not visit the United States until 1979, and then his highly technical discourses on Buddhist philosophy baffled his listeners, especially those accustomed to the brisk epiphanies of Zen, the Buddhist tradition in vogue at the time. No celebrity glamour attended the Dalai Lama's initial visits to the country where he was to achieve his greatest fame. The Dalai Lama's Western fan club began to grow only after he received the Nobel Peace Prize, in 1989.

His popularity seems to have been helped, at least partly, by a romantic idea of Tibet promoted in the 1930s by James Hilton's novel *Lost Horizon*, an account of Westerners chancing upon Shangri-La, a valley near the Himalayas populated by a harmonious and pacifist society. Frank Capra's movie version of 1937 (which inspired Franklin D. Roosevelt to anoint his presidential retreat in Maryland Shangri-La, before the prosaic Dwight D. Eisenhower renamed it Camp David, for his grandson) opens with the lines 'In these days of wars and rumours of wars, haven't you ever dreamed of a place where there was peace and security, where living was not a struggle but a lasting delight?' Despite an ample Tibetan history of brutality, Tibetans are still primarily seen in the West as a blessedly pre-modern people, who naturally possess rather than pursue happiness.

Iyer acknowledges this romantic misconception as a political problem for Tibet: 'It feels—or we need to make it feel—more like Shangri-La than a place that could have a seat at the United Nations.' Often, too, the Dalai Lama seems ready to oblige. His decision to simplify and secularize Buddhist teachings has brought him a much bigger audience than the Japanese Zen masters or the Tibetan sages, such as Allen Ginsberg's guru Chögyam Trungpa, who preceded him to the West. But the gentrification of an ancient and often difficult philosophy has not been achieved without some loss of intellectual rigour. In bestselling books by the Dalai Lama, Buddhism can appear to be a ritual-free mental workout, but the form that religion takes for the geshe student cramming the 322 volumes of the Tibetan Buddhist canon is considerably more severe.

The Dalai Lama can claim the sanction of the Buddha, who is said to have altered his teachings in order to reach a diverse audience. Still, there are some limits to the Dalai Lama's pragmatism, however mindful he is of contemporary liberal sensibilities. He supports full legal rights for all minorities, including gay men and women. But, citing Tibetan texts, he remains disapproving of oral and anal sex. ('The other holes don't create life.') Disapproving of sexual laxity and divorce, he can sometimes sound like a family-values conservative.

None of his compromises, however, have aroused as much bitterness as his decision, first announced in 1988, to settle for Tibet's 'genuine autonomy' within China rather than press for full independence. As the Dalai Lama sees it, countries must pursue their interests without harming those of others, and Tibetan independence, in addition to being an unrealistic ideal, needlessly antagonizes Beijing. This stance has failed, however, to convince the Chinese that he is not a 'splittist'; they have accused him of having 'masterminded' the latest disturbances. It has also made many Tibetans suspect that what makes the Dalai Lama more likable in the West—mainly, his commitment to non-violence, reiterated during the current crisis—makes him appear weak to the Chinese.

'The more he gave himself to the world,' Iyer writes, the more Tibetans have come to feel 'like natural children bewildered by the fact that their father has adopted three others.' The Tibetan novelist Jamyang Norbu complains that Tibetan support groups and the government-in-exile have become 'directionless' in trying to 'reorient their objectives around such other issues as the environment, world peace, religious freedom, cultural preservation, human rights—everything but the previous goal of Tibetan independence.'

Avidly embracing the liberating ideas of the secular metropolis, the Dalai Lama resembles the two emblematic types who have shaped the modern age, for better and for worse—the provincial fleeing ossified custom and the refugee fleeing totalitarianism. Even so, his critics may have a point: the Dalai Lama's citizenship in the global cosmopolis seems to come at a cost to his dispossessed people.

As China grows unassailable, it is easy to become pessimistic about Tibet, and to imagine its spiritual leader becoming increasingly prey to fatalism. The Dalai Lama's retreat from the exclusivist claims of ancestral religion and the nation state can seem the reflex of someone who, since he first copied out his predecessor's prophecy, has helplessly watched his country's landmarks disappear. The bracing virtue of Iyer's thoughtful essay, however, is that it allows us to imagine the Dalai Lama as something of an intellectual and spiritual adventurer, exploring fresh sources of individual identity and belonging in the newly united world.

Certainly, Arendt's 'solidarity of mankind,' enforced by capitalism and technology, has become, as she observed, 'an unbearable burden,' provoking 'political apathy, isolationist nationalism, or desperate rebellion against all powers that be.' There are few things that Tibetans lashing out at the Chinese presence in Lhasa today fear more than absorption into the ruthless new economy and culture of China. Iyer's book makes it plausible that the boy from the Tibetan backwoods may be outlining, in his own frequently Forrest Gumpish way, 'a process of mutual understanding and progressing self-clarification on a gigantic scale'—the process that Arendt believed necessary for halting the 'tremendous increase in mutual hatred and a somewhat universal irritability of everybody against everybody else.' It is hard to see the Dalai Lama bringing about mutual understanding in the world at large when he has failed to bring it about between China and Tibet. Such, however, are the advantages of being a simple Buddhist monk that he is less likely—indeed, less able—than most politicians to compromise his noble ends with dubious means, even as he, following the Buddha's deathbed exhortation, diligently strives on.

TRAIN TO TIBET

On an evening in December 2006, amid the chaos of Beijing West Railway Station, I stood in line for a train that looked little different from any of the other long-distance services shuffling into the vast Chinese hinterland. And yet the train I was about to board, the new Chinese service from Beijing to Lhasa, in Tibet, runs on the highest railroad in the world. Traversing a region known for earthquakes, low temperatures, and low atmospheric pressure, the railroad, which cost 4.2 billion dollars to build, is an extraordinary feat of modern engineering—perhaps even, as the former Chinese premier Zhu Rongji has claimed, 'an unprecedented project in the history of mankind.' In two days, the train brings you to a region that thwarted some of the boldest travellers and explorers of the past.

The route's prospect encourages the laziest kind of armchair fantasy—of great expanses of the 'roof of the world' rolling into view with silky black yaks grazing in the grasslands and prayer flags fluttering from gold-topped temples. The train is meant only partly for seekers of Tibet's romance, however. Beijing claims that the railroad between Golmud, in Qinghai Province, and Lhasa, which began operation on 1 July 2005, will help speed up the modernization of the country's second-largest region, one of the remotest and least developed. Many critics, meanwhile, have denounced the railroad as a means for the Chinese authorities to strengthen their hold on Tibet, further settling the region with China's ethnic majority, the Han Chinese, and eroding indigenous Tibetan culture. Tibet, which is almost as big as Texas, California, and New York State combined, also holds vast reserves of copper, iron, lead, zinc, and other minerals vital to China's economic growth.

In the long, disorderly line for the train, there were hardly any foreign tourists. I noticed several Chinese officials cutting ahead, dressed in Western suits and trailed by armed soldiers. Polite uniformed coach attendants stood rigidly at attention outside the pine-green cars, but no one asked to see my expensively acquired permit for travel in Tibet.

Once aboard, I found my 'soft sleeper' cabin, the ticket for which had cost about 1200 yuan, or some 160 dollars. Containing four bunk beds, it seemed very cramped. The introduction of luxury rolling stock is scheduled for the end of this year; the cars will feature private suites measuring a hundred square feet, and tickets will cost 1000 dollars a day. Meanwhile, it seemed that any impulse to luxury, or even basic comfort, had been squeezed out of my compartment. Flat-panel televisions, headphones, and a solitary white plastic rose in a narrow glass vase only highlighted its bleak functionalism. The ceiling was very low, and the space between the lower berths was barely wide enough for one person to stand up in, let alone four passengers struggling with severe altitude sickness.

To my relief, no one showed up to share my cabin. Indeed, despite subsidized fares and Chinese claims that 450,000 people took the train in its first two and a half months of operation, the train seemed far from full. I changed into my nightclothes, and hurried to the toilet at the end of the railcar; squat style, it did not promise to stay clean for long. Back in the compartment, an attendant brought a thermos of hot water and then a rubber tube wrapped in a plastic packet. Wordlessly, he showed me how to attach it to the oxygen valve above my berth. The extra oxygen was a necessary precaution—the air in the mountains of Tibet contains 35 to 40 per cent less oxygen than at sea level—but made the compartment look like a mobile clinic.

As the train slid away from Beijing, a PA system came to life. After a long speech in Chinese, a deep voice with a strange American accent unctuously intoned, 'Dear passengers,' and began to relay impressive statistics about the 700-mile railroad extension from Qinghai to Tibet: laid by 100,000 workers over five years, it traverses 340 miles of permafrost, often at altitudes between 13,000 and 16,000 feet. Chinese pride in the railroad is intense, as I knew from a three-hour documentary that had been broadcast on the state-run CCTV channel in 2006. It had detailed the history of successive efforts by Chinese leaders to build the railway, and the struggles and sacrifices of construction workers, and had also asserted China's commitment to bringing 'modern civilization' to Tibet, which it described as 'a once remote and backward place.' It claimed that Tibetans had been 'yearning for decades' for the rail link to Lhasa, and showed Tibetans singing, in Mandarin, of their love for the Chinese motherland.

Such propaganda notwithstanding, the greatest rail construction ventures in history, in the American West and the Siberian East, do not come close to matching the technical achievement of the railroad to the Tibet Autonomous Region (as the land previously ruled by the Dalai Lama has been officially called since 1965). Laying rail tracks across Tibet's permafrost is especially risky, because the surface is prone to melt as temperatures rise. Chinese engineers faced this challenge with innovative cooling strategies. They elevated tracks; they put in a network of pipes to circulate liquid nitrogen and cold air beneath the rails in order to keep them frozen throughout the year; they installed metal sunshades in south-facing locations to deflect warmth from the sun. Although the carriages of the train looked old to me, they had UV-resistant coatings and an eco-friendly wastewater-storage system, and their underbellies were enclosed to protect wiring from snowstorms and sandstorms. A complex mechanism drew in outside air and released nitrogen and other gases while pumping oxygen-enriched air through the train.

I went to sleep early and woke up when it was still dark outside. For hours afterwards, I lay in bed, waiting for light to nibble at the edges of the curtains. The light, when it came, was grey and dirty. Thick mist lay outside, through which the sun appeared as a sickly yellow blur. The view from the window, divided cleanly by the white plastic rose, did not improve as the day leaked away. Mist, smog, and dust stifled the passing scenery; the only colour lay in sheets of blue plastic covering vegetable fields beside the tracks.

Once, a station sign proclaimed a resonant place name: Xi'an. We were in the antique heartland of China, watered by the Yellow River. Occasionally, the train, moving swiftly and smoothly, appeared to be in a gorge; we seemed to be travelling through Gansu, which has some of the roughest landscape in China.

In the dining room, as plain as an office canteen, the officials I had seen cutting in line on the platform were having a noisy meal, voices raised and chopsticks fluttering in the air. Their guards stood at a respectful distance while a pretty Chinese waitress hovered around them.

Fantasizing about this trip, I had often seen myself in the dining car, eating spicy tofu and drinking green tea, as the train to Lhasa ambled to its highest point, Tanggula Pass. But when the waitress finally delivered to me the tattered English version of the menu, it turned out to be resolutely unglamorous, with 'vegetable stock' but no spicy tofu. I settled for fried eggplant and rice.

Back in my compartment after lunch, I called—on my British cell phone, which miraculously worked—a Tibetan exile in Dharamsala, the Dalai Lama's home town in India. My friend had escaped recently, after living for some years near the railroad in Qinghai. He seemed both surprised and pleased to hear from someone travelling through his old haunts. He told me to compare the number of Tibetan passengers and workers on the train with the number of Chinese. He said, 'No one will talk to you, but just go and count the number of Tibetans.'

I had seen some Tibetans, recognizable by their full faces and burning-red cheeks, on the platform in Beijing the day before. They had seemed as anxious as everyone else to get on the train. In the morning, there had been four young Tibetans—in knock-off Nikes and identical raffish suede jackets—in the dining car. The pretty waitress, who had been ingratiating with the officials, was brusque with them, placing a single menu on their table without a glance in their direction, and then ignoring their attempts to get her attention.

I had been tempted to approach them. But I knew from an earlier visit to Tibet, in 2004, that Tibetans seen talking to foreigners, especially journalists, could invite unwelcome attention from the apparently numerous spies, informers, and plain-clothes policemen. Were Tibetans on the train being monitored? I couldn't tell. But the Tibetan in Dharamsala was categorical about the train's purpose: it was meant to help Han Chinese move to Tibet to take advantage of the benefits and concessions offered by the Chinese government; it was also meant to take mineral resources out of the region.

Shortly before boarding the train, I had heard a fierce version of this argument from the Tibetan poet Woeser. In the bleak greyness of December Beijing, at the hotel where I had arranged to meet her, she struck a defiantly ethnic note, wearing a gold-and-red Tibetan jacket with a side opening, suede boots, and orange-streaked silver earrings. I had expected to meet someone bearing the visible strain of state oppression, but Woeser seemed unbowed. Curiosity animated her broad oval face, making her look much younger than her forty years, and she smiled quickly between bursts of fervent speech.

'The train is a colonial imposition,' she said, and she quoted Edward Said's description of imperialism as 'geographical violence.' She told me that Chinese rule over Tibet had grown much more repressive in the previous two years. She added, 'Han Chinese already dominated Lhasa, and since the train arrived in July the city has changed even faster.' Her vehement tone made me look around nervously for likely eavesdroppers.

A recently translated volume of Woeser's and Wang Lixiong's writings, *Unlocking Tibet*, offers a forthright statement about the Chinese challenge to Tibetan culture and identity. She criticizes the manner in which the Chinese government has restored many Buddhist monasteries and temples that had been destroyed during Mao's Cultural Revolution. The Tibetans who flock to these temples seem to enjoy considerable religious freedom, but Woeser, in an essay on the Potala Palace, accuses the Chinese of turning the Dalai Lama's former residence in Lhasa into a mine of 'unlimited commercial opportunities.'

It was hard not to feel that Woeser, awakening late to Tibet's plight, was trying to make amends, through her ardent denunciations of the Chinese regime, for the long years when she was a member of the Tibetan elite, unthinkingly loyal to its Chinese overlords. I was struck by the similarity of her situation to that of a young Tibetan monk she describes in one of her essays: taken by Chinese authorities to a human rights conference in Europe, the politically innocent man is thrown into confusion and sorrow by an angry crowd of Tibetan exiles accusing him of being a 'Communist lama.'

Woeser's outspokenness about Tibet also disconcerted me because I had found it impossible to meet Tibetans in China willing to speak to me, even off the record. Recent reports by human rights organizations assert that Buddhist monks in Tibet are still forced to denounce the Dalai Lama, and Tibetans are prohibited from possessing pictures of him. Woeser seems especially vulnerable. In 1999, Wang Lixiong was detained and interrogated by security officials in Muslim-dominated Xinjiang for more than a month. A policeman, Woeser told me, permanently monitors their apartment.

I asked Woeser if she wanted me to keep some of her remarks off the record. No longer smiling, she spoke rapidly to the interpreter, and then stared expectantly at me as I listened to the translation.

'I don't care,' she said.

Woeser's emphatic rejection of the railroad made me uneasy—in part because I have loved trains since childhood. My father worked for the Indian Railways, and I grew up in sleepy provincial towns, close to railway yards, where the days resonated with the melancholy sighs of loitering steam engines and the contemptuous shudder of express trains speeding to the distant cities of Delhi, Madras, and Bombay. Every morning, slow mail trains delivered early editions of newspapers that had been printed the night before in their metropolitan bases. I often walked to the railway station to meet them. On the platform, where bundles of newspapers and magazines thrown by invisible hands landed with a dusty thud, I watched with awe as the soot-blackened engineers went off duty. There were rumours about their alcoholism and violent domestic habits, but on these mornings they always seemed to be returning home from heroic expeditions.

By the 1970s, steam was giving way to diesel and coaches were being designed in a modern functional style. But you could still find first-class railcars embodying colonial luxury. I travelled on them with my family on long journeys two or three times a year. As we sat in teak-panelled compartments with glass windows, inset mirrors, and embossed-leather seats, the sensation of movement infused eating, sleeping, and reading with a new sensuousness. The unremittingly dark nights, the stationmaster holding an oil lantern on a deserted platform, acquired a fresh mystery; there was great drama in the figures of peasants working in the flat fields under vast skies, and also in the small-town bazaars, whose garish shop signs managed to stoke longing as keenly as the familiar cries of hawkers that erupted at every stop.

Like much else in India, the railways seemed as though they had always been there. In fact, they were introduced in 1851, by the British, part of a worldwide surge in rail construction during the nineteenth century, which gave governments and businesses freer access to markets and resources in the remotest parts of Europe, America, Asia, and Africa. Indian nationalists accused the British of using railways to plunder their most valuable colonial possession. Mohandas Gandhi, whose political awakening began when he was expelled from a first-class rail compartment in South Africa because of his skin colour, condemned railways as carriers of disease and disrupters of self-sufficient rural economies. But Gandhi's political heirs did not share his suspicion of Western-style modernization and development. Railways continued to expand in post-Independence India, binding far-flung towns and villages into the fourth-biggest rail network in the world. In the film *Pather Panchali*, the first in Satyajit Ray's Apu Trilogy, the symbolically charged arrival of the train in the Bengal countryside heralds the displacement of a rural family.

In tradition-bound China, railways initially incited similar anxieties. Mandarins of China's last imperial dynasty purchased the few miles of rail track that had been laid by European traders near Shanghai and tore them up. But the nation builders of Republican China quickly recognized the political uses of the railways. As early as the 1900s, when China had no real authority over Tibet, Sun Yat-sen, the founder of modern China, had outlined a plan to connect Lhasa to the Chinese rail system. However, civil war and the Japanese invasion ensured that at the time of the communist takeover, in 1949, China had only a few thousand miles of track, mostly in the north and north-east of the country.

Since then, the Chinese rail network has expanded dramatically and become one of the largest in the world. Reaching Golmud, in Qinghai, in 1984 and Kashgar, in Xinjiang, in 1999, it has economically integrated these remote provinces, making them available for large-scale resettlement by Han Chinese immigrants, and strengthening Beijing's political control.

The link from Golmud to Lhasa, across the almost impassable Kunlun Mountains, which form a natural boundary at the north of the Tibetan plateau, has been the most ambitious of China's rail ventures. In 1889, visiting a country deeply humiliated by Western powers, Rudyard Kipling had wondered, 'What will happen when China really wakes up, runs a line from Shanghai to Lhasa . . . and controls her own gun-factories and arsenals?' China has now woken up.

Later in the afternoon, when I walked through the train, the Tibetans seemed fewer and more subdued. Most were in the cheapest, 'hard seats' carriage, tickets for which cost around fifty dollars. Built with scant regard for the human form, the hard seats encouraged a bolt-upright posture for forty-seven hours. The Tibetans had already slumped into a miasma of cigarette smoke and a faint smell of yak butter.

Many of the Chinese were grouped in the 'hard sleeper' compartments, tickets for which cost around a hundred dollars. Empty instant-noodle cups lay on the floor, the PA system was turned up high, and people shouted into cell phones. It was hard to spot potential immigrants among them. Was it the young rake with quasi-punk hair and Lenovo laptop, or the middle-aged man with the *People's Daily* open on a battered leather briefcase? In one cabin, six teenage girls sprawled on narrow bunks, bored faces turned towards the door. There were more of them in the next cabin—two neat rows of equally listless expressions.

With the world outside obscured, a mood of lethargy and irresponsibility seemed to be spreading through the train. In the dining car, the guards, who had been stiffly solemn before their Chinese bosses, were flirting with the waitress. The coach attendants huddled in another corner of the car, smoking.

The commentary droned on: 'Dear passengers, tea is a common drink among Tibetan people.' I listened for a while, hoping for something like the story I had heard on the CCTV documentary of construction workers on the railroad stopping to let migrating antelope pass. But the PA system dealt mostly in bombast. Such-and-such a bridge or tunnel was a 'masterpiece' in the history of rail construction; the railroad was to help develop Tibet in a 'scientific, harmonious way.'

Neither modern science nor harmony seemed to have played much part in the development of the industrial city of Lanzhou, whose outskirts began to drift past the window in the afternoon—an assemblage of rusting machinery, slag heaps, and landfills; of chimneys and brick kilns belching thick smoke; of concrete tenements whose broken windowpanes were held together with cellophane and old newspapers. Western modes of mass production seemed to have recreated in China the squalor of nineteenth-century British coal and mill towns.

China's urbanization—arguably the most expansive and swiftest in history—has already exacted a steep environmental price from Tibet, whose rapidly melting glaciers feed the biggest rivers in Asia. The Marxist faith in the human ability to use technology to conquer nature means that there is no restraint in China on the Faustian fantasy of gigantic public projects, as demonstrated by the Three Gorges Dam, on the Yangtze River, which has already displaced 1.4 million people. When speaking of the railroad to Tibet, the Chinese sound like the true inheritors of the old European zeal for science and industry, as assured as colonial officials of another era were of their superiority over apparently benighted natives.

The railroad's frailty had become apparent in the weeks following its opening. Chinese engineers, however ingenious, had not fully reckoned with global warming, which was raising temperatures faster than expected, and the foundations of the rail line had already begun sinking into the permafrost by the end of July. Thawing could cause tracks to bend and slump, and bridges to crack. In late August 2006, a dining car derailed 250 miles north of Lhasa, with no apparent effect on the train's oxygen supply system. I tried not to think about the journey's likely perils as I drifted off to sleep for the second night on the train.

While I slept, Qinghai, a barren, inhospitable land settled by Chinese political prisoners in the 1950s and 1960s, passed in the night. The train steadily gained altitude. When I awoke, just after we passed Golmud, the air felt thin, although oxygen was now pumping hard into the compartment. Groggily, I opened the curtains and then sat dazzled before a startlingly white landscape—its forbidding aspect tempered and endowed with heartening intimacy by the unearthly radiance of Tibetan light.

All through that morning, the train twisted and climbed through the Kunlun Range, between mountains with needle-sharp peaks and sunny slopes. Occasionally, the mountains retreated, and then treeless valleys opened alongside the tracks, scored by streams of a glittering chalky white. The artificial rose in my compartment now appeared translucent.

The train clattered past empty railway stations and huts with corrugated tin roofing; they looked like temporary dwellings for construction and maintenance workers. The highway to Lhasa ran alongside us, empty except for an occasional military convoy.

The PA system announced the Tanggula Pass, the highest point of our journey. At 16,640 feet, a thousand feet higher than Mont Blanc, the pass is higher than the altitude at which light aircraft fly. I had a mental image of the pass based on visits to other high passes in Tibet: the snowcapped mountains arrayed imperiously against the blue sky, supervising subsidiary ranges that stretched in rich layers below them. But I couldn't tell when we passed Tanggula. None of the cairns or prayer flags that frame views of Tibetan passes appeared. The railway seemed to have forgone some of the dramatic vistas offered by the road. It ascended gently to the Tibetan plateau, without any of the hairpin turns and loops of the kind that trains negotiate in the Himalayas.

The snow on the hills thinned, exposing wind-abraded rock. The ground showed through, brown and stony, and then we were in flat grassland with soft brown hills at the edge, their peaks sugared with snow and resembling the conical caps of Tibetan Buddhist sects.

Once, a herd of antelope skipped beside the tracks. Looking for more of them, I saw black nomad tents on a distant hillside. Yaks with white stripes on their backs appeared in the dank yellow grass. The train whizzed past empty stations; on the rare occasion that we stopped, there were hardly any Tibetans to be seen. This seemed the strangest aspect of a rail service designed to benefit local people: their meagre presence outside as well as inside the train.

I read and napped for a while, and then took another walk through the train. I had a slight headache, and my swollen bag of dried apricots popped easily and spilled its contents on the floor. But the altitude was having a deeper effect on many people on the train. The guards I had seen carousing in the dining car looked drained, barely able to focus their eyes on the flat-screen television. In the chair car almost no one sat upright. The hard sleeper, too, was a mess of slumped bodies. A faint smell of vomit lingered in the air. Remarkably clean so far, the toilet in my carriage had begun to overflow.

Outside, a few walled settlements in the Tibetan style began to appear—fortress-like houses with sloping walls; red, blue, and green prayer flags at the turrets; and flat roofs, often topped incongruously with the red flag bearing communist stars. A few miles out of Nagqu, the biggest Tibetan town north of Lhasa, the sun began to set. Long blue shadows crept down from the stony slopes of mountains even as the lingering light set their snow-flecked peaks ablaze.

On the highway, two leather-clad and goggled motorcyclists appeared, zooming through the jagged shadows on the tarmac, shrinking into the distance until they disappeared entirely. We passed a wide lake, the waves at its shore frozen into odd sculptural forms suggesting entrapment and desolation. As the train straightened after a long curving tunnel near Lhasa, a nomad emerged from his tent on a hillside. Fantastically dressed in fur hat, sheepskin coat, high boots, and silver buckles, he stopped and gazed at us—interlopers in his world—with what could have been either fear or disdain.

It was dark when the train, moving swiftly through Lhasa's outskirts, pulled into the great vault of the city's new railway station. The announcements on the PA system bounced off the building's high ceiling, wide platforms, and pedestrian tunnels, and dissolved into meaningless echoes. In the neon-lit concrete wilderness outside, the straggly crowd of tired passengers appeared diminished. The parking lot was several hundred metres away from the main building, and the PLA soldiers with machine guns and the checkpoint on the road leading to the city were reminders of Chinese fears about security in Tibet.

On my first morning in Lhasa, I saw the Chinese-built quarter of the city—a grid of long roads lined by supermarkets, restaurants, bars, and nightclubs—through Woeser's eyes. The old quarter—centred on the Jokhang, the holiest Tibetan temple—long reduced to an oasis in the hectically and garishly expanding city, seemed to have shrunk since my previous visit. But it hadn't lost the atmosphere of a medieval market-cum-pilgrim town: skull-capped and thinly whiskered Muslims from Kazakhstan displayed mosaics of nuts and dried fruit; open-fronted shops sold dried yak meat and blocks of yak cheese; and antique stores sold prayer wheels, semi-precious stones, daggers, and saddles. Mingling with the merchants and the hawkers were the pilgrims, chanting and spinning prayer wheels as they circumambulated the gold-roofed Jokhang. A mysterious euphoria seemed to drive the dusty prostrators in their frayed gloves and knee pads, and the tiny aged matriarch in greasy robes tapping her forehead to the faded silk scarves hanging from the holiest chapel inside the Potala Palace.

In the encroaching Chinese city, new, hybrid identities for Tibet were on offer. The three white arches of the railway bridge over the Kyichu River were apparently designed to evoke *khatags*, the silk scarves that are a traditional Tibetan token of reverence. The railway station itself, a colossal structure with sloping walls of white and oxblood red, seemed to compete, in both size and detail, with the red and white of the Potala Palace, which looms above Lhasa on a large outcrop to the north of the city. Such selective borrowings reflect the fact that, in recent years, Tibet and

Tibetan Buddhism have inspired a cult-like devotion among newly affluent Han Chinese. A stylish Chinese poet I met in Beijing last year blew perfect smoke rings as she lamented the immaturity of China's urban culture, and professed profound interest in Tibet. *Kekexili* (Mountain Patrol), a popular Chinese film released in 2004, craftily encapsulated this new Chinese romance, presenting the Tibetans as a proud, earthy, and honest frontier people. There are shops in almost every major Chinese city selling what a signboard in downtown Shanghai describes as 'Buddhism Accessories': Tibetan prayer wheels, bells, and incense.

In my hotel, the Brahmaputra Grand, glass cases displayed antique guns, swords, armour, metal utensils, Tibetan masks, and statues, while the mostly Chinese staff, dressed in colourful Tibetan costume, greeted guests with an exaggerated bow and a heavily accented *'Tashi delek.'* The hotel, which opened two days before the train to Lhasa's maiden journey, billed itself as Tibet's 'first five-star hotel' and a 'unique museum hotel.' In the marble lobby, whose wall decorations, Buddhist statues, winding staircase, and gold-plated mandala created an overwhelming impression of gaudiness, a wide-screen television replayed endlessly an interview with the hotel's owner, a soldier-turned-businessman from Sichuan. According to a glossy magazine placed in every room, the owner understood 'the law of development of objective reality' and was someone who 'spends all energy throughout his life in inheriting and flourishing Tibetan culture.'

Despite the awkward translation, the words betrayed a kind of truth. From the beginning of market reforms in China, Communist Party bosses, government officials, and

PLA soldiers had grasped more keenly than most people the development of objective reality. Not surprisingly, they were, if not the true inheritors of Tibetan culture, certainly the people best placed to make money out of it.

On one occasion when I met Woeser, she was accompanied by her partner, Wang Lixiong. Wang had risked much, not only by finding fault with Chinese rule over Tibet— something no prominent Han Chinese writer or intellectual in China was known to have done—but also by meeting the Dalai Lama. Wang told me that he thought the communist system in China was in serious peril, that the Party's control over China was in danger of being broken. This did not make him hopeful about the future of Tibet, however. He told me that he had taken the train to Lhasa last November. On the journey, he met a Tibetan woman who had left her Tibetan village to see the world and had ended up as a singer and dancer in a travelling show run by a Han Chinese. Realizing after some years that she was getting old, she had opened her own show, in the city of Yangzhou. She told Wang that she was returning to her native village to find more girls there who could be 'ethnic exhibits.'

Woeser thought that these privileged and ambitious Tibetans did not exceed 10 per cent of the Tibetan population. In one of her essays, she recounts a conversation with a young Tibetan entrepreneur seeking to develop Tibet's tourist industry, who grandly proclaims, 'We are going to be the city eating up the villages.' But it seemed that few young Tibetans were well placed to take advantage of the new economic environment. The infusion of Han

Chinese, privileged by both ethnicity and language, had left the teahouses and barbershops in the Tibetan quarter thick with the unemployed and the idle. One evening in a restaurant near the Jokhang temple, I met five young English-speaking Tibetans so overwhelmed by bitterness at their situation that they forgot, briefly, about the punitive consequences of talking to foreigners.

Dressed in jeans and big fluffy jackets, they appeared as if they might have been more at ease in the Chinese quarter's discos than in the Tibetan quarter. But an old-fashioned courteousness lay behind their coolly modern appearance; they belonged to a very different class from the Tibetans I had seen in the nightclubs near the Potala Palace on my previous visit. Children of barley farmers in villages north of Lhasa, they lived crammed in small rented rooms in the city.

Looking for an unobtrusive place to talk, we went up to a restaurant's second floor. A young Chinese couple were already seated there, and a moment of unease followed. The couple were most likely tourists; romantically self-absorbed, they barely glanced at us. The Tibetans, after a few appraising glances, became indifferent to them, probably confident that the Chinese wouldn't be able to follow a conversation in English. But I found myself nervously surveying the menu, remarking, pointlessly, on its variations on yak meat, and then abruptly talking of the Dalai Lama's embrace of vegetarianism during his exile in India. None of the Tibetans ordered meat, and they declined my offer of beer; they did not drink alcohol. I asked if they were religious, and they nodded. Did they go to temples? They nodded again. Conversation flowed only after the Chinese couple left.

The Tibetans had known one another since their early teens, when they left Tibet and made a dangerous journey together across high mountain passes to India. They spoke nostalgically of their time in India, especially of the school run by and for Tibetan refugees in Dharamsala. Their stay abroad had expanded their sense of possibility, but it had also brought a painful awareness of their place in the world. They had learned English in India, but this skill, valuable anywhere else in China, had proved to be of little use when official pressure on their families forced them to return to Tibet. Speaking passionately, and often all at the same time, they described how Chinese authorities worked hard to prevent Tibetans from escaping to India—some 3000 succeed annually—and how they periodically harassed Tibetans who had returned.

In any case, my companions couldn't have benefitted from Tibet's market economy without fluency in Chinese. Even exams for the job of tour guide were conducted in Chinese and covered Chinese rather than Tibetan history. Higher education in China was far too expensive for this group, and they had none of the connections that Tibetans, however well educated, needed in order to obtain good government jobs, or to avoid being posted to the cold border regions. Their only option was to eke out a living off tourists in the summer season, as translators and guides, and then spend much of the winter on their families' farms.

They had, they told me, almost no contact with the local Chinese, and they saw Lhasa as a city divided, as much psychologically as physically, into the Chinese and Tibetan quarters. Mutual wariness, rather than outright hostility, had so far governed the relationship between the two communities. But the train, they felt, could change that. They had little doubt that it was meant to benefit only the Chinese. Travel by road and air had been too arduous or expensive for likely Chinese migrants, who mostly tended to be poor. The train had already speeded up Han Chinese immigration to the city, where Tibetans were now in a minority. Every day, according to the Tibetan government-in-exile, more than 5000 visitors came to Lhasa, of whom some 2000 stayed. The effect on the local economy was already being felt. Rent for modest rooms of the kind they lived in had doubled.

Our voices resonated in the empty, dimly lit restaurant. It was New Year's Eve, but the lanes near the Jokhang had acquired a wintry desolation early in the evening. When we emerged into the night, there was a long wait for a taxi, but the Tibetans insisted on seeing me off. Quietly standing in the cold dark lane, they suddenly appeared adrift in their own city.

Returning to my hotel, I found PLA cars and green-uniformed soldiers blocking the driveway. Alarmed, I went in to discover ballroom dancers crowding the lobby, which had been cleared of much of its Tibetan decorations: the hotel had decided to celebrate the Western New Year. Local Chinese officials in suits sat stiff-necked on sofas, watching women in long black gowns solemnly twirling around the marble floor as a synthesizer produced an approximation of the *Blue Danube* waltz. The uncertain and experimental nature of the event became more evident when the dance floor abruptly emptied and a heavily made-up Nepalese girl,

not more than sixteen years old, in a white miniskirt, began
a kind of pole dance to the tune of a Bollywood film song.
As if completing a scene from a colonial past, the Tibetan
and Nepalese staff looked on blankly from the sidelines.

I left after the Nepalese girl threw off her jacket. In my
hotel room, I switched on CCTV's New Year's show to find
an overweight woman in an orange tracksuit singing a song
about the railroad to Lhasa titled 'The Road to Heaven.'
Woeser later told me that 'The Road to Heaven,' an adapted
folk song sung by a half-Tibetan pop star named Han Hong,
had been played interminably on radio and television in
Tibet for a whole year before the train arrived in Lhasa. In
2004, Han had also performed in Potala Square. In fact, she
had planned to helicopter onto the roof of the Potala Palace
for the performance, and had been dissuaded only after a
campaign on one of Woeser's influential blogs, which has
since been shut down. Judging by the English subtitles, 'The
Road to Heaven' consisted of a series of slightly ominous
banalities: 'people of all nationalities come together,' for the
train 'was like a dragon crossing the mountains,' 'bringing
warmth of the motherland to the frontier,' whose arrival
would make 'barley and butter tea taste sweeter.'

On my last day in Tibet, I visited a young farmer in his
rural home, some sixty miles from Lhasa. The Tibetans
I had met had sent him to accompany me to the Ganden
Monastery, on one of the hills near Lhasa. On the way, I
asked him if I could visit his village instead. Much to my
surprise, he immediately agreed. It was a bright morning,
cloudless, with only a few wisps of mist lingering around
the hills in the remote distance. The farmer joked about
Chinese attempts to get families in his village to fly the

communist flag and display pictures of China's president, Hu Jintao. Tibetans were apparently still required to take seriously the old-fashioned propaganda that much of inland China has outgrown.

It was with something like pride that he showed me around his old family house and introduced me to his parents and younger siblings. The courtyard where a huge Tibetan mastiff sat tethered, the hay-strewn shed where cows were being milked, the long living room with the coal stove and a fridge and a television set (both emblems of modernity covered decorously with embroidered cloth), the flat roof with an unrestricted view of the hills: this, he seemed to say, was the life that he and his family had created, without any help from the Chinese.

Nowhere was he more self-assured than in the prayer room, to which he took me last. Pausing in what was evidently the best-tended part of the house, he let me absorb its aura of sacredness. The Tibetan love of colour and baroque decoration was on full display in the panelled chests painted with floral designs, the thick frescoed columns, the *thangkas* representing scenes from the life of the Buddha, the sashes hanging from the ceiling, the pile of Tibetan scriptures bound in bright-yellow silk, and the row of silver lamps before an extravagantly gilded shrine.

On one relatively bare wall was a poster, the mandatory portrait of Hu Jintao. It was even bigger than the largest of the thangkas, but in this portrait the Chinese president had been Tibetanized: he wore a khatag, and his figure was superimposed over images of the Potala Palace and ecstatic Tibetan dancers in traditional costumes. Smiling conspiratorially, the farmer pointed to one of the panelled chests. Inside, he said, was a picture of the Dalai Lama. The farmer, growing more cheerful by the second, told me that all his neighbours had one, too.

It was a defiant gesture, like that of the nomad who had watched from outside his tent as the train went past. And when I returned to Lhasa later that morning the city, overwhelmingly defined by the Chinese, appeared more clearly to be an exception. It seemed that there were many more Tibetans like the young farmer, asserting traditional ways of life against change imposed from Beijing—Tibetans whose loyalty to their faith and identity had been tested by successive political setbacks, and who would now struggle to survive the arrival of the railroad in Lhasa.

THE BONFIRE OF CHINA'S
VANITIES

Soon after I met Yu Ha one cold afternoon at the state-run Friendship Hotel in Beijing, he cheerfully began to describe the incipient international fame of his most recent novel, *Brothers*, one of China's biggest-selling literary works. He had just returned from Hong Kong, where the novel was shortlisted for the Man Asian Prize; he was leaving soon for Paris to receive an award for the book, which had just been translated into French. With the breezy insouciance that unbroken success creates, Yu then began to recount a somewhat irreverent memory of Mao Zedong's death.

Though nearly fifty, Yu, who wears his hair short and spiky, looks relatively young. He speaks in emphatic bursts, his face often flushing red, and he is quick to laugh. It was, in fact, his boisterous laugh that almost got him into trouble on the morning of the solemn announcement of Mao's death. Responding to orders that blared out from loudspeakers, he assembled with hundreds of other students in the main hall of his small-town high school. 'Funereal music was played, and then we had to hear the long list of titles that preceded Mao's name, "Chairman," "Beloved Leader," "Great helmsman . . . ,"' Yu recalled. 'Everyone loved Chairman Mao, of course, so when his name was finally announced, everyone burst into tears. I started crying, too, but one person crying is a sad sight; more than a thousand people crying together, the sound echoing, turns into a funny spectacle, so I began to laugh. My body shook with my effort to control my laughter while I bent over the chair in front of me. The class leader later told me, admiringly, "Yu Hua, you were crying so fervently!"'

He paused, and then jumped thirteen years to a memory of another momentous—and more traumatic—event in China's modern history. In the spring of 1989, when tens of thousands of protesters filled Tiananmen Square, Yu was living in Beijing, partaking of the cultural excitement and political hopefulness of post-Mao China. Already a major figure in the city's artistic avant-garde, Yu biked every day to Tiananmen Square to express solidarity with the student protesters.

As Yu described the widespread civilian support for the students, a note of passion entered his voice, and the menu he had elegantly snagged off a passing waiter lay open and unread in his lap. 'The word "people" was much used in the Cultural Revolution,' he said. 'It is a very loaded term in China, it is used a lot, but until the mass protests in 1989 I did not realize what the word meant.'

His voice grew louder as he recalled the bloody suppression and aftermath of the protests. I became nervous. Yu, a short, thickset man with bulging eyes, could easily pass unnoticed in a crowd of Chinese peasants and workers, but he does not exactly strive for self-effacement. We were sitting in the corner of the hotel lobby, partly concealed by a large pillar and surrounded by a thick fog of cigarette smoke. Yu, a restless chain-smoker, insists on ignoring China's new ban on smoking in public places.

The hotel was full that day of young executives from nearby IT offices, any one of whom might have recognized Yu, who is frequently mentioned as a likely candidate for the Nobel Prize in Literature. Though official repression of the memory of Tiananmen has ensured that few young Chinese know much about the struggles for democracy waged in the 1980s, cyber-savvy youth of the kind we were surrounded by are still likely to take a sternly nationalistic line with a Chinese writer or intellectual criticizing the events of June 1989 to a foreigner. Indeed, as Yu spoke, a trendily dressed young woman looked up from the glowing screen of her laptop to squint at him.

Yu seemed totally oblivious to potential eavesdroppers. His face was red as he came to the end of his memory of 1989. Turning to me, he said: 'Sorry to take off like that. But this was a big turning point for all of us. After June 1989 people in China lost interest in politics. In 1992 Deng Xiaoping made his famous "Southern Tour," calling for faster market reforms, and the economy started to take off. The ideals of nation and socialism began to look empty. People became focused on making money.

'I, too, began to enjoy the fruits of capitalism,' he added, and laughed.

Yu was only partly joking. For someone who started out in China's brief moment of counterculture in the 1980s as a writer of bleak, experimental, and defiantly unsaleable stories, Yu has gone on to receive an ample share of the fruits of capitalism. Published in two parts in 2005 and 2006, *Brothers*, which traces the fortunes of two stepbrothers from the Cultural Revolution to China's no-less-frenzied Consumer Revolution, has sold more than a million copies in China, not counting the probably higher sales of innumerable pirated editions.

Certainly, foreign readers will find in its sprawling, rambunctious narrative some of China's most frenetic transformations and garish contradictions. *Brothers* strikes its characteristic tone with the very first scene, as Li Guang, a business tycoon, sits on his gold-plated toilet, dreaming of space travel even as he mourns the loss of all earthly relations. Li made his money from various entrepreneurial ventures, including hosting a beauty pageant for virgins and selling scrap metal and knock-off designer suits. A quick flashback to his small-town childhood shows him ogling the bottoms of women defecating in a public toilet. Similarly grotesque images proliferate over the next 600 pages as Yu describes, first, the extended trauma of the Cultural Revolution, during which Li and his stepbrother Song Gang witness Red Guards torturing Song Gang's father to death, and then the moral wasteland of capitalist China, in which Song Gang is forced to surgically enlarge one of his breasts in order to sell breast-enlargement gels.

The reasons for the novel's commercial success seem clear. It invokes the widely experienced violence and suffering of the Cultural Revolution while also drawing on another resonant theme in China: the outlandish lifestyles of the rich and famous, especially nouveau-riche entrepreneurs like Li. Li represents the country's new cultural icons, whose large appetites for money, women, and cars keep the innumerable Chinese bloggers and Internet chat rooms transfixed with both admiration and revulsion.

Other writers have dealt with the Cultural Revolution and the counter-revolutions of post-Mao China—the wealthy entrepreneur in Chi Li's *Coming and Going*, one of the country's most successful novels and TV series, also provoked much fascinated ambivalence among middle-class Chinese and the many millions more aspiring to be. But Yu brings to his potent mix of market-tested subjects the ambition, energy, and flair of a born provocateur. He seems less interested in representing modern-day China through mimetic realism than in evoking it through a bawdy semi-fantastical narrative, in which human bodies are frequently and gruesomely violated in recurring scenes of debauchery, brutality, and death.

Yu's provocations may have succeeded better than he hoped; enraged critics have made *Brothers* one of China's most controversial novels in recent years. Yu, who is one of the very few literary writers to have flourished in the new China, always seemed a bit suspect to puritanical critics. But *Brothers* has aroused a special malice among many readers, both online and in print, who accuse Yu of caring more for profit margins than for literature. When the second part of the novel came out in 2006, a famous literary critic at Beijing University, who championed Yu's short fiction in the 1980s, told me that the former avant-gardist had learned how to work China's new marketplace and 'make money.' Other reviewers doubted Yu's grasp of the details of Chinese life. Online forums debated with special vigour whether it would have been possible for a man in a small Chinese town in the early 1960s to spy on women's bottoms in a public toilet and then, in the process, slip and drown in a cesspool.

An anthology of criticism titled *Pulling Yu Hua's Teeth* charged the author of *Brothers* with several crimes: selling out to the very forces of commercialism and vulgarity anatomized in his novel; promoting a negative image of China and Chinese writers to the West; sinking into 'a world of filth, chaos, stench and blackness, without the slightest scrap of dignity'; being a carpet-bagging peasant who gives himself literary airs.

'Good people are not rewarded,' one critic writes, 'the kind do not die a good death, scoundrels take the upper hand, love proves false, only money is praised, but there is nothing behind money but lasciviousness and ugliness.' Opening the teeth-pulling operation with an article claiming that Yu's writing consists of four bad teeth—a black tooth, a yellow tooth, a false tooth, and a carious tooth—the book systematically excavates Yu's dentures over four parts, ending with a conclusion titled 'It's Not the Toothache but the Pain That Kills You.'

Yu betrayed no signs of post-operative stress when I asked him recently about the reaction to his book. He dismissed *Pulling Yu Hua's Teeth* as 'sensationalism' and robustly rejected the accusation that he performs for a Western audience. 'My books are more popular in China than anywhere else,' he said. 'If they weren't, these critics would have a point.'

When I first met Yu one evening in Shanghai in 2006, he confidently described to me his vision of *Brothers* as a social and moral critique of China's evolution. Yet he was suffering from a version of post-publication angst common among authors—the cankerous feeling that his work, and its vision of China lurching between political authoritarianism, extreme poverty, consumerist excess, and moral depravity, was not being taken seriously enough. High sales and popular acclaim had not taken the sting out of the venomous reviews. But almost three years of a sustained critical assault on *Brothers* seems to have hardened Yu. He now sees the attacks in sociological rather than literary terms, as exposing a fault line between generations, and his detractors as typical of China's new nationalists—people too young to have any memory of their country's previous traumas but obsessed with boosting China's image as a rising power vis-à-vis the West.

'The main reason that the book was attacked is because it exposes the dark side of China,' he told me when we met again in Beijing. 'A highly respected critic in Fudan University, Chen Sihe, pointed this out. "Look at the critics who are attacking this book," he said. "They are all young. Older critics have a more ambiguous take."'

Yu added, 'Younger writers don't like to see books that reveal the dark side of China; they live very comfortable lives; they don't believe in the dark side of China; they are not even aware of the hundreds of millions of people still living in extreme poverty.'

Yu himself seems to have rarely turned away from the dark side of things. He first became known in the late 1980s as a writer of surreal short fiction whose raw violence—in one story, a four-year-old strangles his cousin, a baby, in order to 'enjoy the explosive crying'; in another, a young girl is hacked to pieces—brashly defied the hygienic pieties of socialist realism to which China's state-supported writers were expected to conform.

Yu switched to melodramatic realism in 1992 in his novel *To Live*. This atrocity-rich tale of a forbearing peasant whose son dies after a blood transfusion to save a party official was turned into an internationally successful film by Zhang Yimou, China's most prominent director. It won the Grand Prix at the 1994 Cannes Film Festival. Both *To Live* and his next novel, *Chronicle of a Blood Merchant* (1995), in which a peasant traffics in his own blood to supplement his meagre income, remained resolutely focused on the tragic aspects of China's modern history. But it was not until Yu travelled to the West that he began to think about a broader fictional canvas that would depict China's chaotic present as well as its past. In 1995 he went abroad for the first time, to the French seaside town St Malo, for a literary festival. 'The foreign journalists there,' he recalled, 'would often ask me about the Cultural Revolution, and it occurred to me what a barbarous and bizarre experience China had had.'

Almost miraculously, *Brothers*, which contains graphic descriptions of the violence of the Cultural Revolution, including the suicide of a man who hammers a nail into his skull, managed to escape Chinese censors. Yu said he profited from his experience with Zhang Yimou, who cannily altered the story of *To Live* in order to make the film version palatable to Chinese authorities: among other things, Zhang made the son's death seem like a tragic accident. 'As he made the changes I became very impressed by how well Zhang

Yimou seemed to understand the Chinese Communist Party. But the film still got banned. After that, I stopped caring about what the censors would think.'

It was his publishers rather than the state censors who wanted cuts in *Brothers*. But they relented after Yu threatened to withdraw his book. 'They knew,' he said, 'that the book would sell; they are willing to take more risks with the censors because they are not state supported any more and have to fend for themselves in the marketplace.' For Yu the publication of his novel is a sign of slow but steady progress in China. 'Ten years ago, *Brothers* could not have been published,' he said. 'It may take another ten years for a movie to be made out of it.'

We were sitting with Yu's wife, Chen Hong, a poet who now devotes most of her time to looking after their son, in the living room of the apartment they rent in West Beijing. We were surrounded by the marks of a temporary existence: new Ikea-style furniture, mismatched curtains, piled-up books, and a general air of neglect. Yu explained that he and his wife were waiting for their son to finish school before moving to Hangzhou in his ancestral province, Zhejiang. He didn't like Beijing; it was too big and impersonal. The neighbouring apartments, for instance, housed 'hair salons,' often a front, in China, for brothels, with bright neon lights. 'I tell my friends we live in a red-light district,' he joked, and his wife, a woman with a delicate pale face and loose long hair, broke into a melodious laugh.

One room in Yu's austere apartment is reserved for surfing the Internet, which is probably the most revealing window on modern China. But Yu said he spends more time in his study, another stark room with a laptop computer on a clean desk. He added that he didn't need to rely on the Internet; he had personally experienced the weird mutations of China's consumer culture described in the novel. He remembers turning on the television in the 1990s to find nothing but beauty pageants: every town in China seemed to host them.

He disputes the charge that the details in the novel are far-fetched; reality can be equally, sometimes even more, gruesome in China. 'After the book was published, an academic friend wrote to me to say that his father had also killed himself by hammering a nail into his skull,' he said. 'Three readers said that their father's corpse had to be mutilated in order to fit into the coffin. A *New York Times* journalist who interviewed me in 2006 thought that businesses offering hymen reconstruction were extremely unlikely; he then discovered that they existed all over China.'

When I asked Yu if he had ever contemplated breast enlargement, like Song Gang in *Brothers*, he and his wife laughed. But both grew sombre as Yu recalled his childhood, no less infected by the grotesque for being relatively untouched by the chaos of the Cultural Revolution. Born in 1960, Yu grew up in a small town called Haiyan in Zhejiang province (a breeding ground for many Chinese artists and intellectuals including Lu Xun, the pioneer of modern Chinese literature). Despite the Cultural Revolution, Yu recalled, life was generally monotonous—except when a criminal was to be executed, when 'the whole town would become as lively as festival time.' Yu remembers the executions as the 'most thrilling scenes of my childhood, seeing the criminal kneeling on the ground, a soldier aiming a rifle at the back of his head and firing.'

His father was a doctor—but this makes him sound grander than he was, for he worked, Yu said, wearing a bloodstained smock in one small room and lived with his family across the road. Their home also faced a public toilet, where nurses often dumped tumours, and the local mortuary. 'On hot summer days, it was cool inside the mortuary,' Yu recalled, 'and since the corpses were deposited only at night, I often took a nap there. Sleeping at night in our home, we would be woken by the sound of people crying.'

Yu now attributes the relentless bleakness of his early fiction to his childhood exposure to brutality and death. 'I was unable to steer my writing away from bloodshed and violence,' he said. 'Writing during the day, I'd have one character killing another, characters dying in pools of blood. At night, asleep, I would dream that I was about to be killed by someone else.'

Yu never went to college. 'My entire education was encompassed by the Cultural Revolution,' he said. 'I went to school in 1966 and came out in 1976, so I never received a proper education.' Then, like many 'barefoot doctors' in China in the late 1970s, Yu underwent only some very basic training before he became a dentist.

He claims he became a writer because he hated his job: 'the inside of a mouth is one of the ugliest spectacles in the world.' In the early 1980s he was living in a small town between Shanghai and Hangzhou. From his window he often observed workers of the local Cultural Bureau, the Chinese state's salaried writers and artists, loafing in the streets. 'We were all very poor in those days,' Yu recalled.

'The difference was that you could work hard to be poor as a dentist, or you could do nothing and still be poor as a worker in the Cultural Bureau. I decided I wanted to be as idle as the workers in the Cultural Bureau and become a writer.'

Yu wrote a short story and sent it off to a literary magazine in Beijing. An enthusiastic phone call from its editor soon put him on the path to paid idleness at the Cultural Bureau. Yu seems to have relished manipulating the communist system to his own ends. 'I was deliberately late on the first day at the bureau office,' he told me. 'Later I would only go once a week, and then finally only once a month to collect my salary.'

In 1993 the royalties from *To Live* enabled Yu to leave his job altogether. 'My friends,' he recalled, 'say I have enjoyed the best of both ideologies: first receiving a writer's stipend under socialism and now royalties in the free-market regime.'

Though Yu's account of his beginnings as a writer is light-hearted, from the first his works of fiction provoked serious critical attention. Published in such major literary magazines as *Zhongshan*, *Shouhuo*, and *Shanghai Wenyi*, his stories, with their surreal violence and cruelty, seemed to deftly summarize China's history; their metafictional devices also spoke of a formal ambition rare among Chinese writers. As early as 1991 the critic Henry Zhao predicted that Yu was 'destined to occupy a long page in Chinese literature.'

Remarkably, Yu seems to have had as little apprenticeship in writing as he had in dentistry. Books were hard to come by during the Cultural Revolution, or they would circulate in mutilated form, like the torn copy of a novel by Guy de Maupassant, which Yu read the middle of ('I remember it had a lot of sex,' he said) without knowing its title or author.

His formative reading experience was provided by the big character posters of the Cultural Revolution, in which people denounced their neighbours with violent inventiveness. 'I remember,' Yu said, 'walking home from school and reading each poster as I walked along. I was not so much interested in the revolutionary slogans as in the stories.'

He had never cared much for Chinese writers; only later did he come to appreciate Lu Xun's resolve to diagnose Chinese society and culture through literature. Like many of his peers recoiling from socialist realism, Yu was drawn to the icons of Western high modernism whose work began to appear in translation in China in the 1980s, in particular Kafka, Bruno Schulz, and Borges. The delicate fictions of the Japanese writer Yasunari Kawabata were also a great early influence. 'Kawabata taught me the importance of detail,' Yu recalled. 'I would buy two copies of his novels whenever I saw them. One to read and the other to keep in pristine condition on my shelf.'

So why did he abandon avant-garde experimentalism? Yu says he discovered that his characters had their own lives, which he could not control. By the early 1990s, when almost all major works of international fiction were being translated into Chinese, he was also reading more widely, particularly novels by V.S. Naipaul and Toni Morrison. But there seem to have been extra-literary reasons, too, for the general retreat from aesthetic radicalism among Yu's generation. The critic Chen Xiaoming, who teaches at Beijing University, once told me that by 1992, as China's economy hectically expanded and the state began to withdraw its cultural subsidies, publishers were increasingly forced to sink or swim in the marketplace. In the new era of mass culture, which TV dramas and popular music dominated, there were fewer takers for avant-garde fiction, and its practitioners had to improvise or face irrelevance.

This sounds true: Su Tong, one of the more famous avant-gardists in the 1980s, turned to writing historical romances. In an apparent concession to his commercial times, Yu scripted an episode for a TV show titled *China Models*. 'It was for the money,' he jokingly admitted to me. But he also claims that he was led to a more populist aesthetic by a new idea of his social responsibility as a writer. As he sees it, boldly experimental writing of the kind he and other writers produced in the 1980s was a rejection of the official orthodoxy of Mao's notion that literature ought to serve the communist regime's political ends. 'We wanted to say,' Yu told me, 'that writing is not in the service of anything other than itself.'

Yu claims that he was forced to reconsider his stance of aesthetic autonomy after the events of 4 June 1989, and reconfigure his notion of the relationship between writer and society, especially as he confronted the problems created by China's breakneck modernization in the 1990s. This meant embracing the old Chinese model of the writer as social critic and a pared-down style of cinematic brevity and much earthy humour. It meant, too, writing about China's large but invisible majority in the age of globalization: peasants and workers in villages and small towns.

Yu now looks back wryly on his reputation as a militant advocate of *l'art pour l'art*. He said he had recently been persuaded to conduct a public conversation with Alain

Robbe-Grillet during the latter's visit to Beijing. He didn't think much of the high priest of the nouveau roman, to whom he was often and inaccurately compared in the past. 'He was just an old codger,' Yu said, and laughed.

Expressing a preference for engagé over ivory-tower literature is unlikely to endear Yu to left-leaning readers in China. 'If the right-wingers,' Yu said, 'hate *Brothers* for its depiction of capitalism in China, the left dislikes it for its depiction of the Cultural Revolution.'

I put this to Wang Hui, the most prominent of intellectuals described as part of China's New Left, which maintains that many of China's peasants and workers have yet to reap the benefits of the newly globalized economy. Wang is an old friend of Yu's and wrote the foreword to a collection of his essays. (It was Wang who first encouraged Yu to begin writing essays in the late 1990s, publishing them in *Dushu*, the magazine he edited until 2007.) Yu told me that, broadly, he shared the New Left's criticism of Chinese-style capitalism, its tendency to create wealth in the cities while bypassing the countryside. Wang, however, seemed reluctant to wholeheartedly endorse *Brothers*.

'The first part reproduces the conventional "grand narrative" of the Cultural Revolution as a time of unrelieved suffering and betrayal,' he told me. 'I actually find the second part more interesting, because the author is no longer in control of his narrative. But, you know, we are old friends, and we haven't really discussed this book.' As he said this, Wang put an arm around Yu. We were at a restaurant in West Beijing that serves the cuisine of Zhejiang, Yu's native province. I had travelled to it in a taxi with Yu and noticed a strain of writerly competitiveness in his terse responses to my questions about contemporary Chinese novelists: he read mostly Mo Yan, Wang Anyi, and Su Tong. No, he didn't much read young Chinese writers or the Chinese Nobel Laureate Gao Xingjian, who lives in a suburb of Paris. Ma Jian, the author of the blackly satirical novel *Beijing Coma*, who lives in self-imposed exile in London, is barely known in China. He was more interested in foreign authors; he had recently read Ian McEwan's novel *On Chesil Beach* and also introduced a collection of the British novelist's stories in Chinese translation.

Yu spoke warmly, though, of Wang, whom he first met in Beijing in the 1980s and who is one of the very few people he sees frequently. At the restaurant they sat together, presenting a study in contrasts: Wang, unfailingly thoughtful, and Yu, as jaunty as ever. Yet they radiated an easy mutual regard, built upon the shared experience of the tumultuous late 1980s in Beijing and amusement at how significantly things had changed in their own lives since they were provincial students during the Cultural Revolution. Wang seemed to cherish the mischievous—what he called the 'joke-making'—side of Yu.

They had just returned from a trip to Nepal, where they went white-water rafting together. Yu chortled as he recalled his attempts to hold on to his boat amid the swirling waters. 'It's very dangerous,' he said, 'very dangerous.' But he grew visibly aggrieved when I asked him if he followed the Olympic Games in Beijing. The organizers promised to sell tickets online on a first-come-first-served basis, and he tried to buy them as soon as they were made available. But he wasn't able to get the best seats for the basketball matches and then found empty rows in the stadium whose neatness hinted at early block sales to party bigwigs. 'Typical Communist Party corruption,' Yu bellowed, and for once I was glad for the loud Muzak playing in the restaurant.

He fell silent after this, chain-smoking in his quiet but tense manner, as Wang spoke of the Western financial crisis and its implications for China's export-oriented economy. The stock market was in a steep decline; factories on the coast were closing. The discussion seemed to bore Yu. When I remarked that President Hu Jintao's then imminent visit with President Bush was very likely an exercise in futility, he said, 'These politicians are mostly a waste of time.'

He perked up only when I asked him what he thought of Zhang Yimou's contribution to the opening ceremony of the Beijing Olympics. He said he felt sympathetic to Zhang, who is often accused of selling out to communist authorities as well as to commercial interests. 'He would have reached the end of his career very quickly had he persisted in making films like *To Live*. He had to live with the realities of Chinese society. And it is different for film-makers. I can always publish in Taiwan if I am restricted in China. In China, too, the political atmosphere has gone back and forth from closed to open, and I have been lucky in hitting the troughs.'

Later in the taxi home, sitting next to the driver, Yu spoke of a threat to artistic expression in China newer than state control. 'I am really worried about the new nationalism,' he said. 'Anything slightly critical of China appears in foreign media, and the nationalists are swarming online, attacking it. I tell these angry youth that the *New York Times* doesn't criticize China as much as it criticizes America.

Basically they are ignorant. They think the American media is always praising American presidents. The problem is that the younger generation hasn't lived through poverty, collectivism; it is lacking in restraint, its references are very few, the experience is so limited.'

We were moving down Beijing's stately avenues, past the quasi-imperial grandeur of its postmodern architecture. Yu seemed eager to return to his sparsely furnished study and the room with the Internet. Earlier that day at his home he spoke of how his son, who has known only post-Mao China, would nevertheless witness extraordinary transformations in his own lifetime since the capitalist economy was bound to collapse. Yu barely looked out of his window as he said: 'These young nationalists have no sense of ambivalence, no idea of life's ambiguities. But when times are hard, their attitude will change, become more mature, and because capitalism in this form cannot go on in China, it has to end, those hard times will come soon.'

PART 3

ECHOES FROM THE MAINLAND

HONG KONG: THE QUEST
FOR CULTURE

Hong Kong is a great clamour. Arriving after a long flight from London, I felt as though I had stumbled into a feverish old dream of the Orient. The city is defined by an overwhelming intensity of life, an excess that is rendered more confounding by the familiar linear background of a Western-style metropolis. Crowds flow ceaselessly on the pavements and elevated walkways and mill about in the cathedral-like malls; radios and television sets blare from the grilled windows of dollhouse-like apartments; giant video ads loom and wink above the waiting phalanxes of commuters at striped crossings; and the noise of electric drills follows you everywhere until even the plump, glossy ducklings that hang quivering in restaurant windows appear to have been infused with the city's special vitality.

But Hong Kong, which was raised out of bare rock into glittering city state by capitalism in just over a century, doesn't take long to reveal its implacable inner logic. From Norman Foster's giddily spacious airport to César Pelli's twin International Finance Centre towers to the humble pedestrian underpass in Kowloon that diverts the unsuspecting flâneur to a Louis Vuitton store, all of it has been ingeniously designed to inject fresh ecstasy into the immemorial human need to make—and squander—money.

As I wandered Hong Kong on this visit, the city's handover to communist China in 1997 seemed oddly distant. British-ruled Hong Kong, Mao Zedong had famously quipped, had been 'a pimple on China's backside.' And as the date of the island's return to mainland rule approached, China's communist leaders seemed intent on squeezing the capitalist pimple out of existence. Deng Xiaoping's promise—'One Country, Two Systems'—did not seem very sincere to many people. In a 1995 cover story *Fortune* magazine provocatively announced 'The Death of Hong Kong.'

Nearly two decades later, the city continues to thrive, disregarding, yet again, the predictions of demise that have marked its existence—from the Japanese invasion in 1942, the communist takeover in China in 1949, and the US trade embargo on Mao's China to the Cultural Revolution and the Tiananmen Square massacre in 1989. Democracy seems a receding dream for Hong Kong's seven million citizens, many of whom suffer too from severe economic inequality of Latin-American severity and some of the world's most polluted air (karmically poisoned by factories in the Pearl River Delta financed, in part, by Hong Kong investors). But the taipans—the foreign traders and businessmen who made the city the world's great entrepôt to China, whose descendants still dwell in their white villas on Victoria Peak—have rarely been happier.

Hong Kong, with its reliable legal and financial systems, has proved to be the perfect gateway to its big neighbour, whose communist rulers, themselves in the midst of a radical experiment with capitalism they insist on calling 'socialism with Chinese characteristics,' have adjusted happily to Hong Kong's laissez-faire traditions. Although its economy has cooled somewhat, along with most of the rest of the world's, the city's stock market has nonetheless set new records, largely because of Chinese companies that now account for just over half of its capitalization. Hong Kong has surpassed New York and rivals London as the world's biggest market for initial public stock offerings. Property prices have risen sharply. Only London, Moscow, New York, and Istanbul have more billionaires.

Consequently, I saw more Rolls-Royces on the streets than ever, and the racecourse in Happy Valley was overflowing with local plutocrats in jewels, minks, and chinchillas (yes, pelts remain a sought-after accessory in humid Hong Kong). One evening at the ultra trendy Kee Club in Hong Kong's own SoHo, I may have been the only person worrying about the steeply rising tab as vintage Veuve Clicquot flowed with abandon across several tables. In the end it wasn't clear who paid—the brash tycoon from the local Indian business family or the slick French exporter visiting from Shanghai—and it did not seem to matter.

Foreign businessmen and Chinese fleeing the chaos of war and revolution on the mainland laid Hong Kong's economic foundations. Together, they also seem to have prepared the city better than most metropolises for the previous decade of hectic globalization—for unrestricted capital flows, immigration, and unabashed consumerism. Events beyond its control—the East Asian financial crisis of 1998, SARS in 2003, and Avian flu—have temporarily broken the city's stride. But Hong Kong, blessed as though with supernaturally good fortune, recovers with dazzling swiftness.

I often found myself fixated by the view of Kowloon and mainland China from my hotel room in one of the new steel-and-glass monoliths that strut on reclaimed land in Central, ahead of the downtown's already quite futuristic skyline. At dawn and late in the evening, the rusty junks, barges, and sampans becalmed on the jade-green sea and the vintage old green-and-white boats of Star Ferry criss-crossing Victoria Harbour could have come out of etchings and watercolours by the British officials who founded Hong Kong in the nineteenth century. Something of the place's primeval wildness would be hinted by the misty outlines of the vast archipelago (Hong Kong is only one out of 234 largely uninhabited islands) on the coast of China. But Kowloon across the shrinking harbour was always ablaze with neon.

Traditionally low-rise due to the old airport in its midst, Kowloon is now free to partake of Hong Kong's real estate boom; and the International Commerce Centre, the third tallest building in the world, was going up on freshly reclaimed land in Kowloon. At night a signboard shone forlornly underneath the looming cranes, proclaiming the building site to be the 'West Kowloon Cultural District.' This reclaimed harbour-front land is where, at least as originally planned by the Hong Kong's Special Administrative Region government in 1999, the largest urban arts and cultural district in Asia, several times bigger than the Lincoln Center, was to sprawl. A master plan by Norman Foster offered a beguiling fantasy of museums, performance venues, art schools, galleries, and studios cowering under a transparent canopy. The project was soon tainted by allegations that the government was colluding with real estate developers. But it did not fail to reveal the deep new desires of Hong Kong's rich and powerful.

Apparently satiated with wealth and luxury, they have developed cultural ambitions, and often come up with the wherewithal to fulfil them. In 2004 the Hong Kong Philharmonic, the city's biggest cultural event, acquired a world-class conductor, Edo de Waart. In 2007 Gore Vidal enthralled audiences at an International Literary Festival. The same year Man Investments, the sponsor of the UK's Booker Prize, established a new Hong Kong-based prize for Asian literature. The city, which showcases some of the more adventurous work of I.M. Pei and Zaha Hadid, is now known for its Architecture Biennale as well as its international modern and contemporary art fairs.

Hong Kong has long produced a distinctive cinema. Local cineastes will tell you proudly how local director John Woo influenced Quentin Tarantino and how Martin Scorsese's *The Departed* derives from the Hong Kong crime-thriller trilogy *Infernal Affairs*. But Hong Kong's government has grander plans to present the city as an emblem of cultural as well as economic globalization. Official websites, and banners, buses, and billboards across the city proclaim Hong Kong to be 'Asia's World City.' Peter Gordon, a columnist for the *Standard*, the island's highest-circulation English newspaper, summed up local longings for international eminence when he wrote that 'Hong Kong's role of "Asia's World City" could be just a stepping stone on the road to becoming "the world's second capital" after New York.'

Such extravagant visions invite a snigger—especially from those who have known Hong Kong as a staunchly philistine city, whose bars and prostitutes made it an R&R centre during the wars in the Pacific, Korea, and Vietnam. Indeed, when you are standing in the heart of the obstreperously commercial island, it is hard not to wonder whether Hong Kong *needs* culture at all.

Certainly, it has no lack of opportunity for leisure and entertainment. Hong Kong's very own Disneyland with Chinese characteristics, such as feng shui, opened in 2005 on Lantau, the biggest island in the archipelago. For seekers of luxury, few grand hotels in the world combine Oriental sumptuousness with Occidental conveniences as elegantly as Kowloon's Peninsula Hotel. Indeed, no place in any of the British Empire's old possessions in Asia—India, Singapore, Sri Lanka—still radiates as much imperial confidence and self-sufficiency as Hong Kong's Foreign Correspondents Club, which occupies the premises of an old ice house on one of Central's winding hilly roads.

A helicopter briskly transports one to Shenzhen, where Nick Faldo, Greg Norman, and Vijay Singh have helped design the world's largest golf facility. On Macao's seafront, which is reached in an hour by ferry, miniature replicas of Beijing's Forbidden City and Lhasa's Potala Palace stand handily close to a hotel-cum-casino of monstrous Las Vegas proportions. Picture-postcard fishing villages on Lamma Island amply fulfil the craving for the pastoral that periodically overtakes one in the midst of Hong Kong's unrelenting human density. The beaches on the island's own relatively uncluttered south side are still remarkably clean; and the colonial-style veranda of the rebuilt Repulse

Bay Hotel is a good place to while away a lazy afternoon.

Hong Kong is no longer the capital of Cantopop, the popular Western-style music that once thrilled the vast Chinese-speaking world: the king of easy listening Andy Lau is now better known for his tough-guy roles in such films as *Infernal Affairs* and Johnnie To's *Election*. Though no longer as seedy as before, the nightlife of Hong Kong, immortalized in the 1960 film *The World of Suzie Wong*, still flourishes in the cramped alleys of Lan Kwai Fong, a hilly neighbourhood near Central's business district and SoHo. The elevated pedestrian escalator that snakes past this area offers fascinating glimpses of squeezed-in lives in tower blocks (potted plants, flickering televisions, washing poles, mah jong tables, smells of Chinese herbs), and the sighting, rare in Hong Kong, of human repose while the subterranean arcades in subway stations, especially at East Tsim Sha Tsui, where the MTR line meets with the KCR, are equally unforgettable spectacles of light and energy.

Then, too, Hong Kong has terrific food, arguably the most cosmopolitan variety in Asia, due to the immigrants and expatriates who have brought to the city their own regional culinary traditions. A dim sum breakfast, one of the city's quintessential experiences, can still be reliably had at Fook Lam Moon in Wanchai. For the gastronomically more ambitious, the twelve-course meal at Sichuan Cuisine Da Ping Huo on Hollywood Road is accompanied with Xiaoxing opera. Chefs such as Michelle Garnaut and Opia's Teage Ezard have taken their Australian art of inventive fusion to impressive heights. Food courts in the big shopping malls like Pacific and IFC briskly dispense healthy juices and smoothies but *dai pai dong*, open-air stalls specializing in seafood, at the Temple Street Night Market in Kowloon's Yau Ma Tei neighbourhood are as tempting as the stunningly perfect counterfeit Prada bags and pirated box-set DVDs of *The Wire*. Afternoon tea of delicate English cucumber sandwiches in the lobby of the Peninsula Hotel remains a treat. A short walk away on Nathan Road, a humble South Indian canteen serves the softest idlis outside of Chennai.

Hong Kong's easily consumable cosmopolitanism probably deepened the government's self-congratulatory mood during the tenth anniversary of the handover to China, when the sound bite 'Asia's World City' was amplified ad nauseam. Still, economic success, though continuously underwriting galleries and bookshops, has yet to incite an explosion of new writing or ideas in the island. Though long blessed with more artistic freedom than China and Taiwan, Hong Kong has yet to produce a world-class writer—the inaugural Man Asian Prize was won by a writer from mainland China. The cultural vacancy makes the city's innumerable vast malls often seem full of people to whom, in the withering description of John Chan, essayist and former editor of *City Times*, once Hong Kong's coolest magazine, 'nothing has happened'—nothing at least compared to the fraught historical and political experience of their ethnic counterparts in China and Taiwan.

As Leo Lee Ou-fan, professor of Chinese studies at Hong Kong University, puts it, 'a society without radical protest and intellectual fermentation is a boring place.' 'The culture here is all about winning and losing money,' I was assured by Augustine Mok Chiu, one of the city's respected theatre directors, who gamely agreed to appear in a list of the 'beautiful losers in HK arts and culture' published in the inaugural issue of *Muse*, Hong Kong's boldly highbrow features magazine. The Taiwanese novelist and Taipei's minister of culture, Lung Yingtai, echoes this sentiment. 'In Hong Kong,' she wrote in a scathing article in the local *Apple Daily*, 'economic benefit is the core value for all decision-making, and development is the sole ideology.'

With the vast, rich hinterland of China to draw upon, Hong Kong is at least theoretically better placed than the desert Arabs of Dubai and Abu Dhabi to buy culture for local consumption. And yet no jaded robber barons, Hong Kong's own Fricks and Carnegies, have expressed a visible interest in building or stocking museums. Even the discovery of contemporary Chinese art, which was expedited by such Hong Kong-based connoisseurs as David Tang, the founder of Shanghai Tang, and Johnson Chang, the owner of Hanart, Hong Kong's leading art gallery, has turned into a lucrative multibillion-dollar business in which Hong Kong-based auction houses, surpassed only by those in London and New York, act as clearing houses for private collectors.

The city has little regard for its own architectural heritage—or what remains of it after decades of depredations by real estate developers. 'Cities,' wrote Lewis Mumford, 'are products of time. They are the molds in which men's lifetimes have cooled and congealed, giving lasting shape, by way of art, to moments that would otherwise vanish with the living and leave no means of renewal or wider participation behind them.' Some feeling for their vanishing landmarks may have prompted the protestors in Hong Kong who in December 2006 stormed the old Star Ferry pier and hung a banner around the clock tower that pleaded 'Preserve Our Collective Memory.'

Nonetheless, the government pulled down the charming old building (an act of vandalism comparable to the destruction of the old Penn Station in New York), replacing it with a faux-Edwardian structure that is conveniently linked by elevated walkway to the IFC shopping mall. Government House in Central and the Western Market are among the old buildings that still stand in Hong Kong, whose blithe self-purging verifies Karl Marx's famous dictum about the ruthlessness of capitalistic progress: 'All that is solid melts into thin air.' In 1993 the then newly constructed Ritz-Carlton hotel was almost demolished before it received a single guest because the multinational consortium that bought it thought they would make more money selling office space in a taller building.

But then a city built almost entirely by emigrants, and seen by many of them as a place of transit, cannot escape a certain rootless quality. This lightness of being partly explains why Hong Kong never developed a distinctive cosmopolitan culture of its own—unlike its sister port city Shanghai, which was simultaneously built by foreign businessmen (and, though overwhelmed recently by a nexus of politicians and developers, has actually managed to preserve some of its old neighbourhoods). It also explains why Hong Kong seems ever eager to be imprinted by the culture of its rulers—whether British or Chinese.

For decades under the British, Hong Kong was a standing reproach to backward and musty China, its shiny affluence and consumerism envied by the poor cousins to the north. But in recent years, the city has experienced a reverse phenomenon. Cantopop now seems an exception, and, like much Hong Kong cinema, it has wilted in the face of competition from mainland China, where Mandarin is the majority dialect. Rather than sending its movie and pop music stars to the north, Hong Kong now adds superfluous lustre to the actresses, astronauts, concert pianists, models, and Olympic athletes who have already attained idol status in China. In the Central business district mainlanders educated overseas are more prized than their English- and Cantonese-speaking peers. Taxi drivers do crash courses in Mandarin, which was once rarely heard in the territory, in order to accommodate the Chinese tourists who account for just over half of Hong Kong's 25 million annual visitors.

'Hong Kong,' Perry Lam, editor of *Muse*, told me, 'is suffering from a serious confusion about its identity today.' Again, this may be because unlike Shanghai where the humiliations of foreign rule spurred Chinese literature and art as well as nationalism, Hong Kong did not nurture anything resembling a political opposition, which is often a prerequisite for indigenous cultural production, if not quality. As Perry Lam put it, 'what explains much about Hong Kong is that over a century of British rule did not produce a single anti-colonial hero. The closest we have come to a hero is Bruce Lee—and he was from San Francisco!'

Lung Yingtai believes that Hong Kong has yet to break from the culture of its colonizers, or to even examine their 'aesthetic tastes,' 'value system,' and 'historical viewpoints.' Even Peter Gordon who asserts that Shanghai's monolingualism and lack of intellectual and cultural freedom makes Hong Kong the Asian 'front-runner to be New York City's alter-ego' believes that setting up massive performance

venues, as planned for the West Kowloon Cultural District, is
no guarantee of cultural and intellectual merit. He concedes
that the city needs to do as well in literature and ideas as
it has in films and music and also needs to 'strengthen its
individuality rather than meekly conforming with the rest
of China.'

This may be too much to ask of the older, historically
innocent beneficiaries of Hong Kong's great luck—the
immigrants who fled China for Hong Kong in the 1940s and
1950s. Struggling for mere survival, they understandably
could not realize whatever urge they felt for dissent or
individual cultural expression. As in early twentieth-
century America and Australia, it is their privileged children
and grandchildren who are likely to overcome Hong
Kong's intellectual and cultural backlog. And there are
encouraging signs in the city's present identity crisis and
the related groping for the most obvious forms of culture,
not to mention its political restlessness, as manifested
in mass commemorations of Tiananmen, and frequent
demonstrations against Hong Kong's puppet government.

On my last evening in the city, I took the Victorian-era
tram to the Peak, which scales the rocky hillside more or
less vertically and opens up breathtaking vistas of the island
and surrounding seascape. It was foggy at the top, but the
city's abundant neon shone through. Here, defiantly looming
out of the faint outlines of the vast archipelago on the coast
of China, Hong Kong seemed to me more than ever the
apotheosis of capitalist modernity: a strange utopia, already
prefigured by Singapore and Dubai, city states where free
enterprise coexists frictionlessly with authoritarian politics
and ersatz culture. Still, in that rare moment of silence and

solitude, I felt convinced that a society of such material plenitude would eventually foster longings that could not be appeased by the mere accumulation of goods—a historical lesson that may be useful to remember as Hong Kong hurtles, as apparently heedlessly as ever, towards the future.

MONGOLIA: FALLING OUT
OF HISTORY

Arriving in Mongolia on the Trans-Siberian Express from Beijing, I wondered where everyone was. In China, there had been crowds everywhere, the dense human mass overwhelming even to someone from India. But just miles after we crossed the border with China, an eerie void defined Mongolia.

This shouldn't have been so strange—after all, the Gobi Desert covers much of southern Mongolia. But when I thought of Mongolia I pictured the multitudes of horsemen that swept across Central Asia and Russia in the thirteenth century, all the way to Central Europe, creating the greatest land empire the world has ever seen.

All through that cold morning, pastureland rolled past my train window. I saw an occasional *ger*—the white circular tent that is the Mongolian version of the Central Asian yurt—and horses accompanied by a cowboy with an *uurga*, the Mongolian lasso. And then there was emptiness for hours on end.

The blank landscape seemed to have subdued the

Chinese attendants in my coach. Huddled with their pals over beers in the dining car, as the Trans-Siberian Express began its long journey from Beijing to Siberia via the Gobi Desert, they had barely glanced up as I stumbled through my phrasebook-aided request for hot water. In the bright Mongolian morning, they seemed withdrawn.

The Russian couple in the compartment next to mine also looked sullen. They'd had a terrible night. At the border crossing the night before, the Mongolian immigration officer had told them that their visas had expired and had threatened to throw them off the train into what seemed, literally, the middle of nowhere. Sitting in my compartment, I had heard their tearful pleadings. Then, even the Chinese attendants looked sympathetic.

It had finally been sorted out, after a delay of almost two hours. The Mongolian officer relented and gave new visas to the Russians. He may have been bluffing after all. The Chinese attendants looked relieved, the Russians grateful, if worn out by their ordeal.

It was an odd scene—the assertive Mongolians, the subdued Chinese, and the terrified Russians. It hinted at great historical shifts and ironies: the hierarchies of the Cold War, when Mongolia was a satellite state of the Soviet Union, had been overturned. But it was after a few days in Mongolia, with a greater understanding of what it meant to be a modern Mongolian, living in a country sandwiched between Russia and China, that the fuller meaning of what I had witnessed would become clear.

Though surrounded by giants, Mongolia itself is no slouch. It is twice the size of Texas, but with a population of fewer than 3 million people—it has the lowest population density in the world. More than a third of Mongolians reside in the capital city, Ulaanbaatar, which lies on a plateau surrounded by high mountains. It was only late September when I arrived, but it felt like December in the Himalayas, the air full of the smell of snow. Temperatures can drop by 55 degrees in a single day, and on the evening I arrived I left my hotel unprepared, and caught a chill.

I had imagined myself leaving Ulaanbaatar immediately for the northern borderlands, where the Mongolian steppes yield to the Siberian taiga, into a purer void than I had seen from my train. As it turned out, my cold confined me to Ulaanbaatar for a few days. This was not a loss; the city, which is small and easy to walk around in, holds plenty of surprises for the flâneur. I had imagined something more Chinese, or Asian: a staging post or a market town, with nomads on horseback and crimson-robed monks in its narrow alleys. In 1924 Mongolia had been only the second country in the world after the Soviet Union to go communist. If I was unprepared for the Soviet, faux-European architecture of Ulaanbaatar, and the signs in Cyrillic everywhere, I was even less ready for the gridlock traffic on broad avenues, the new cafés, beer bars, beauty salons, and discos packed with both expatriates and trendy Mongolian youth, or the cranes everywhere, one of them constructing Mongolia's first five-star hotel. Being a vegetarian, I had prepared for the austerity of Mongolia, stocking up on processed cheese and crackers in Beijing. I realized I had wasted my time when I found myself on Peace Avenue, the city's main thoroughfare, surrounded by multi-ethnic cuisine and fusion restaurants and department stores and supermarkets.

These images of luxury seemed far away when I woke up every morning in my room at the Ulaanbaatar Hotel and saw a statue of Lenin dominating the view from my window. With its high ceilings, chandeliers, marble staircases, and generally unresponsive staff, the hotel itself seemed to conform to a Soviet idea of luxury. Neoclassical buildings ringed the massive Sukhbaatar Square, a wilderness of cement named after the Mongolian nationalist who rid his country of Chinese influence in 1921, only to saddle it with the Soviets. One building in garish pink stood out in particular. This was the State Opera and Ballet Theater, which wouldn't have looked out of place in St. Petersburg, part of a Russian fantasy of Europeanness.

Much of this, I learned, was the work of the Mongolian communist Yumjaagiyn Tsedenbal and his Russian wife, Anastasya Filatova, who together ruled the country from 1952 to 1984, consolidating Soviet influence with an iron fist, especially in the communist-style command economy where the government owned all the means of production and restricted private business. They further cleansed Ulaanbaatar of Chinese influence.

Even before their reign, the Soviet Union had cast a dark shadow on Mongolia—communism had managed to recreate here the cruelties and absurdities it had inflicted on people in the Soviet Union and Eastern Europe. One afternoon in Ulaanbaatar I wandered into the Memorial Museum of Victims of Political Persecution. It had been set up soon after 1990, when Mongolia rid itself of communism and embraced democracy. I was shown around by Bekhbat

Sodnom, the director of the museum, who turned out to be the grandson of Peljidiyn Genden, Mongolia's prime minister in the early 1930s.

Genden was shot dead on Stalin's orders after he repeatedly defied the Soviet dictator's orders to purge Mongolia of allegedly anti-communist and rightist elements, such as the Buddhist clergy. More Mongolian leaders would be executed before Stalin found those who were prepared to follow his instructions. The museum contained much evidence of the terror Mongolia had known in the 1930s. The first floor had photos of some of the thousands of Mongolians killed during that time. On the second floor I was abruptly confronted by a display case housing a pile of skulls pierced with bullet holes. I winced; my host looked unperturbed.

Sodnom felt, he told me later, that visitors needed to face the true scale of the tragedy inflicted on Mongolia's Buddhist culture and identity by the Soviet Union and its Mongolian allies. Death squads travelling around the country had executed more than 20,000 monks and destroyed more than 700 monasteries. They had also wiped out the country's entire fledgling intelligentsia, to the extent that as the British journalist Jasper Becker pointed out, only 'five people were left in the entire country with more than high-school education.'

Given that almost every other ethnic nationality between Russia and China—Kazakhs, Uzbeks, Kyrgyz, Tajiks, Tibetans, Uygurs—was absorbed into one of the two communist empires, Mongolia's uninterrupted existence as an independent state cannot but be considered an achievement. Still, walking around Ulaanbaatar, I marvelled at the evidence of an extraordinary historical reversal: how Russia, which once feared the Mongol hordes, had later managed to completely dominate Mongolia.

The Mongols, known to the Russians as Tartars, either ruled or threatened Russia for much of the second millennium. Mongols lived in many Russian towns and intermarried with Russians. Many famous Russians, such as Boris Godunov, Gogol, even apparently Lenin, were said to have Mongol blood. The Russian state itself, as it began to develop in the sixteenth century, was a successor to the empire created by Genghis Khan's conquests. (Soviet communists and their Mongolian supporters reviled the great Mongolian hero.)

Since the collapse of communism, Genghis Khan has made a triumphant comeback. Many statues of Lenin and Stalin have been taken down, and Genghis Khan now stands everywhere in Ulaanbaatar; his bearded face is on currency, billboards, matchboxes, and shop signs. In November 2012, the Mongolian government raised 1.5 billion dollars in international markets by selling a bond called 'Genghis.'

I was in Ulaanbaatar when Mongolia's president spoke at the UN General Assembly in New York, upholding Genghis Khan as a model of efficient and humane governance. As I read the speech in the *UB Post*, Mongolia's English-language weekly, I imagined representatives of the Central Asian republics, as well as Afghanistan, Iran, and Iraq, rising in protest and reciting the names of cities—Samarkand, Herat, Kandahar, Nishapur—devastated by the Mongols.

But the revisionists have been at work on Genghis Khan. The modern version of the legend of the man now comes to us expunged of its extreme cruelties. Certainly, the mass murders committed by Stalin and Hitler in the twentieth century have made Genghis Khan appear a moderate.

This may come as a relief to Mongolians. For certifiable heroes such as Genghis Khan seem to act as glue for a national identity that has fragmented since 1990. Poverty and deprivation during the communist era had united Mongolia; stagnation had ensured a degree of stability. But, as in Russia, the transition to a free-market economy since 1990 has caused much confusion and distress.

According to the foremost American scholar of Mongolia, Morris Rossabi, the country may have had a successful transition to multiparty rule, but economic disparities continue to widen between those few who can take advantage of the foreign presence in Mongolia and the many more who can't. The crime rate has tripled since 1990 in Ulaanbaatar, and pawnshops have flourished.

Mongolia's urban-based rulers often declare that they want their subjects to give up their nomadic way of life and move to the cities. But, walking around Ulaanbaatar, it soon became clear to me that the city's new comforts and luxuries—the cafés, bars, and discos—were confined to the expatriate population and a small number of the Mongolian nouveau riche.

In the suburbs, former employees of state enterprises languish in dingy Soviet-era apartment blocks, or, even worse, in gers without running water or sanitation. Ulaanbaatar's smog, which I had attributed to rapid industrial growth, is largely the result of the coal-burning stoves of the suburbs.

It is hard to see how things could improve soon. The country's economy, previously heavily dependent on foreign aid and investment, has been boosted by the discovery of copper and gold. The Oyu Tolgoi ('Turquoise Hill') or 'OT' copper-and-gold mine, which is partly owned by Rio Tinto, a British-Australian mining behemoth, is expected to contribute one-third of GDP by 2020. An ongoing quarrel between the Mongolian government and Rio Tinto may delay national prosperity, or it could turn Mongolia into a kleptocracy, like another previously dirt-poor and now resource-rich country—Angola.

Certainly, as it grows wealthier, Mongolia grows more dependent. It needs extensive foreign assistance in order to exploit its apparently large deposits of coal, iron, tin, uranium, copper, gold, and silver. Mongolia's neighbour China, which is perennially in need of raw materials, could help. Almost all of Mongolia's exports—minerals, cashmere, wool, milk products—go to China, which is also the largest investor in the country. The country's massive coal and copper deposits are also destined for China. But relations between the two countries remain cool. They are now complicated by a nationalistic Japan, which seeks a broad anti-Chinese coalition in the region, and plans to enlist Mongolia in it. Japanese Prime Minister Shinzo Abe visited Mongolia in early 2013, speaking, flatteringly but unconvincingly, of a 'strategic partnership' with a country that shares 'the values of freedom, democracy, the rule of law and basic human rights.'

Since 1990, Mongolia has also hosted the kind of foreigner who offers economic sustenance as well as cultural identity: the Christian missionary from the United States. I had been reading about the American churches that, denied the opportunity to evangelize in populous but

rigidly closed China, have turned their attention to other
parts of East and Central Asia, particularly Korea, Japan, and
Mongolia. Almost all the major denominations and sects are
represented in Mongolia, and, although no reliable census
figures are available, they have apparently found many 'rice
Christians' among the Mongolians—people eager to convert
in exchange for food and shelter and the possibility of travel
to the West.

Agizul Sosor, programme manager of the Tibet
Foundation, which works for the revival of Buddhism in
Mongolia, told me that 'the new generation of Mongolians
is very consumeristic. They want cars, jeans, stereo systems,
and satellite TVs, and they will go to whoever gives it to
them. But very few people can have these things; the rest
can only watch with envy and malice.'

One Sunday morning I went to a service at a Mormon
temple on the outskirts of Ulaanbaatar—one of many in
the city. The temple's white steeples rose cleanly out of the
usual roadside cluster of apartment blocks streaming with
clotheslines. Mongolians wearing fake brand-name jeans,
sneakers, and anoraks filled the austere chapel. 'They are
good kids,' one of the very young Americans sporting a
crew cut and an extremely earnest expression informed me.

It turned out that he was from Utah and had just returned
from two years in the Mongolian countryside—'without
heating,' he added. The other American Mormons there
seemed equally virtuous. They denied that they were
in Mongolia to convert people; they were there rather
to educate and train Mongolians into economic self-
sufficiency. The Mormon Elder, a bald, severe-looking man,
complained that their church often got a bad name because

of the Seventh-Day Adventists and Baptists, who use cash inducements to convert Mongolians to Christianity.

Buddhism, which encourages a suspicion of desire, might seem the perfect antidote to such materialistic practices, particularly because it was once woven into the fabric of everyday life in Mongolia, its rituals and mantras ever present during marriages and funerals.

Much like Tibet, Mongolia was an ecclesiastical state—indeed, it was the sixteenth-century Mongolian ruler Altan Khan who inaugurated the lineage of the Dalai Lama (Dalai is a Mongolian word meaning 'ocean'). In the pre-communist era, almost every family sent a boy to the local monastery to be trained as a monk. But two generations of Mongolians lived without any experience of their traditional religion.

Since 1990, more than 100 monasteries have reopened, and the number of monks is rising. The Tibet Foundation is only one of the many organizations working to promote Mongolia's traditional religion. One afternoon I visited the Ganden monastery, which now has more than 500 monks.

Inside Migjid Janraisig Sum, the main temple in the monastery complex, middle-class pilgrims bowed before the new 85-foot-high gilded statue of Avalokiteswara, a replacement of the statue removed by communists in 1937 and taken to St. Petersburg. The chief abbot, Venerable Baasanswren, a large, jolly-faced Buddhist clutching a mobile phone, told me that the first novice monks after communism had to travel to Buddhist monasteries in India—a journey that parallels one made by the great medieval figures of Mongolian Buddhism. Some even went to Tibetan masters living in Europe and America. The first of these monks were just now returning, and training others. They were also learning the traditional Buddhist art of thangka painting.

The abbot would pause now and then in the conversation to help himself to snuff, which he kept in a Kodak film container. Speaking of the Christian missionaries, he became visibly angry, and I noticed the translating monk hesitate, leaving out the more un-Buddhist sentiments from his leader's outburst. The missionaries, the abbot said, gave free computer education, clothes, and food to Mongolians in an attempt to bribe them into their alien religion.

But what he didn't tell me was that the Buddhist monks who controlled Mongolia before the communists had hardly set a high moral example. Monasteries were centres of corruption, and the clergy was widely hated by Mongolians. Bogd Khaan, the last spiritual leader of Mongolia who died in 1924, was often drunk for days on end. I was not surprised to learn that Choybalsan, one of Mongolia's more repressive Stalinist leaders, had spent his childhood unhappily in a monastery.

I was relieved, finally, when my cold improved and I was able to leave Ulaanbaatar. For years, I had thrilled at the mention of the word Karakorum, and it was to this ancient capital, now called Kharkovin, that I now set off.

Unfortunately, the only practical vehicle on Mongolian roads is the environmentally challenged SUV. But I had reason to feel grateful for it as we left the city's industrial suburbs and moved into the countryside. The road, uneven at best, often disappeared, and then the knuckles of my

Mongolian driver, gripping the steering wheel, would go as white as the dust kicked up by our bouncing, bucking Pajero.

Occasionally, small hills appeared in the distance. Their smooth sides showed pointillist dark and white spots, which would then reveal themselves as gers surrounded by herds of sheep and horses, often supervised by handsome men with weather-beaten faces and lassos. But for many miles on the long straight road there was no vehicle or human being in sight, and the sky, streaked white by jet planes, seemed more eventful than the undulating grassland.

Such a total absence of the known world and its familiar features is initially oppressive. But it can be soothing once you get used to it. For a few hours that day I felt that nothing mattered; all ambition, vanities, and egotisms faded, and the sense of smallness and insignificance imposed by the vast blank landscape seemed utterly natural and true.

It was early afternoon when we drew into a ger camp. The white tents lay next to a bright icy stream, where a raw wind made it clear why Mongolia is considered colder than neighbouring Siberia. But it was remarkably warm inside my ger, once the brazier was lit, and the adjustable flap sealed the top of the felt tent. Inside the ger that served as the local restaurant, I surprised a couple of middle-class English ladies sniffing at a Mongolian lunch. Mongolian cuisine, usually mutton in watery gravy, is not the most distinguished feature of the country, and I stuck with the processed cheese and crackers I had bought in China.

Somewhat fortified, I ventured late that afternoon to Erdene Zuu Khiid, a sixteenth-century monastery. The oldest monastery in Mongolia, it was originally built out of the ruins of the capital and has been destroyed and rebuilt many times. When I walked through the gates with their floating Chinese eaves, there was hardly anyone in its vast walled compound. The chapels housing the statues of the Buddhas were under lock and key, and the shadows of temples lay sharp on the ground. I saw a young monk in the distance, trying to ride a bicycle, and his exuberance only seemed to add to the solitude of the monastery.

Beyond the monastery to the east lies the ancient capital of Karakorum, built by Genghis Khan's son and successor, Ögödei, its boundaries marked by four turtle-shaped rocks. The city was abandoned after Kublai Khan decided in the late thirteenth century to move the capital to what is now Beijing. But its fame lasted long enough to reach the ears of Marco Polo, who mentioned the city in an account of his travels through Asia. In 1254, William of Rubruck, a Franciscan monk sent by Louis IX to meet the Mongol Khan and make an alliance against Muslims, became the first European to visit the city.

What he saw didn't impress him much. The Mongol nomads did not produce great architects. But there was no mistaking the extraordinary power that radiated from Karakorum—the power that spread and made Karakorum a household name in places as far away as Iran and India.

To leave the monastery compound and re-enter the unfenced expanses of Mongolia; to be told by the Mongolian hawkers selling fake archaeological finds and trinkets that the dusty land of scrub and wild grass where I stood was indeed Karakorum, with no distinguishing sign except for the remaining turtle-shaped rock; to remember that this was once the centre of the world, was to be given a unique historical lesson.

Encircled and diminished by Russian and Chinese powers, and waiting now for Western tourists and investors, modern Mongolia seems very far from its adventurous past. No longer the originator of earthshaking events, or even a valued pawn in the Cold War, it faces the uncertain future of small countries with narrow economic bases everywhere. Grappling with inequality, pollution, and political instability, it may look to Genghis Khan's exploits for emotional succour. But nationalism based upon a memory of the past rather than achievements in the present is usually shallow. Sooner or later, Mongolia will have to make its peace with—and learn to depend upon—China.

This is not as humiliating as it sounds: the American economy, after all, also depends on China. I thought again of the faded grandeur of the Mongols a few weeks after leaving Karakorum when I read the surprising news that George W. Bush, who is not known for his frequent-flier mileage, had visited Mongolia, mostly to thank the country for its contribution to the war effort in Iraq.

In a speech at Ulaanbaatar, Bush offered the curious theory that Mongolians were like Americans: hardy frontier people. It wasn't clear whom the president's speechwriter had wished to compliment—the Mongolian hosts, whose ancestors had once known 'full spectrum dominance,' or the powerful visitor, who had been aspiring to it. For the Mongolians' frontier days were long past, and if the memory of their extraordinary conquests spoke of anything now, it was of the transience of nations and empires, and the impermanence of human glory—the melancholy but important truth that Mongolia's great emptiness still holds.

TAIPEI: THE FORGOTTEN
CHINESE

It should take less than two hours to fly from Shanghai to Taipei. But there were no commercial flights between the two cities in 2008. Coming from mainland China, I had to go south to Hong Kong in order to reach Taiwan's capital, and the trip took almost a whole day. So close and yet so far; and every hour I spent getting to Taipei—at airports, on flights—heightened my sense that I was travelling to a remote place that had dropped out of time.

Taiwan's giant neighbour certainly helps create that impression. I had been to China many times but, gripped by the sheer energy and scale of the country's modernization, I had paid little attention to the small island off its southeastern coast.

Of course Taiwan, which parted ways with communist China in 1949, has been modern for a long time. It had built an industrial economy by the 1970s, when China was still a largely rural and poor country coping with the devastation caused by Mao Zedong. Very prosperous in terms of per capita income, Taiwan does not suffer from the extreme economic inequality and environmental devastation that increasingly darken China's future.

Culturally and politically, too, Taiwan is in some ways ahead of China. Taiwan's pop music is hugely popular and influential across East Asia, and film-makers like Edward Yang (director of *Yi Yi*) and Hou Hsiao-hsien (*Flowers of Shanghai*) are revered around the world. After remaining politically stagnant during forty years of continuous martial law, Taiwan experienced a popular citizen's movement that turned the island into a democracy in 1987—the first anywhere on Chinese soil. Today, its population of 23 million contains a large and well-educated middle class.

Yet Taiwan has no place at the United Nations or any other international organization. Even countries that maintained diplomatic relations with it for decades have abandoned it for China; Taiwan's democratically elected leaders are unwelcome in most countries.

The Taiwanese I meet in the United States and Europe often lament their country's exclusion from the international community. Shortly before leaving for Taiwan, I spoke to Lung Yingtai, one of the island's leading writers. Lung spent years in Europe and America before returning in the 1990s to participate in Taiwan's democratization. In 2012, she became Taiwan's minister of culture. 'We used to think of China as a backward and isolated place,' she said. 'But it is Taiwan that is now isolated, through no fault of its own. It really makes me very sad.'

I remembered her words as I journeyed to Taipei. Arriving late at night, I prepared for a melancholy city resigned to its marginal status. But there was nothing mournful about the garish thickets of throbbing billboards

I saw as I drove in from the airport. Passing the crowded night markets, through the smells of seafood and the sounds of good-humoured haggling, I felt as though I had arrived in another great Chinese city, a counterpart to Hong Kong and Shanghai.

Opening the curtains in my hotel room the next morning, I saw a sprawl of utilitarian concrete blocks enclosed on all sides by green hills. Compared to the slick kitsch of Shanghai, Taipei's modernity initially seemed a bit dated, belonging to the 1970s. But within this ageing cityscape stood Taipei 101, the second tallest building in the world. Resembling an elongated pagoda at the top, it rose shiny tier by shiny tier out of a haze of pollution into the blue sky. It dwarfed the landscape.

Self-consciously grand architecture usually leaves me cold. During the days that followed, I made no attempt to get to the top of Taipei 101. Yet I often found myself standing at my hotel window, arrested by the big, beautiful apparition above the grey city. It spoke eloquently of Taiwan's prosperity, and I came to see that it represented the national ambition of a fascinating country and people that had been unfairly shunned by the world.

Taiwan's identity is deeply rooted in Chinese culture. Almost 85 per cent of the island's modern population consists of migrants from the Chinese provinces of Fujian and Guangdong, and almost 75 per cent speaks the Minnan dialect of Fujianese. But as the example of the United States proves, settler populations eventually find their own ways of defining themselves, breaking with the mother country. Taiwanese self-perception has changed particularly swiftly over the past twelve years: according to a survey in the *Economist*, the number of those identifying themselves as Taiwanese has doubled to 41 per cent, while those who see themselves as purely Chinese have dwindled to 6 per cent of the population.

But it didn't take me long to discover that many Chinese traditions—condemned as 'feudal' and 'bourgeois' in communist China—never faded in Taiwan, and are actually experiencing a revival. One of the most popular television shows in Taiwan features a puppet theatre called Budaixi, whose costumes and plots draw on ancient Chinese sources. And if you are a Sinophile, the best reason to visit Taipei is the National Palace Museum. With jade-green tiled roofs and yellow walls that loom dramatically out of a mountain valley north of downtown Taipei, it holds one of the largest collections of Chinese artefacts and artwork in the world, including the famous *Jade Cabbage*—a piece of jade carved to resemble a head of cabbage—and a boat carved out of an olive pit. Much of the best Asian art resides in Western museums. But China, which was never fully conquered or occupied by a Western country, managed to hold on to much of its heritage, and a lot of it was carted away to Taiwan in 1949 by Chinese nationalists fleeing the communist army of Mao Zedong. Renovated in 2007, the National Palace Museum can lay claim to being the Louvre of Asia.

One afternoon, I walked from the busy and smoggy Xinsheng South Road into Taipei's famous Wistaria Tea House—and into a world where time had been ordered to stand still. Music from Chinese lutes floated through the room; sunlight streaming in from wood-framed windows and skylights and bamboo curtains created dappled patterns on the tatami mats. Green moss clung to the dark red-brick walls. In the small Japanese garden at the back, a spring bubbled quietly amid little ponds and stone tables.

The teahouse's owner, Chow Yu, who resembles the wispy-bearded sage of Chinese landscape painting, performed a serving ritual, mixing teas and warming miniature pots and bowls with delicate and elegant gestures. Teahouses in imperial China, he explained, were places where the literati gathered. No other traditional culture venerates writers and intellectuals as much as the Chinese. Chow explained that he uses only the ceramic ware favoured by the scholarly class in old China: Yixing, which best retains the flavour of tea.

But Wistaria is connected as much to Taiwan's eventful modern history as to the classical past. Built in 1921, the two-storey building was originally Chow's family residence. 'Many writers and intellectuals would gather here in the 1950s to talk about art and politics,' he said. 'It was dangerous, because Taiwan was under martial law and we could have been accused of sedition.' After Chow turned the building into Wistaria in 1981, it became the favourite watering hole of intellectuals and politicians who participated in the movement for democracy in 1987.

Taiwan has moved on. Its democracy is now a raucous and unruly affair, with two main parties—the Chinese Nationalist Party and the Democratic Progressive Party, colour-coded blue and green, respectively—that periodically assault each other with allegations of corruption and incompetence. But Wistaria remains popular among the city's literati. Joining me for a light lunch of steamed vegetables and hot-and-sour soup that afternoon were Chen Hao, a television talk show host, and Yang Ze, an editor at the *China Times*, Taiwan's leading daily newspaper.

Like the cities of Italy and France, Taipei abounds in literary bookstores, the kind that have Philip Roth rather than Dan Brown in the window display. Ze confirmed my impression of a small but cultivated reading public. Newspapers, he told me, publish literary supplements every day. The flow of translations from foreign literatures is brisk. Speaking of his own love for literature, Hao was embarrassed to admit that he worked in television. Laughing, he said, 'I despise television. I really do!'

I asked Hao and Ze about the windows with metal security grating that I had seen on apartment buildings everywhere in Taipei. 'It reflects the general sense of insecurity of the recent refugees from China, as well as of the Taiwanese who have long been residents here,' Hao said.

He and Ze went on to speak about politics with a frankness that slightly alarmed me; it would have been inconceivable in mainland China. They explained how modern Taiwan remains the unfinished business of the civil war that raged in China in the early twentieth century. Since 1949, when the Chinese nationalists fled to Taiwan, the country has remained in a sort of limbo. American support for Taiwan's separate identity has steadily dwindled since President Nixon travelled to Beijing in 1972 and began to normalize relations with China. But Taiwan is prevented from being absorbed into what Chinese communists call their 'motherland' mainly by the US Seventh Fleet, which still patrols the narrow strait between Taiwan and China.

'Because Uncle Sam protects us from Big Brother,' Ze

said, 'we have been heavily influenced by him in many respects, more than we have been influenced by Japan, which ruled Taiwan from 1895 to 1945. American movies and music were very important to all of us who grew up after 1949. There were scholarships to American universities, and almost every educated Taiwanese aimed to study in the United States. Many of those who went as students settled down there.'

Meeting other Taiwanese, I discovered a reverse trend in progress: large numbers of those educated or formerly settled in Europe and America are returning to the island. Along with East Asian countries like Singapore and Malaysia, Taiwan was among the first movers of globalization, well before the word became widely known. It also helped bring mainland China into the web of global trade and investment. Taiwanese money routed through Hong Kong accounted for a large part of the initial foreign investment in China in the 1980s and 1990s. The chance to do business with the fastest-growing economy in the world is bringing many Taiwanese expatriates back to Asia.

In a posh club adjacent to Taipei 101, I met Joanna Lei, a businesswoman who was also an influential legislator for the Chinese Nationalist Party. We sat in a private room into which waiters dressed from head to toe in black discreetly brought one delicately flavoured dish after another; the Chinese love of good food was evident in the loud gay voices eddying around the club, and chopsticks fluttered over steaming plates of fish and vegetables.

Travelling to the United States as a student, Lei had risen from research editor at ABC Television to senior executive. She was, as she herself put it in a strong American accent, 'one of the highest-ranked Asian-Americans in the media industry.' In the late 1990s, she terminated a promising career trajectory and returned to Taiwan. 'I was half-fulfilled in America,' she said. 'I wanted to see what I could do in Taiwan.'

Lei hasn't found it easy to negotiate Taiwan's highly charged and sometimes nasty politics. When I met her, she was fighting to clear her father, a former defence official, of corruption charges. The rise of China, she said, has crudely polarized Taiwanese society into people who want greater integration with China and those who want independence. She herself hopes for integration.

Indeed, as I discovered, the issue of reunification with China is a Taiwanese obsession. All my conversations in Taipei inevitably veered towards it. When I reported Lei's views to Lin Cho-shui, a former legislator from the Democratic Progressive Party, he responded sharply: 'Taiwan is a democracy and China is a dictatorship. How can the two come together?'

Perhaps, as the writer Lung Yingtai suggested, China will have to catch up with Taiwan and become properly democratic before unification can happen. Many Chinese intellectuals and activists, she claimed, see Taiwan as an inspirational model for democracy in China.

It was Wen C. Ko, one of Taiwan's leading venture capitalists, who outlined the most likely and practicable scenario. Sitting in his company's boardroom in Neihu, an upscale business district, he said the inexorable forces of globalization would bring about a gradual and peaceful unification. Taiwanese companies, many of which had offshored much of their work to the mainland over the past decade, are now physically relocating to the Chinese coast, he explained. The close intermeshing of business interests is likely to improve political relations. There are already signs of a thaw: chartered flights between Shanghai and Taipei have been allowed. Taiwan is letting more tourists from the mainland visit.

Looking at it from a business perspective, Taiwan's absorption into China could make sense. Still, as Ko's son Patrick pointed out, Taiwan's youth (almost one-fourth of Taiwan's electorate is under thirty) is far from embracing China's imitation-modern culture. One afternoon I went to a performance of traditional Taiwanese opera at the Red House Theater, in the Ximending area. Built by the Japanese in 1908, the red-brick octagonal building was recently renovated, like many old structures in Taipei. Stylishly dressed young people filled the café on the first floor and the theatre on the second, sitting impressively still during the ancient and—to my ears at least—somewhat long-winded two-hour performance.

It is as though democratization has allowed the Taiwanese to rediscover all the many aspects of their identity. The proof that Taiwan's cosmopolitanism was imprinted not only by China and the United States but also by Japan shone vividly in the narrow pedestrianized streets of Ximending, Taipei's Times Square. Here, stalls selling manga comics, Japanese video games, and American baseball caps alternate with food carts peddling oyster noodles and 'stinky tofu,' a fermented bean curd with a smell that makes it strictly an acquired taste.

Youth also dominate the crowd of worshippers at Longshan temple, the city's most revered site. It's in Taipei's oldest district, near Snake Alley, one of the more famous night markets, where snakes are sold as food. An incongruous sight in their jeans and high heels and name-brand handbags among the temple's fantastically gilded and lacquered pillars and walls, men and women in their late teens and twenties kneeled, bowed, and held up smouldering incense sticks with a touching devotion.

Patrick Ko, who like many upper-class Taiwanese was educated in the United States, told me that Buddhism has experienced a big revival in Taiwan, which now has the largest number of nuns in the world. Indeed, Buddhists from Taiwan are now transmitting their teachings to the mainland—a reversal of the historical process that had originally brought the religion to Taiwan. And Buddhism in Taiwan has an even more special aspect: it is less introspective and more oriented towards social welfare than Buddhism in the United States. Buddhist organizations run nurseries, orphanages, hospitals, retirement homes, and clinics; they are an important presence in Taiwan's civil society.

Patrick himself seemed affected by the strong current of idealism running through contemporary Taiwan. While in his twenties, he could have joined his father's company, easing himself into an Asian elite. Instead, he had chosen to teach in a small school in Nepal. 'I know many people my age,' he said, 'who don't want to join the rat race and make money, who want to do something more meaningful with their lives.'

It is as though Taiwan, having already known a degree of material prosperity, is now experiencing a countercultural moment. Certainly, Taiwanese like Patrick who have never lost their Chinese traditions seem to be embracing an ennobled sense of their identity and their role in the world.

In that way, they are ahead of many Chinese, who, while savouring their newfound wealth, seem to be stuck in a version of the American 1950s, with all the familiar traits of conspicuous consumption and conformity.

The world is still likely to prefer China over Taiwan. The island is fated to be always thought of in relation to its powerful neighbour. But the Taiwanese themselves seem undeterred from their pursuit of a separate identity. And when after leaving the island I thought of it, the image that came most readily to mind was of Taipei 101. Despite its beauty, the building had initially seemed pointlessly tall in an otherwise flat and sprawling city. But I now realized that it not only reflected Taiwan's wealth and modernity; it also proclaimed the dignity of an isolated people, and their determination not to be forgotten.

KUALA LUMPUR: BEYOND THE
MELTING POT

One evening last fall I was walking through Chinatown in Kuala Lumpur, Malaysia, when, suddenly, in the midst of Cantonese restaurants, shops selling knock-off designer bags and food stalls hawking exotic-looking meats, I came across the wholly unexpected sight of a Hindu temple with a voluptuous gate tower: a riot of gilded idols and precious stones and wafts of thick incense.

I walked on, under a freeway, past a pretty north Indian-style mosque, and, abruptly, the narrow vertical signs and single-column ideograms of Chinese shops gave way to something intensely familiar: I was in a south Indian market town, all gaudy silk and glittering jewellery shops.

Bollywood music blared out of speakers at Saravanaa Bhavan, the restaurant where I sat, savouring *bisi bele bhath*, a deliciously spicy south Indian concoction of lentils and rice. The pavement was hectic with flower and garland sellers—the kind of sweet-smelling chaos that lines the approaches to Hindu temples in India. But the waiters were glued to the TV screen, which showed a horse race in Hong Kong.

The contrasts made me think of the word 'Indochine,' which the French used to refer to the tracts of land separating Asia's two major countries. But Kuala Lumpur (or KL, as it is commonly known), the capital of Malaysia, which lies almost exactly between two of the world's oldest civilizations, gives the word a more contemporary and urgent resonance. It hints at Asia's own attempt at cosmopolitanism, at finding ways of living with cultural diversity in an interconnected world: a challenge that people in almost every country now share.

In recent years, Malaysia seemed to be running away from it. Until 2003, it was led by the authoritarian-minded Mahathir Mohamad, the author of many disturbing racial theories and rigid enforcer of discriminatory laws against ethnic Chinese and Indian minorities. Protests by Mohamad's victims were ruthlessly crushed.

This recent record belies Malaysia's long exposure to the fluid identities created by globalization. The Malay Peninsula has long been at a major crossroads of history. Well sited between the Indian and the Pacific Oceans, its ports attracted Chinese and Indian merchants and Arab adventurers from the Red Sea long before the Europeans arrived to trade in the sixteenth century. A few miles south of KL, the famous city of Malacca still speaks of its Dutch, Portuguese, and British past. To the east of the Malay Peninsula lies the island of Run that the British ceded to the Dutch in 1667 in exchange for an island that, initially called New Amsterdam, we now know as Manhattan.

But the sense that never leaves you in India or China— of being embedded in history, of being surrounded by the debris of the past—vanishes in KL. There were days when rain and mist veiled the city's tall silvery buildings as well as the thickly forested hills in the distance, and I could imagine the land to be as empty and untenanted as its first explorers may have found it.

I kept promising myself to go up the Petronas Towers, the world's tallest buildings until recently, for panoramic views of KL and its surrounding green hills. From up there, I imagined, I would see Asia's own New World, a space only faintly inscribed with human endeavour and aspirations, a late arrival in history, and a still fresh and uncluttered setting for generations to come.

This wasn't just pure fantasy: the only people who have continuously inhabited the main Malay Peninsula are aboriginal tribes; the rest came from elsewhere, the majority as late as the nineteenth century, such as the men from China and India who came to plant rubber and mine tin, and stayed back.

KL started life as a tin-mining encampment—the side product, like many cities in the New World, of the nineteenth-century scramble for commodities and easy wealth; the city's name literally means 'muddy estuary.' Built pell-mell, the city lies thinly on the ground, radiating out from a small historical downtown and business district into hilly suburbs. There is something Los Angeles-like about its snaky freeways and bad public transportation. The promiscuity of its architectural styles is very LA, too. It's not what one expects in a major Asian city, which either wears a patina of its premodern past (Delhi, Beijing) or carries the clear impress of its founders (Mumbai, Hong Kong).

One afternoon I stood in the middle of KL's old colonial

quarter, now renamed Merdeka (Independence) Square, where the country's first prime minister declared liberation from British rule in 1957. To the west was the Royal Selangor Club, whose mock Tudor facade would have been at home in the English county of Suffolk. St. Mary's Cathedral, on another side, reminded me of the Anglican churches that cast a melancholy shade over English cemeteries in the hill stations of India. But the strangest structure of all faced me across the square: the Sultan Abdul Samad Building, whose profusion of onion domes, cupolas, colonnades, and arches made it seem like a Moorish fantasy gone crazy.

The capital of an oil-rich Muslim country, KL is full of the solemn emblems of modernity: skyscrapers, five-star hotels with vast atria, and imposing shopping malls. (At some point, I stopped marvelling at the patient queues outside a new Uniqlo store.) Indeed, you could suspect that this is a tropical Dubai, another glamorous mirage in the middle of nowhere.

Certainly, Penang, to the north, has classier architecture; Singapore, the British-built city state south of the Malay Peninsula, can boast of a more orderly cosmopolitanism; and Hong Kong has always made more money. But while those places have lost their Johnny-come-lately airs, KL retains its charming frontier-town raffishness. The countryside, the landscape of thick river and dense forest that is commemorated in the fiction of Joseph Conrad and Somerset Maugham, still feels close. Just a few minutes from downtown, you can drive through stretches of fine parklands with massive rain trees.

And it remains a city of immigrants: the population is more than one-third Chinese, contains a sizable group of Indians, and has an underclass of labourers from Java, Sumatra, Bangladesh, and Nepal. Unlike their counterparts in Hong Kong or Singapore, immigrants here don't cower out of sight while the rich splurge at Hermès. In fact, they give the city its particular vitality.

The city's gritty working-class past never feels remote. Chinese labour and entrepreneurial energy created the city, and half of its population is Chinese (the other half consists of Malay Muslims and Indians). The melancholy lives of their Cantonese, Swatow, Hakka, and Hokkien ancestors are still evoked by the tiny shophouses of Chinatown: narrow two-storeyed buildings with open-fronted shops on the first floor, and divided residence on the projecting second floor that shades the pavement from sun and rain.

China projects raw power across Asia today, binding big as well as small economies to its export juggernaut. But for much of the nineteenth and the first half of the twentieth centuries, China exported its poorest people to Southeast Asia and beyond. There is something moving about the Chinatown temples, earliest attempts by the Chinese immigrants at a sense of community and spiritual solace. Thick with dragons and joss sticks, they commemorate old Chinese clans. A statue with a Western-style top hat at Chan See Shu Yuen temple commemorates the relationship with Western traders that made the Chinese the most successful immigrant community in KL.

KL was also notorious for its Chinese triads, and at Old China Café, amid the pulley lights, feng shui mirrors, marble tabletops, and bentwood chairs from the 1930s, you can imagine the top-hatted gangsters suavely plotting a shipment or even an assassination. In today's Chinatown, meanwhile, the hawking of fake Rolexes and Burberry bags is perhaps the most brazen illegality. Still, in the narrow buildings with dungeon-like rooms above open storefronts, you can sense the vulnerability and desperate diversions—the gambling and prostitution—of lonely immigrants far from their homes in southern China.

The Indians, who remain relatively impoverished, live even closer to their past. One evening I went with the Malaysian leader Anwar Ibrahim to a celebration for Deepavali. Anwar, as he is called, is a thoughtful man. He had broken with his mentor Mahathir Mohamad in the late 1990s, and suffered long imprisonment on false charges. He had returned to Malaysian politics with a new programme for racial harmony. He talked about V.S. Naipaul whom he had met on the latter's travels to Malaysia.

'He sees Islam as a threat,' Anwar said, 'religion in general as something to be discarded. You won't be able to understand places like Malaysia if you think that.'

Anwar moved easily through the vast hall packed with Indians impassively watching a young couple on stage belt out popular Tamil songs. There was an overpowering fragrance of perfumed oils and sandalwood incense. The men were dressed in white dhotis, or unstitched cloth wrapped at the waist, and the women, often with kohled eyes, wore jasmine garlands interwoven into oiled hair and diamond and gold studs in their noses and ears. Their saris were magenta, pink, and green.

Garish papier-mâché gateways and twinkly lights adorned Brickfields, KL's Little India, whose canteens serve some of the spiciest food east of Venice. One evening, as I sat in one of them with the Malaysian writer Amir Muhammad, drinking the milky sweet tea called *teh tarik* (pulled tea), a large, traditionally dressed Tamil family arrived. Their mood was festively gluttonous, and the staff duly responded. One group of waiters unfurled large banana leaves on the tables, sprinkling them with water; others arrived with serving bowls and then proceeded to set down steaming curries, daubing bright patterns on the leaves with as much assured fluency as an artist engaged in action painting. The scene could have been from Madras circa 1950.

But the identity that KL tries to project most forcefully is Malay and modern; and there is a disquietingly sectarian aspect to this assertion.

Government policy of affirmative action favours bumiputra—literally, 'sons of the soil'—in education, business, state employment, and even the arts. Parties have divided along racial and ethnic lines. 'Malaysia,' Muhammad told me, 'is one of the most racially conscious societies in the world.' (This can have a certain dark humour. A line from *Atomic Jaya*, a satirical play from 1998 by Huzir Sulaiman, one of KL's highly respected writers, goes: 'The Chinese do the work, the Malays take the credit, and the Indians get the blame.')

But Malay nationalism has grown less funny in recent years, often in tandem with political Islam. It often uses the modern spaces of KL to make its points. Sometimes, the effect is not wholly incongruous.

Unlike the Chinese and the Indians, ethnic Malays were traditionally a people of the countryside, and a semi-rural settlement stands right next to KL's Golden Triangle business district, immune to the boom in property prices around it. The squat houses, some on stilts, are of weathered timber and tin. The straight lanes between the houses are lined with frangipani, bougainvillea, coconut and date palms, and banana trees thick with fruit.

Food stalls here sell some of the best street food in KL: curries and grilled fish, fried pancakes, satay, and, most important, the national dish, *nasi lemak*: rice, peanuts, cucumber, anchovies, and sambal in coconut cream. In the nearby bazaar you can find Malay shops specializing in batik, *songkok* (headgear for men), prayer mats, and robes. You can also come across Malay medicine men selling herbal concoctions that can apparently cure all ailments. If this sounds too un-Islamic and faintly heretical, there is a big mosque nearby, speaking of a globally assertive faith.

The impressively maintained National Museum most vividly embodies the Malay quest for a usable and dignified past. More than the exhibits themselves, I found intriguing the groups of formally dressed Malays in high-collared shirts, silver-threaded sarongs worn like kilts over their trousers; they looked eager to be instructed in their nation's history.

Nothing, however, is more eloquent with aspiration than the Petronas Towers, until 2004 the tallest buildings in the world. Their minaret-like shape is a defiant Islamic claim upon the modern world and an assertion of Malaysia's place in the comity of nations. But as Anwar has written, Asia 'is in the process of coming into being. The long and intense process of self-definition and self-understanding is just beginning.' Cities such as KL and Mumbai are already the site of much ideological contestation and debate. KL's paternity, for instance, is disputed. Historically attested wisdom had the founder as the Chinese Yap Ah Loy, the largest landowner in the mid nineteenth century. But the nationalist Malays like to think it was the Malay aristocrat Raja Abdullah, and so Yap Ah Loy's name has been virtually excised from textbooks.

But such sectarianism does a disservice to KL, which contains the cultures of Asia and the West in startling new juxtapositions. Consider, for instance, its old railway station, another Moorish extravaganza, partly obscured by a freeway and painted a dazzling white. The curves and planes of its pavilions and archways are still blindingly clear. It is as though Gaudí had been let loose in KL.

And whatever the intentions of the Malay nationalists, the shiny new buildings speak less of Malay identity than of a city where people know how to be rich, and learn how to spend money. Visiting the city in the 1930s, the French writer Jean Cocteau complained of 'an atmosphere of over-rapid luxury, a glut of gold.' It still exists, nowhere more garishly than in the malls near the Petronas Towers, each vying to be more elegant than the rest, where white-robed Arabs, reluctant to travel to Western countries, stand checking their BlackBerrys while their wives, covered head to toe in black, shop for lingerie.

Freeways lead out of the rotting city core to the suburbs in the hills, where big SUVs hide behind foliage rich with jasmines and jacaranda. Here live the millionaire businessmen and the diplomats in burglar-alarmed homes with sprinklers swishing away and Filipino maids in the kitchen. Here are the smart cafés and restaurants where you can find practically every major cuisine respectably represented.

At dinner one evening in the elegant suburb of Damansara Heights, the city's lights ablaze below us, guests argued passionately about Malaysia's frustratingly racial politics and small-minded politicians, who, they say, keep the country from realizing its full potential. Our host, Karim Raslan, one of the shrewdest pundits on Southeast Asia, cited it as one of the reasons why he spends half of his time working and living in Indonesia.

It was left to me, an outsider, to point out that Malaysia was a country still relatively untouched by the many violent conflicts of class, caste, ethnicity, and region that make the rise of India and China less self-evident than it looks. Malaysia is a middle-income country with a small population (28 million). There are no cruel disparities between rich and poor here; KL has none of the utter destitution that blights the downtowns of Indian cities. Though flawed and rowdy, Malaysia's democracy is preferable to the nanny authoritarian state of neighbouring Singapore; and it has lately thrown up some promising young politicians and activists eager to move beyond the petty concerns of their elders.

Two of the country's most famous rising politicians—Khairy Jamalauddin and Anwar's daughter, the American-educated Nurul Izzah, known as the 'Reformist Princess,' who represents the posh KL suburb of Bangsar (described by the local wit as 'The Republic of Bangsar') in the Malaysian Parliament—belong to different sides of the political divide. Both told me that they were determined to carve a post-racial future.

And there are signs that this may be more than a fantasy. In the pivotal elections of May 2013, the Malay-dominated ruling Barisan Nasional coalition returned to power with a 133-seat majority in the 222-member parliament. Khairy Jamalauddin, an outspoken critic of Mahathir's racial policies, was appointed a minister in the new cabinet. More remarkably, Anwar's Pakatan Rakyat coalition garnered more than 50 per cent of the vote. Preferred by urban Malays as well as ethnic Chinese and Indians, Anwar demonstrated that the old race-based politics is challenged by increased urbanization, and the priority many voters give to disparities of income and class over race.

Malaysia's old racial consensus is fraying. Broader political enlightenment will obviously take some time. For now, KL's thinkers and writers forge their own, somewhat lonely paths in a materialist city that is not hospitable to activities other than making—and spending—money.

At an Indian restaurant off Bukit Bintang, I met the writer Bernice Chauly. Like many urban Malaysians, she is a striking product of Indochine: her father was north Indian and mother, Chinese. KL, she said, was an unsatisfying place for her. At the same time, she liked her marginal position within it. As an individual artist, she felt more freedom to do what she liked in a non-competitive realm.

The visual arts are more connected to a rapidly growing economy, and they're experiencing a mini-boom here. The clean white spaces of Bangsar's Valentine Willie Fine Art Gallery express a confidence that I first came across in Hong Kong's galleries, just before Chinese art rose to international prominence. Its director of programmes, Eva McGovern, who left a job at the Serpentine Gallery in London to work in KL, told me that the region around Malaysia—Indonesia, Philippines, Singapore, Thailand—was being knit together very fast, helped by low-cost airlines that flew to small cities and towns not only in China but across the vast Indonesian archipelago (much of which shares the Malay language with Malaysia). Artists can be discovered and exhibit their work in a way that was nearly impossible before, she said. KL is now embedded into a wider Southeast Asian sphere of culture.

It's true that KL won't become famous overnight for its culture—even if, like Abu Dhabi and Qatar, it frantically buys up a lot of it. For now, this remains a city of modest pleasures, of malls and night markets. Indeed, its most resonant message to the world is to eat well and variously.

Nevertheless, KL's place seemed assured, notwithstanding Malaysia's sluggishness, in a new emerging idea of Asia. It now carries the sediment of far too many different cultures and societies to retreat into provincial obscurity. Certainly, an experiment with important consequences for the future is being worked out in this particular New World; and it may be nothing less than a new way of being a modern Asian, of having multiple identities, and being reflexively cosmopolitan.

I did not, finally, go up the Petronas Towers. Perhaps I did not need the static geographical overview of this inescapably fluid and hybrid city, 'where,' as Amir Muhammad writes in one of his essays, in words redolent of the island formerly known as New Amsterdam, 'everyone comes from elsewhere; therefore, everyone owns and shapes it to become something much greater than the sum of our individual origins.' Instead, I went walking through the old entertainment hub at Bukit Bintang. Colorfully seedy with backpacker hostels, massage parlours and malls, it crackled with all the languages I can recognize, and more: Bahasa Indonesia, Filipino, Urdu, Bengali, Arabic, and Persian, as well as English spoken with a variety of accents, from the broad Australian to the singsong Sri Lankan and the lovely Malay lilt. And I left KL convinced that here in the heart of the new Asia, the city is working out a way of being reflexively cosmopolitan, truly Indochine.

INDONESIA: DEMOCRACY
REDEFINED

In 1929, the Indonesian poet and historian Sanusi Pane travelled to India. It was a pilgrimage of sorts for the young nationalist. Pane had been educated in a Jakarta school inspired by Rabindranath Tagore's experiments in pedagogy. Like many anti-colonial Southeast Asians riveted by Gandhi's campaign for self-rule, he hoped that India would offer a way to achieve national wealth and power that avoided the means—large-scale violence, dispossession, and extensive environmental despoliation—deployed by Western nations. 'A free India, built upon a Western basis,' he wrote, 'would be of little worth . . . Must we forever be satisfied with what has been left behind by others and found worthless, trudging behind in the wake of other nations?'

This anxiety of perennial belatedness was to acquire a rich irony in the postcolonial era. India, though apparently democratic and non-aligned, failed to become a proud exemplar of intellectual and economic autonomy. Wealth and power came to authoritarian countries where local elites had adopted colonial tactics of coercion and ideological deceit. For many upper-caste or middle-class Indians observing Southeast Asia's embrace of global capitalism in the 1970s and 1980s, their own country seemed to have not only missed out on this chance of enfeebling its uneducated, unproductive, and potentially dangerous classes; it had handed them the right to vote periodically, entrapping top-down economic growth in the morass of electoral democracy and purely rhetorical socialism. We were dazzled by Lee Kuan Yew's no-nonsense, squeaky-clean technocracy in Singapore; transfixed by images of Southeast Asia's mildewed colonial port cities being transformed into glittery business megalopolises; and we admired our own authoritarian-minded politicians—such as Indira Gandhi and her son Sanjay—who proposed to clean up and 'beautify' Indian cities sullied by the poor. And so, in 1995, three years before Suharto was ousted, Indonesia could entice an untutored visitor like myself from India.

To arrive in a country that once belonged to the Hindu–Buddhist *ecumene* was to drift into a pleasurable hallucination, where minor figures recalled from childhood readings of the Ramayana and the Mahabharata, loomed over city squares or were miniaturized in *wayang* (shadow puppet theatre). It was to marvel how, unlike the British in India, the Dutch had inflicted few obviously self-aggrandizing monuments on a country they pitilessly exploited. Squatters flourished in the decaying colonial district of Kota in old Batavia, where the colonialists had once created their own fantasy of home with mansions, canals, and cobblestoned squares. The language of foreign usurpers had been discarded; a new national language, Bahasa Indonesia, had helped pull the archipelago together; and, though the Nehruvian discourse of nonalignment, secularism, and socialism had been eagerly abandoned in India, the newspapers still spoke reverently of Pancasila, the national ideology of social harmony that Suharto vigorously promoted.

To be an Indian in Indonesia in 1995 was also to witness a new postcolonial promise of deliverance from poverty and squalor after the failures of the first generation of autarkic leaders. Indonesia seemed far ahead of India in its collective embrace of a form of capitalism honed in the once much-despised West. Envied by Asia's *Time*-reading elites, a new business district of glass and steel had risen in Jakarta (actually facilitated by hired thugs who used murder and rape to evict tens of thousands of squatters, renters, and landowners from *kampongs*, urban villages). Accustomed to the austerities of made-in-India goods, the shabbiness of our counterfeit modernity, I remember being struck by the shops abundantly stocked with international brand names, the number of working women in the cities and towns, and the material possessions of even factory workers, who had scooters, televisions, and fridges (if not unions). Even the small-town hotels were of a high standard; and the golf courses and suburban villas spoke of a prosperity that in India was still a dream.

In a major shift in the 1980s, the Indian government embraced big businessmen, discouraged labour activists, and emphasiszd rapid wealth creation to the detriment of equitable and sustainable growth; and an authoritarian-minded Hindu right-wing movement had emerged in time to protect the advantages of the old rich—the country's corporate families—while boosting the fantasies of a growing aspirational class. GDP growth rates accelerated after India's deeper integration into the global economy in 1991; they helped exalt the 'free market' in India as another Hindu deity, one whose propagandists claimed would shower—presumably through the great trickle-down miracle—prosperity on all. Meanwhile, the country's biggest and oldest corporations found better ways of enriching themselves through alliances with a business-friendly political class, affording themselves the best pickings among the country's wealth of minerals, land, and forests. By the end of the decade, Anglo-American affirmations of India as 'a roaring capitalist success story' (*Foreign Affairs*) would be replaced by anxieties in the *Economist* and the *Financial Times* that the country was breeding Russian and Latin American–style oligarchies while growing ever more authoritarian. Big industrialists such as Tata and Ambani now openly push for the Hindu nationalist Narendra Modi, who brims with business-friendliness, to be made prime minister, despite his complicity in the murder of more than 2000 Muslims in 2002. In 1995, however, I knew little about the deeper lessons India could have learned from Indonesia's experiments in crony capitalism and neo-liberalism.

Superficially at least, the pothole-free toll roads in Java and Bali; the shopping malls; the private TV channels, controlled but scoring easily over the state TV's dreary didacticism; the skyscrapers; and the totems of early globalization everywhere—pirated software, cloned watches, cassettes, Japanese comics, and CD-ROMS—denoted a country that had taken a long lead over India in the Asian scramble for capitalist modernity.

We remained generally unaware of the contradictions and tensions building up in Suharto's Indonesia, although there were signs such as the brutally repressed Tanjung Priok riots in 1984 in northern Jakarta's port area where anti-government posters showed a prominent Chinese crony pouring US dollars into Suharto's gaping mouth. This smouldering rage among the permanent underclass of those left behind and destined never to catch up would finally explode after the Asian financial crisis in 1997, making the country synonymous with urban riots, terrorist plots, car bombs, widespread ethnic violence, earthquakes, fires, volcanic eruptions, and tsunamis, not to mention Islamic beards. Indonesia has undoubtedly burnished its international image in recent years. The number of foreign correspondents in the country has grown; and, moving on from laggardly India, investors and financial and management consultants have set up new echo chambers of optimistic projections about another 'rising' Asian economy. According to the much-cited Boston Consultancy Group, more than half the country's 242 million people will qualify as middle class or richer by 2020. This may prove to be as much boosterish fantasy as the BCG's and McKinsey's predictions about India in the past. For now, however, domestic consumption among an overwhelmingly young population—60 per cent of Indonesians are under the age of thirty—accounts for more than half of Indonesia's economic growth.

The traditional mainstay of the economy—abundant natural resources—is doing better than before in the age of globalization. Selling off its coal, oil, palm oil, and gas, sparsely populated East Kalimantan had emerged as one of the republic's richest provinces with the highest GDP per capita in Indonesia—some 8500 to 9000 dollars. The Chinese and Indian demand for commodities has endowed small cities like Makassar in Sulawesi and Palembang in Sumatra with gated communities and Louis Vuitton. More disconcerting mutations await visitors in other parts of Indonesia. Large parts of Sumatra, ravaged by slash-and-burn investors, resemble a lunar landscape, and smoke from land-clearing fires by palm-oil prospectors extends as far as the cities of Malaysia and Thailand, prompting doctors in Kuala Lumpur and Singapore to warn people with respiratory diseases to wear masks. Bandung, once famous for its invocations of Afro-Asian solidarity, is now known for another kind of interconnectedness: low-cost Air Asia flights from Singapore and Malaysia that bring in hordes of shoppers looking for cut-price deals at fashion designer outlets.

It is also becoming clear that while outsiders focused obsessively on the cornucopia of democracy and global capitalism in post-Suharto Indonesia, older, established business groups and families have used their proximity to politicians to garner an even more disproportionate share of national resources and income. Nearly half of the country's population continues to live on less than 2 dollars a day, largely employed, if at all, in the exploitative informal sector, which includes scavengers sifting trash dumps for recyclables and ill-paid wage labourers toiling at hazard-rich construction sites. Corruption scandals have blighted the reputation of all major political parties and figureheads, sending many (though not enough) members of parliament to prison. In a recent survey, a majority of interviewed Indonesians said they preferred life under Suharto, with its minimum guarantees of public health, security, and affordable basic goods.

Disenchantment with old-style politics has made Joko
Widodo, Jakarta's new governor, the most popular politician
in Indonesia today. Widely tipped to be the country's
next president, Widodo, better known as Jokowi, is an
outsider, with no known links to big corporate groups or
established political parties. He grew up in a riverside shack
in the central Javanese city of Surakarta; his father was a
truck driver, his mother a bamboo seller; he was the first
member of his family to attend university. He flourished
as a furniture exporter before deciding to enter Surakarta's
electoral politics. During his seven years as its mayor, Jokowi
turned the city into an instructive example of what he calls
'bottom-up' governance. This was particularly remarkable
since Surakarta is known in Indonesia as *sumbu pendek*
(city with a short fuse). Jemaah Islamiyah, the extremist
Southeast Asian group with links to al-Qaeda, originated in
the city, which also provided a base to the militants linked
to the bombings in Bali in 2002 and 2005. Surakarta had
witnessed vicious attacks on the ethnically Chinese and
business-minded community in 1998 (as the Asian financial
crisis intensified, Javanese everywhere exposed to rising oil
prices, food shortages, and unemployment took out their
frustration on an old and perennially defenceless target: the
Chinese who comprise less than 5 per cent of the population
but, during the three decades of Suharto's rule, controlled
70 per cent of the country's economy).

Jokowi energetically courted an insecure people by
choosing a Chinese as his running mate (and then fending off
a smear campaign about his propinquity to infidels). In a city
of small merchants and traders, he made it easier to procure
business permits and licences. In a country notorious for

corruption and crony capitalism, he favoured small food-cart owners over global convenience store chains and shopping malls. He peaceably relocated unregulated street vendors to a new marketplace, enhanced access to public health services, and championed small and medium-size industries against local and foreign corporations.

He had also supported such traditional crafts and industries such as batik. These, he told me, should not only be able to compete with mass-produced goods from China; they ought to play an important role in deepening regional identities (a distinctive feature of central Javanese culture). This form of localization—deliberately counterposed to the socioeconomic ruptures and steep environmental costs of global capitalism—seemed like a necessary experiment in a populous, diverse, and largely agrarian society that had to find its own way of being modern. Not surprisingly, Jokowi, first elected in 2005 as mayor of Surakarta, had won re-election in 2010 with the kind of majority vote— 90.9 per cent—often claimed by Central Asian tyrants.

In the elections in Jakarta in 2012 (where Jokowi again chose a Christian running mate) the many underprivileged migrants-cum-entrepreneurs from rural Java helped him upset the calculations of establishment parties and politicians. But Jakarta, not to mention the vast Indonesian archipelago, poses a different order of challenge altogether to Jokowi. The city's low-lying slums populated by rural migrants are exposed to periodic, uncontrollable floods. Consumer capitalism in the world's largest Muslim nation has bequeathed to Jakarta's ten million residents polluted air, gridlock traffic, and venality on a fantastic scale. The city's previous governor, a mustachioed holdover from the

Suharto era of plunder, possessed a Van Gogh in addition to the more typical Hummer and Harley Davidson.

A populist figure like Jokowi, however, does seem an attractive throwback to a moment of postcolonial idealism, speaking, as he does, of an economy configured to serve the *rakyat*—the people—rather than enhance profits and growth rates, and of the need to replace 'top-down' with 'bottom-up' governance. As early as the 1970s, Indonesia's most lucid modern thinker Soedjatmoko was warning against fast-growing disparities between the Javanese political centre and the resource-rich periphery, and between rural and urban areas. 'We will have to turn developmental thinking upside down' he argued; the poor must have 'first claim to the total national resources of the country.' Extreme inequalities doomed the prospects of democratic politics in the country. For a 'crowded, hungry and competitive world' leads to increasing 'pressures toward greater authoritarianism and oppression' and 'human freedom is certainly the first victim of such a future.'

Soedjatmoko, and his inconvenient reminders that social justice is the fifth principle of Pancasila, was ignored—and he eventually exiled himself from Indonesia. By the 1970s, Western-style capitalism seemed to be working nicely together with authoritarian regimes and American client states in South Korea, Taiwan, Thailand, the Philippines, and Singapore. Prefiguring their later Gadarene rush to China, multinational corporations identified Southeast Asia as the site of abundant natural resources, labour, and low wages. While India stagnated under a protectionist regime, parts of post-World War II Asia were rebuilt with copious American investment and aid. The historical role of the military in developing societies, Samuel Huntington wrote in *Political Order in Changing Societies* (1968), a warning against the chaos caused by social and economic modernization, 'is to open the door to the middle class and close it on the lower class.' And, as part of an implicit Cold War bargain, military and business elites across Asia joined hands to squash labour activism and disenfranchise the rural poor.

Religious solidarities were recessive for much of this time. I remember an incipient Hindu nationalist from my first visit in 1995. Drinking beer at a hotel near the ninth-century temples of Prambanan, where colossal productions of the Ramayana are held, he blurted out his muddled impressions: 'It doesn't look like . . . it doesn't feel like a *Muslim* country.' But then unlike Pakistan, which mainly supplied our images of impoverished and fanatical Muslims, Indonesia didn't think of itself as a Muslim country—not until its postcolonial political and economic upheavals. Residues of pre-Islamic beliefs and practices—Hindu–Javanese syncretism and even animism—clung to the traditionalist faith of the majority: the *abangan*, in Clifford Geertz's broad description. The major divisions were between classes and regions. In the country's first—and remarkably free—elections in 1955, the communists and the secular nationalists did as well as the Islamic parties. Indonesia's early problems, greater than in many much less diverse territories expediently stitched together by colonial administrations, were of governance: how to consolidate a rickety political construct menaced by both internal dissent and the geopolitical stresses of the Cold War.

The novelist Richard Wright, visiting Bandung's Afro-Asian conference in 1955, thought that this wasn't necessarily 'a Right or Left issue.' The important thing was to find 'the *engineer* who can build a project out of eighty million lives, a project that can nourish them, sustain them, and yet have their voluntary loyalty.' But effective socio-political engineers and nation builders were in short supply everywhere in Asia and Africa. Sukarno, Indonesia's first president, was no different, exalted to power by his long anti-colonial battles, but lacking all experience in administration or institution building. Faced with the miserable legacy of colonialism—unemployment, low literacy, and rising inflation—he was doing by 1955 what many others in his position were doing and would soon do: he spoke of the evils of imperialism, of continuous revolution, and the noble idea of Indonesia; and he charmed many of his compatriots.

Watching the familiar spectacle, Wright concluded: 'Indonesia has taken power away from the Dutch, but she does not know how to use it.' This was a harsh verdict. Sukarno's task in Indonesia was particularly vexed. Unlike Nehru, Sukarno inherited no 'steel frame' bureaucracy or professional armed forces from the departing rulers. Wartime occupation by the Japanese and the long war against the Dutch had devastated the colonial economy. Sukarno had to contend with, among other political groupings, a politically and commercially ambitious military; and he was increasingly forced to rely on his generals to quell CIA-backed separatists in Sumatra and Sulawesi (Suharto himself rose to prominence in various counter-insurgency operations in Sulawesi and West Papua). The power of the generals grew—in inverse proportion to the health of the economy—as Dutch-owned businesses nationalized by Sukarno came under their control.

Sukarno, increasingly exasperated by electoral democracy, scrapped the liberal constitution in 1957, and replaced the elected parliament with one appointed by himself. Seeking a counterweight to the military, which by then was developing close links with the Pentagon, he began in the early 1960s to encourage their natural adversaries, the Partai Komunis Indonesia, then the largest communist party in the 'free world,' while speaking of a broader anti-imperialist alliance with Hanoi, Beijing, and Phnom Penh. The polarizations of the Cold War also marked the countryside, where Partai-supported landless farmers and sharecroppers faced off against landowners and small-town bourgeoisie aligned with the Nahdlatul Ulama, the more traditionalist of the two Muslim organizations in the country.

Sukarno was playing a dangerous game by empowering both the generals and the communists, and invoking an ideology he termed 'Nasikom': an attempted synthesis of nationalism, Islam, and communism. As Indonesia's economic crisis intensified—with inflation rising to 600 per cent—an assault on the generals in September 1965 by Sukarno's supporters, followed by a counter-coup by Suharto, led to his downfall. Blaming communists for the coup and the general disorder in the country, Suharto swiftly sidelined Sukarno. He then inaugurated his 'New Order' with a blood rite: in one of the twentieth century's biggest unpunished crimes over half a million suspected communists were murdered in 1965–66, many of them ethnic Chinese accused of links with Mao Zedong's China. Many of the killings were along the political fault lines that had developed before 1965: landholding feudal elites and small-scale bourgeois versus peasants and workers. The military, with considerable stakes in agricultural and other businesses, zealously participated in the extermination of left-wing pests. When not directly engaged in mass murder, army officers gave support to the members of Ansor, the young wing of Nahdatul Ulama, a large Islamic social organization established in 1926 and based in East Java.

Having physically decimated the left in Indonesia, Suharto consolidated his rule, adapting the authoritarian structures of Sukarno's 'Guided Democracy' to those of the 'New Order.' There was no question of representative democracy; Suharto's intellectual consigliere, Ali Murtopo, a close reader of Huntington's *Political Order in Changing Societies*, worked out the 'floating mass' theory, whereby the population was to be depoliticized and fragmented: 'people in the villages,' he ordained, 'will not spend their valuable time and energy in the political struggles of parties and groups, but will be occupied wholly with development efforts.' The government would now ensure order and stability, and keep communists and other troublemakers at bay, while the rakyat were tasked with higher economic growth, assisted by rural electrification, rigorous population planning, and a green revolution, and exposed to the sensuous pleasures of consumerism. (Pramoedya Ananta Toer, Indonesia's greatest modern novelist, was only slightly guilty of hyperbole when he claimed that 'the post-1965 Indonesian society was constructed on two pillars: entertainment and fascist oppression.')

All state institutions were purged of communists and their sympathizers, and staffed with loyalists from the military.

Suharto also appeased the generals by letting them fashion for themselves an elaborate system of extortion: a variety of organizational structures and managerial roles in state-owned and private enterprises, cooperatives, corporations, and even charitable foundations. The country's valuable resources—minerals and timber—were thrown open to Japanese and American investors. A new rent-seeking class of Indonesian middlemen and fixers emerged while the poor suffered from pollution and fires, and loss of livelihood through the depletion of forests and fisheries. The Paris Club of lenders including Americans, the Japanese, and Western Europeans expressed their gratitude by rolling over debts and coughing up money for Indonesia's development budget. They also funnelled some of the largesse via the World Bank and Asian Development Bank. The Japanese, the single largest private investors in the country, paid large bribes to Suharto's family and friends. Heartened by Suharto's business-friendly and anti-communist posture, the Americans acquiesced in the Indonesian invasion and occupation of the former Portuguese colony of East Timor in 1975. In the subsequent four years, about one-third of island's entire population was killed by gunfire, napalm, or starved to death.

Suharto also made Indonesia safe for civilian and military capitalists by putting real and likely dissenters in prison, and by banning independent trade unions altogether. Indonesia's political culture had long been marked by mass mobilizations, a history that went back to the armed rebellions of peasants and plantation and port workers initiated by the Partai in 1926 and 1927 and an abortive rebellion in 1948. Now, thugs on retainers, part of an anti-civil society actively fostered by Suharto, stood ready to break up demonstrations, or beat up activists: the tradition of vigilantism and mob violence inaugurated in the 1960s that blights Indonesia to this day. Suharto kept alive the bogey of communism, well after the end of the Cold War. With one eye on his Western patrons, who insisted on some minimal gestures to democracy in the free world, Suharto also designed a system of sham elections in which Golkar, the government's party that included all civilian bureaucrats, soldiers, policemen, various 'technocrats,' and journalists, easily won two-thirds majorities.

But it would be too simple to say that simple predation by the propertied classes, as in Marcos's Philippines, and state terror underwrote Suharto's reign. Indonesia's economy grew an average 6.5 per cent from 1967 until it contracted cataclysmically, by 13.6 per cent, in 1998. A culture of bribes and extortion flourished, but it wasn't incompatible with high GDP growth. Development subsidies by the West and Japan ensured the rise of living standards even before Indonesia turned into an export-oriented country; an oil boom starting in the 1970s helped. Rural incomes were boosted by the introduction of high-yield rice varieties. Literacy rates rose from abysmal levels.

Monopolies in cement, oil, timber, telecommunications, media, and food came to be enjoyed by an indigenous business class, which included Chinese-Indonesian groups as well as Suharto's own family members (Suharto didn't trust other Indonesian business families). Local companies in Aceh were allowed to strike deals with ExxonMobil while Freeport and Rio Tinto acquired mining rights in Papua. Military rule in Indonesia opened the floodgates to the corporate class, and small windows to the middle class. Not surprisingly, many among the salary earners and the urban petty bourgeoisie supported Suharto (and can still be found mourning the demise of his 'stable' regime). Suharto's Golkar party partly ensured that some of the loot trickled down to low-level officials. Even conservative Islam was eventually brought into Suharto's patronage networks.

However, Suharto's careful sharing of spoils with a select few eradicated any lingering notion of a national project or idea: one dedicated to the welfare of the rakyat. By the 1970s the nation-building ventures that had galvanized the anti-colonial struggle had developed cracks everywhere in Asia and Africa; the first generation of idealists and visionaries such as Nehru, Nasser, and Nkrumah were being replaced by authoritarian-minded figures (Sadat, Indira Gandhi) striking deals with local business and feudal elites. But Suharto presided over a more radical reorienting of the national mood.

In 1988, the Indonesian playwright and publisher Goenawan Mohamad braved censors to write nostalgically of Sukarno, who had died in disgrace in 1970: 'When Bung Karno was alive, Indonesia still had the ideals of a Kshatriya who owns no credit card, no BMW and no Black Drakkar aftershave. In Bung Karno's time, Indonesia was still felt as an aim, a reason to fight, a cause. Now we don't seem to be like that—and we feel that we have lost something.' Indonesia, Mohamad wrote, was now merely a name for a territory populated by 'stomachs, ambition and anxiety.'

Indeed, Suharto had bet on that outcome: a 'floating

mass' divided by its private pursuit of food, wealth, and status was at the basis of his regime's security and stability. What finally tripped him up, along with Marcos, Park Chung-Hee, and other pro-American Asian strongmen, was the gross inequity and fragility of the system he had created. The last years of privatization and financial liberalization under Western pressures saw Suharto and his family at their most rapacious. (The general himself had 73 billion dollars in various bank accounts by the mid 1990s; and his son Tommy had energetically scammed the exchequer, exceeding even Sanjay Gandhi, his fellow Asian dynast and motorphile, by manufacturing in Korea a 'national car' called the Timor). The final looting was led by Chinese conglomerates and a few *pribumi* (indigenous) families, which, helped by subsidized credit from the state and foreign investors, swallowed banks and lucrative units of state-owned enterprises. It was during this time that some of Indonesia's best-known Chinese businessmen and corporate groups—Salim, Mochtar Riady, Bob Hasan, Prajogo Pangestu, and Nursalim—acquired or established new companies.

Having entered the age of financial capitalism early, debt-laden Indonesia was also among the first to be exposed to its hazards in 1997. The currency lost nearly 80 per cent of its value following the Asian financial crisis; per capita income collapsed. Banks imploded; millions lost their jobs. The foreign direct investors, who had been underwriting Suharto's economic 'miracle,' predictably fled the scene. The IMF, which had exhorted liberalization, deregulation, and globalization, stepped in as usual with a harsh 'rescue package' of subsidy cuts, leading to food riots; IMF came to mean 'I Am Fired.'

Suharto, who had styled himself *Bapak Pembangunan* (father of development), and staked everything on economic growth, could not survive a crisis in which more than one-third of the population slid under the poverty line. A widely circulated photograph of IMF director Michel Camdessus, arms crossed, looming over a seated and clearly suppliant Suharto invoked for many Indonesians the racial humiliations of the Dutch era. And Suharto seemed to have lost his immunity as he faced the first major protests against his rule.

Radical students, inspired by the left-wing movements of the early twentieth century, and working quietly with urban factory workers, were at the forefront of many of the biggest demonstrations. Mass violence erupted across the archipelago after soldiers fired at protestors at Trisakti University in Jakarta on 12 May 1998, killing four students and injuring dozens. (One of the leading presidential contenders in 2014, Prabowo Subianto, Suharto's son-in-law and head of Kopassus, the notorious special forces, was implicated in this incident.) In many instances, the military tried to redirect public anger away from Suharto's regime by organizing mob assaults on the relatively affluent Chinese. But Suharto's position was untenable. Following a five-day occupation of the parliament by students and workers in May 1998, he resigned.

His appointed successor, an engineer called Jusuf Habibie began *reformasi* promisingly by removing press censorship, which released a torrent of public hatred for the former leader, freeing political prisoners, and eventually ending

Indonesia's disastrous twenty-four-year occupation of East Timor in 1999. He also inaugurated an ambitious experiment in decentralization, delegating power from the centre, where it had been tightly held since the days of Dutch, to some 470 districts and cities. Habibie's successor, Abdurrahman Wahid, a blind Islamic leader of the Nahdlatul Ulama, a charitable organization with nearly 30 million members that run *pesantren* (boarding schools) and hospitals, participate in elections, and exercise a great deal of social prestige and political power in rural areas, signalled a real break with the New Order. Gus Dur, as he was popularly know, boldly apologized for the killings of communists by members of his organization; he also proposed to lift Suharto's ban on Marxism-Leninism until he was thwarted by military pressure and angry Muslim groups. He helped build better relations between Muslims and Christians, and between the Nahdlatul Ulama and Muhammadiyah, the other large Muslim organization in Indonesia, which advocates a non-syncretic, Arabia-tinted Islam. For all his erratic ways, which finally led to his impeachment in 2001, Gus Dur recognized that a society deeply fragmented by violence and greed had to do a lot more than hold elections that day-tripping Western statesmen, UN observers, and journalists could then hail as a sign of democracy.

There were early signals, such as the mobs in Jakarta cheering gang rapes of Chinese women, that reformasi was not revolutionary and probably didn't even amount to reform. Sukarno's daughter Megawati Sukarnoputri, the republic's fifth president, assumed an aloof maternal posture as president—probably to mask her lack of political skills—while the military reverted to brute force against the separatists on outlying islands, especially in Aceh. On her first official visit to New York, she arranged for a special showing of *The Phantom of the Opera* for her entourage. Abandoning her working class and urban poor constituency, she stood by while her husband openly cut deals with retired generals and businessmen from the Suharto era. Reformasi had turned into *restorasi* when in 2004, one of Suharto's pro-American military confidantes General Susilo Bambang Yudhoyono, was elected president, and was soon joined at the top by figures from the military, business community, and conservative Islam.

'I would give a C to democracy in Indonesia,' a young legislator said as we talked one evening in Jakarta. He had been presented to me as a 'rising' politician. But, once assured of anonymity, he spoke with uncharacteristic frankness—even dramatic irony. His own party, Suharto's Golkar, now renovated and run by one of the country's richest businessmen, is proof, he said, that the oligarchs and bureaucrats who had previously used the centralized state apparatus to guarantee their privilege had adapted to a more open and competitive political system. It didn't take long after Suharto's exit for broader alliances to emerge and for the old elites to use popular consent to protect their political and economic power. Elections are now the main source of power and legitimacy. Those still serving in the military, too, have made effective use of democracy and decentralization to expand their business interests, often working together with local politicians and *preman* (hoodlums); the police, separated from the armed forces, are now their competitors in the business of selling protection, and have fought a number of pitched battles around the archipelago. Many retired generals and former cronies of Suharto established political parties, which, bereft of principles and ideas, are machineries aimed at the capture of state power.

One clear manifestation of this continuity with the past is the prominence in Indonesian politics of old faces, such as Prabowo Subianto, one of Suharto's American-trained army henchmen, and previously married to Suharto's daughter—intermarriage was one form the circulation of elites in Indonesia took. While rearranging its power and privileges, the old elite has also sought to extend them to a few more people—just enough to stave off mass discontent. The spoils are now trickling down to provincial and district levels. Local politics has become more important than national politics. People are more interested in becoming a bupati (head of regency, one of Indonesia's administrative divisions) than an MP because bupatis control access to local resources; it's a lucrative gig. Most people coming into politics are crassly motivated. 'I tell my cadres how to write, how to tweet,' the Golkar office holder said, 'but they are only in it for the money.' Under Suharto, corruption was centralized. Now it's everywhere.

And this kind of decentralization has gone well with Indonesia's integration into the global economy. The bupati I met one afternoon at the Hyatt Regency in Yogyakarta couldn't stop boasting of his various friends among Korean, Thai, Japanese, and Australian investors. Like many of his peers, he was a grateful child of the New Order; he had joined the state-owned life insurance company and then worked his way to the top. He smiled ambiguously when asked if he had supported Suharto's resignation in 1998. 'It was a gentlemanly act,' he said, 'it had stopped the country from descending into further conflict.'

The bupati, intellectually bland but plainly shrewd and single-minded, reminded me of the oft-repeated joke that post-Suharto Indonesia was a country with many mini-Suhartos. Armed security officers heralded his appearance, striking a minatory note with their uniforms and guns in the Hyatt's marbled lobby, which that afternoon brimmed with cheerful, flag-waving tour groups bound for Borobudur. And then the man himself—in his late sixties, grimly accessoried in the contemporary style of Asian plutocrats with a Mont Blanc pen and designer eyeglasses—led an entourage of khaki-uniformed personal assistants, who stood half-bent with solicitude around our table as he unfolded glossy brochures and maps of various projects in his region.

He had invested most of his energies into the possibility of building a steel industry in Java through a joint venture with an Australian firm. This involved setting up one mining operation and thirty-five iron-ore processing plants. He complained that his plan to create jobs and industrialize Java was not getting the green light from the environmental ministry. But why, I asked, does he want to industrialize Java? He had a ready answer: agriculture is unprofitable in a land with too many small farmers. Java has to rely more on manufacturing and services. He stared blankly when I asked him about the likelihood of educating the young population for jobs in the industrial sector. Does he plan to set up more colleges or vocational training institutes? He consulted briefly with his assistants, and then told me that the foreign companies investing in Java will train them.

Later, my interpreter, a soft-spoken young Javanese man, couldn't hold back the contempt he felt steadily rising through the meeting with the bupati. The various projects I was told about, he said, are all pretexts to siphon off public and private funds. But the bupati was no different from others he knew. The system doesn't encourage honest people. If you want to be a bupati or governor of a province, you have to pay party bosses vast sums to secure their support, advertise your candidacy, and bribe voters on polling day. The money for all this comes inevitably from business elites who, dismayingly out of pocket, are determined to have you do their bidding after your election. So the axis of business, government, and the military that was once dictated solely in Jakarta has now been reproduced at local levels. At its best, the devolving of state authority and financial power has produced a confident and innovative politician like Jokowi. At worse, it has created a multitude of fiefdoms in the vacuum of 'substantive' democracy. Even local military commanders have used the weakening of a central authority, and the end of subsidies from above, to become self-financing: their clients in protection rackets range from real estate speculators and illegal loggers to human traffickers and drug traders.

Still, many people told me, the much feared Balkanization of Indonesia—the intensification during the last days of Suharto and afterwards of old separatist insurgencies in the provinces of Aceh, West Papua, and East Timor—has been staved off with the promise of regional autonomy. Local elections are now held all the way to the village level; indeed, Indonesia has organized three free and fair elections since the downfall of Suharto in 1998. The media, which grew rapidly after the fall of Suharto, are relatively free, if not exceptionally critical or analytical. Even the long silence over the mass killings of 1965 is now slowly and fitfully being broken. Last year, a special issue of *Tempo* magazine, produced to coincide with the release of the documentary film *The Act of Killing*, disinterred the grisly logistics and motivations behind the slaughter. Corruption remains a big problem but a new agency, the Corruption Eradication Commission, has sent a few powerful politicians and businessmen to jail.

For almost everyone I spoke to among the elite the big news out of Indonesia, one that seems to obscure all its ailments, is now economic. 'I am bullish, bullish, bullish,' Fauzi Ichsan, chief economist at Standard Chartered Bank, said. There were sepia-tinted pictures in his elegant home of Sutan Sjahrir, the country's first prime minister, an avowed socialist, and one of the revered names of Indonesian modern history. It turned out that Sjahrir was Fauzi's grandfather: 'He was a Javanese aristocrat, who gave away all his lands, and so I had to become a banker.' Fauzi's own commitment to Indonesia is recent. He was a bond trader in Singapore when Suharto fell. Visiting Jakarta during the big demonstrations, he narrowly escaped being fired upon by the police, and for some years he stayed away. 'This place was hell,' Fauzi said, 'Indonesia looked like it would fall apart. There was no one to pull it together.' But now the country is pulling ahead. 'Democracy was "trial and error" and decentralisation was chaotic. People were fighting among themselves, and Islamism was on the rise. But, strangely, everything worked, and is still working. The infrastructure had to be built from scratch, but if you are a European or

American investor you have no alternative but to come to Indonesia.'

This is what the British financier Nathaniel Rothschild felt when in 2011 he set up a mining company called Bumi in association with the Bakrie Group, one of the biggest family-owned conglomerates in Indonesia. Rothschild wanted to find a way to lure foreign investors to an emerging market while ensuring that the unreliable locals play by the rules and regulations drafted in the City of London. The deal unravelled amid allegations of financial irregularities that tainted both European financiers and the Bakrie brothers (the eldest of whom, Aburizal Bakrie, is another presidential candidate in 2014). There were other stories of collaborations turning sour, Indonesia's increasingly opaque rules, and its rising economic nationalism. Nevertheless, Jakarta's five-star hotels and restaurants, though usually adjacent to the kampongs with miniature shacks and open sewers and alleys just wide enough for motorbikes, echoed with the boosterish talk by hedge fund managers and diplomats.

It was quite a contrast to meet Antonius Benny Susetyo one afternoon at the food court of one of Jakarta's downmarket shopping malls. Susetyo is a Catholic priest, and he spoke of the working class and the poor, and their near-total exclusion from the bonanza of GDP growth. The pastor, popularly known as Romo Benny, became famous after he publicly confronted Aburizal Bakrie in 2006. One of Bakrie's companies was associated with the oil and gas drilling that in 2006 accidentally created the world's biggest mud volcano in East Java. Benny demanded that the government seize Bakrie's assets to compensate the thousands who had lost their homes and jobs. One possibly related consequence was a near-fatal assault on Benny in 2008. He has only become more vociferous since then in his criticisms of the country's elite.

The country's economic growth has been built on 'hot money' from abroad, he said, which only benefits 10 per cent of the population. Others dismissed Benny as one among a minority of carpers in human rights organizations and other NGOs, pissing on the parade of a country that was—and I heard this often in Jakarta—is set to replace India as the 'I' in BRICS. Indeed, Yudhoyono, coming off his recent stewardship of the Association of Southeast Asian Nations, has been trying to project Indonesia as a global power, one with which both China and the US are eager to form strategic and business partnerships. An expensive nation rebranding campaign on CNN hails the 'golden moment' for 'Remarkable Indonesia.' Barack Obama had triumphantly 'returned' to Jakarta, with a rousing speech at the national university that received as many ovations as Binyamin Netanyahu's speech to the US Congress. The US had also decided to sell air-to-surface missiles to Indonesia's military after years of condemning the latter's human rights record. Paul Wolfowitz, a former ambassador to Indonesia, had urged Obama to 'cement a closer relationship with an ally in the fight against Islamist extremism'. And days after Obama's visit to Jakarta, senior Chinese officials had shown up, bearing 6 billion dollars in new aid.

In this race for geopolitical advantage, the Americans can count on many eager and longstanding local allies. Yudhoyono, like many of Suharto's generals, was educated in the United States. The technocrats who managed the economy under Suharto were referred to as the 'Berkeley Mafia.' University and think tank fellowships, Ford Foundation grants, and year-abroad programmes immunized the country's elite to the reflexive post-9/11 wariness of America in many Muslim and non-Western countries. The Chinese, on the other hand, have had to overcome a long legacy of mistrust; and their own 'soft power'—sourced largely from the Chinese business community—in the country has to be very cautiously wielded, if at all.

In 1965 Suharto's regime blamed the People's Republic for arming the masterminds of the 'communist coup.' The Chinese Embassy was promptly sacked and diplomatic relations with the country were suspended until 1990. Suharto also banned Chinese schools and calligraphy, and forced members of the minority group to change their personal names to more Indonesian-sounding appellations. Denied citizenship, or left in limbo, many Chinese left for the 'motherland' that centuries of settlement in the archipelago had rendered utterly alien. But China stopped exporting communist revolution in the late 1970s. It sought markets and commodities; and it had on its side the 'bamboo network' of overseas Chinese, one of the world's great economic powers.

Suharto was shrewd enough to recognize early on the way the local Chinese were able to attract foreign capital and use their overseas networks to move to high growth areas. Singapore, Hong Kong, China, and even the United States. One of his early chums was Liem Sioe Liong, the head of Salim Group, featured in the 1984 poster pouring dollars into Suharto's mouth. The financial clout of such ethnic Chinese —as opposed to that of indigenous businessmen—posed no political threat to him; and in the late 1980s, seeking to check the power of the military, he moved closer to them.

One monument to that intimacy lies a few miles west of Jakarta: an American-style suburb called Lippo Village that includes a hospital, university, cyberpark, golf course, museum, and basketball court. It was built on what was once a rice paddy by Mochtar Riady, one of Suharto's cronies and beneficiaries. Riady had started out as a bicycle trader after World War II, then bought a bank, before founding the Lippo Group, a conglomerate that is now thought of as the General Electric of Indonesia. In the 1980s, Lippo was among the first of the Indonesian-Chinese groups to go global: it branched out from banking to telecommunications, was assisted by the Suharto's loan and export and import policies, and spread from Indonesia to Hong Kong, Singapore, and finally the motherland.

After resumption of normal diplomatic ties with China in 1990, Riady toured the country for eight months by car, building more networks. 'China at the moment is terrible,' he reportedly said, 'but in another 10 years it will be incredible . . . Now we're starting to lobby, to get to know people, and then we'll start moving.' And so Riady did later in the decade, investing in second-tier Chinese cities that Western corporations were reluctant to invest in. Globalization posed some challenges, especially where local practices clashed with strict regulatory regimes. In 1996 Mochtar Riady's son and heir was caught funnelling illegal donations to Bill Clinton's presidential campaign and a paranoid American press floated rumours of Lippo's links with Chinese military and intelligence. But Lippo's influence and prestige suffered its biggest loss after the fall of Suharto. A frenzied mob of

10,000 people, apparently egged on by Probowo, torched and looted the Lippo Village super-mall, then the largest shopping centre in the country, killing eighty-six people.

The Riadys soon recovered. Encompassing a range of ventures from property to supermarkets and newspapers, Lippo is now one of the biggest family-owned Asian business empires. That doesn't show, however, in the sober demeanour of one of Lippo's scions, John Riady. Still in his twenties, Riady was prepared for membership of the global business elite at Georgetown, Wharton, Columbia, Harvard, and Oxford, followed by the usual anointment at Davos. But he returned to teach law at his family's university in Lippo Village. His spare and dark academic office seemed in deliberate contrast to the cheeriness of the American-style campus, where frisbees whirled below billboarded exhortations to embrace Jesus. He spoke earnestly to me of empowering the poor, of bringing skills to underprivileged Indonesians through a wider network of schools, colleges, and hospitals. This was not just about corporate social responsibility: the rich have a duty to help the poor.

Riady was in a penitential mood, I had been told, trying to atone personally for his father and grandfather's long years of unabashed cronyism. In general, the third generation of Asian tycoons, to which John Riady belongs, are moving away from the bamboo networks and opaque practices of their fathers and grandfathers, and trying to build shareholder-friendly companies. But Riady's philanthropy is also a hedging strategy: he and his family are identifiably Christian and rich in an increasingly Islamic and poor country.

A casual proposal by his father to set up more Christian schools in villages was greeted with angry demonstrations by Muslim groups, which accused Lippo of secretly converting Indonesians to Christianity. Even Jokowi, who had Chinese Christian running mates in both Surakarta and Jakarta, has been accused of being an infidel. The experience of inequality and deprivation amid the signs and intimations of great wealth have put many nerves on edge; and the ethnic Chinese are the default lightning rod. Most Indonesians, Romo Benny said, are turning to religion out of great frustration. The terrorist attacks in Bali and then Jakarta, the work of marginal radicals, and extensively covered by the international media, were actually a sideshow to the growing moral and political appeal of a largely non-militant yet deeply conservative Islam.

The millions of young people flocking to Jakarta from the countryside missed out on the traditional pesantren education that many of their parents had known. Marooned in the big anonymous city, they have found new sources of moral authority and solidarity in groups such as Majelis Rasulullah, or Prophet's Assembly, run by a charismatic preacher wearing long silk robes. Even many old leftists have embraced Islam. As we were driving one rainy evening from Surakarta to Yogyakarta, Goenawan Mohamed recalled a communist poet who had returned to Indonesia after a long exile in Holland, and then left soon afterwards: all his old friends were going on Haj, and he feared that if he stayed longer he too might end up wearing the telltale white robes.

And not just Islam but also Christianity, especially its evangelist exemplars, is part of the massive religious revival in Indonesia. I had been reading about a mammoth revival meeting in the central Javanese district of Temanggung, where the sick and the disabled claimed to be cured by Allah while thousands of worshippers stood in the rain, raising their arms to the heavens. Professional fishers of men like Pastor Romo Benny aren't so happy about the miraculous hauls to be found in Indonesia. 'The challenge for religion,' he claimed, 'is to take sides with the downtrodden, the poor, and the migrant workers and advocate on their behalf.' The new kind of religious preacher, however, thrives on militant disaffection, and often turns it into nihilistic violence against vulnerable peoples. It has become easy, as in Pakistan, for extremist Muslim groups to deploy jobless youth in violent assaults on infidels and blasphemers while politicians look the other way.

Muslim militants have shut down brothels, small-time gambling operations, nightclubs, and bars serving alcoholic beverages. They have also assaulted Christian churches, and prevented the construction of new ones. In the central Java town of Temanggung, not far from the site of the revival meeting, a mob emerged out of nowhere to burn down a Pentecostal church after the local court sentenced a Christian man to five years in jail for distributing leaflets insulting Islam; evidently, the sentence, the maximum allowable, was too lenient. When I visited the church two weeks after the attack, the façade was still black; and the beheaded figures at the Last Supper hadn't been replaced. The pastor and his family, living in a tiny house behind the church, looked fearful of rather than assured by the token policemen at the gate, who hadn't bothered to ask me for my identity. They weren't sure who was among their tormentors, but they certainly weren't locals, and they were highly organized.

They were anxious for me to leave. Their nervousness was understandable. Earlier that month nearly 1000 people, wielding knives and stones, had attacked members of the Muslim minority sect, Ahmadiyah, in West Java's Banten province. A bleak YouTube video showed a mob pummelling what looked like corpses with sticks and rocks while police stood by.

Such incidents have been increasingly frequent, and in the absence of any investigation much speculation centres on the nefariousness of the 'Deep' State: the enforcers of the ancien régime trying, as in Turkey, to enhance their power by discrediting civilian rulers. It's an explanation that sounds plausible. But the Deep State theory leaves out the expedient and growing role of political Islam, and the attitudes to sectarian violence among civilian politicians that extend from 'deadly indifference', according to a new Human Rights Watch report, to active complicity.

The state's expedient tolerance, even encouragement, of Islamic groups dates back to the last half of Suharto's reign. Having suppressed the communists, Suharto had also squashed another potential source of opposition. Islamic groups were required to pledge allegiance to Pancasila, and abandon Islamic symbols and language. Sensing a decline in his popularity in the 1980s, Suharto turned to Islam to legitimate himself, even making a much-publicized pilgrimage to Mecca. Pious Muslims were exalted to important positions within the government and the military, Islamic learning was reinstituted in schools, and the ban on headscarves in schools was lifted. Muslim intellectuals were courted, and Islamic banking encouraged. Suharto underwrote mosques in the neo-Arab rather than the local style. During his last days, he made a last desperate attempt to rally Islamists against reformasi.

But political Islam properly re-emerged only after Suharto was gone, and it's now an element of the ferment caused by competitive systems of democracy and globalization. Broadly conservative, even hardline, the new Islam is part of a global phenomenon, emerging from the Islamic revolution in Iran and the subsequent effort by Saudi Arabia to match the appeal of Shiite millenarianism by funding Wahhabi-friendly organizations, schools, and pilgrimages. Islam has also been helped by a political process growing ever more diffuse and unpredictable with urbanization and the growth of new power centres in cities and small towns. The many political parties have come to be backed by even more numerous and shifting power brokers, including Islamic groups and organizations. The result has been an unseemly scramble for votes and a hectic manufacturing of election 'issues.'

So now it isn't just explicitly Islamic groups that advocate rule by Sharia. All parties claim to be fulfilling an Islamic agenda to gain votes. The old demand to turn Indonesia into an Islamic state, largely regarded as outlandish in the 1940s and 1950s, has gone mainstream. Local governments have enacted laws that required women to be indoors after dark, and men applying for government jobs have to know their Qur'an. Aceh City has considered a proposal to ban women from straddling motorbikes since it 'accentuates' their 'curves.' Bowing to populist pressures, Yudhoyono signed an anti-pornography law floated by Islamists and staffed his advisory body of Muslim clerics, the Ulema Council, with mostly Wahhabis, who have brazenly issued fatwas outlawing the Ahmediya sect.

Democracy and free expression has turned out to be no defence against creeping Islamization, which includes such modern items as 'Muslim' clothing, for men as well as women, Arabic calligraphy, 'Islamic' cosmetics and medicines as well as halal food. Among Indonesian writers and journalists, who had eagerly partaken of the freedoms of the post-Suharto era, the rise of an overtly Islamist politics and culture often provokes a conservative anxiety of the kind found among secular Turkish elites. Complaining bitterly of his five-year-old daughter being made to wear a headscarf at school, a newspaper editor I met didn't take long to plunge into nostalgic longing for the secular strongman who would sort out the fundamentalists. The novelist Ayu Utami spoke more sensibly of Islamism as an unavoidable consequence of Indonesia's globalization—a long process in which Arabic has become as much a language of power as English, and austere and urban visions of Islam have overwhelmed the syncretic Indonesian varieties nurtured in the countryside.

One beneficiary of Islamization has been the Partai Keadilan Sejahtera (the Prosperity and Justice Party). It has grown, with the help of Saudi money, through pedagogic cells on university campuses, and has self-consciously combined the revivalist and social-welfarist orientation of the Egyptian Muslim Brotherhood with Islamic theology drawn from Wahhabism. The Partai received 9 per cent of all votes cast in the elections in 2009 and joined Yudhoyono's cabinet. Its support base is the consumerist middle class—people uprooted from traditionalist forms of Islam.

This was apparent at the 2011 national convention of the Partai at the Sheraton Hotel in Yogyakarta, where baseball caps were as much in sight as pamphlets by Hasan al-Banna, the Egyptian founder of the Muslim Brotherhood. Yogyakarta—even more than the five-star hotel with white women in bikinis around the pool—was a provocative choice. The city is the centre of Javanese mysticism and, with its Hindu-Buddhist and Sufi traditions, anathema for the Wahhabis. It is also the seat of an unelected sultan, whose hereditary gubernatorial privileges, secured by a special clause in the Indonesian constitution, are increasingly challenged by Islamic democrats. I met the chain-smoking son of the sultan's deputy, who despised, in his words, the Wahhabi 'rabble' who wanted to cancel the privileges of the ruling family, and were not above using even the revered Wali saints of Java to entice Hindus away from Hinduism. He feared that the whole cosmopolitan world of Javanese culture was falling apart.

The Partai, however, were aiming at their own kind of internationalism. Delegates to the convention were treated to a wayang performance based on the life of Bhima, the sturdiest of the five brothers in the Mahabharata. More surprisingly, there were also items branded with the coat of arms of the Yogyakarta Sultanate. This reflected some confusion within the party's leadership. One young Partai diehard I spoke to, perspiration staining his white turban, denounced the Sultan Hamengkubuwana for using the title *kalipatullah* (God's Caliph). Apparently, the man was a *kufr* (infidel); the true caliphate had yet to be established.

Certainly, the Partai itself has some way to go in establishing the sovereignty of true Islam. Proximity to a venal establishment had brought its own problems: corruption and even sex scandals. One Partai MP, an especially vociferous campaigner for anti-pornography legislation, was caught watching a pornographic video in the legislative chamber. The *kyai* (leader) of a pesantren near the city of Magellang smiled wryly when I reported my visit to the Partai convention to him. 'They are trying hard to fit in,' he said.

His pesantren was on a narrow lane, on the edge of a roadside settlement, beyond which rice paddies glimmered on all sides. He sat under a huge 3D portrait of Mecca, gently scolding his daughter, who wore a t-shirt emblazoned with a Disney Rapunzel, when she broke into the conversation. His own Islam, he said, came from Arabia, but had 'softened' in Hindu-Buddhist Java. The pesantren he led had always staged wayang; he had sent his pupils to help clean the damaged Pentecostal church in Temanggung.

Outside, in the pesantren's courtyard, the boys sat smoking furiously the clove-scented Indonesian cigarette in their pre-dinner recess time. They seemed eager to talk. Living five or six to a small cramped room, they had something gentle in their demeanour, the courtesies of old Java lingering among the sons of farmers and fishermen, and it was hard to imagine the young Muslims of the region who in 1965 had gone from house to house with lists of communists to kill.

The students themselves know nothing about that past, though books about famous communists such as Tan Malaka are now available. They know a lot more of conditions in Gaza, denoting their membership of the global *ummah*. It's as though the loss of national mission has pushed them to another, vaguer idea of a global community. But however internationalist in appearance, the ummah has actually narrowed the scope of political action—there's nothing the students in Central Java, themselves sunk in the darkness of perpetual 'under-development,' can do about the situation in Gaza or the West Bank.

And, in the meantime, I couldn't help thinking, other more globalized and better-networked groups—the politicians and the businessmen of the Suharto era—have secured an enormous advantage in all aspects of public life. In post-Suharto Indonesia, democracy can't help but become the promise of material improvement and social and economic justice for a politicized citizenry. Instead, globalization has entrenched vast inequalities, threatening traditional livelihoods as well as national sovereignty—to the point where many Indonesians long openly for Suharto's guarantees of security and stability. Far from helping, elections, or the zero-sum competition for state power, have squandered the energies and gains of a popular mobilization against a corrupt and brutal elite. Political Islam, in this context, turns out to be effective only in encouraging private grievances and nebulous ideas of the enemy. The random violence of Islamists against minorities is less a reaction to Christianity or secular modernity than an attempt to create consoling illusions of identity and solidarity at a confusing time.

The older elites remain the maestros of top-down governance, the hidden socio-political engineers, as the rakyat, once invoked by the country's founders as the basis of the diverse archipelago's unity, has succumbed to a long political amnesia. In the end, Suharto's most successful creation was this transnational oligarchy, one defined more by rent seeking than by entrepreneurial dynamism and regard for the rule of law, not to mention notions of fairness and justice. Increasingly fractious but still powerful, it keeps Indonesia at a political impasse. And there's now no social force strong enough to overturn its deeply rooted structures of power.

There seems barely a conception of political life in which trade unions, peasant associations, student and women's groups, and empowered local governments play a role. Jokowi has emerged in this unpromising scenario of post-national politics, the beneficiary of an electorate disgusted by venal and inept politicians. He seems to be trying to use the dispersed and distracted nature of the state to his advantage. Defying the political trend of soft bigotry, he has upheld the rights of Christians and other minorities. Tinged with small-is-beautiful and local-is-superior-to the-global optimism, his invocation of a rakyat-centred economy and the repudiation of top-down governance can seem more than rhetoric; it's as though he's asking the poor themselves—rather than their usual patrons, the centralized state, the free market, and do-gooding NGOs—to remove poverty.

In Jakarta, he started with unannounced visits to slums to hold conversations about health and education; he planned a big drainage system to deal with the periodic monsoon floods that were particularly severe earlier this year; he inaugurated new toll roads and a monorail system to ease the traffic, and build subsidized apartment blocks in South Jakarta for slum dwellers exposed to floods. As though acknowledging Jokowi's populist appeal, Yudhoyono has proposed new rules forcing foreign investors to reduce their stakes in mining companies, which will also be made to process their yields within the country. Fewer beef and horticultural goods will be imported in order to protect local farmers; small traders have effectively lobbied for restrictions on foreign chain stores. Certainly, Jokowi has been well ahead of politicians, and others representatives of a much withered and discredited Indonesian polity, who are still fighting hard to avoid the taint of neo-liberalism, and trying to figure out how to renegotiate their compact with increasingly enraged voters. But he seems to have arrived too late to prevent the fragmenting of politics into a sterile multiplicity of competing elite interests, or to rebuild faith in a democracy fundamentally designed to further empower the rich and the powerful.

JAPAN: LIFE AFTER
ECONOMIC GROWTH

Tokyo was Asia's first modern city. Which may be why it now looks like the continent's oldest metropolis—at least to those accustomed to the shinier buildings, grander avenues, and the more garish newness of Shanghai. Compared to the upstart countries of Asia today, much of Japan presents a spectacle of aged modernity: brown plains marked by a clutter of small houses and criss-crossed by giant power pylons. Even the wild beauty of the country's coastal areas is now touched, after the nuclear catastrophe at Fukushima, with a hint of menace. And it is with some shock that you recall that Japan was where the future once lay, for decades, before its 'bubble' burst in the early 1990s and the country, pushed inward by adversity, became a strange absence in our lives.

While Japan languished within a low-growth economy, China, its formerly poor cousin, unexpectedly became Asia's pre-eminent economic power, and its old domineering mentor, the United States, suffered a severe economic and geopolitical diminishment. Insecurity, brought on by China's rise and America's growing inwardness, is now driving neo-nationalists in Japan to risky geopolitical and economic experiments. China, in turn, now seems fully committed to anti-Japanese nationalism: violent demonstrations, often abetted by the communist regime, erupted in 2005, 2010, and 2012.

While I was in Japan early in 2013, its new prime minister, Abe Shinzo, was promoting an ambitious plan of national renaissance, which looked, particularly to the country's alarmed neighbours, like revanchism. Emboldened by the stock market, which, though well below its peak in the early 1990s, had responded keenly to 'Abenomics,' the prime minister, a conservative nationalist, assured his rapidly ageing electorate that 'Japan is back.' But it was far from clear how this somewhat minatory promise of 'return' would manifest itself: would Japan abandon its status as a great pacifist power, as Abe desired, and assume leadership of an anti-Chinese coalition, or would it become economically regnant again. In any case, it seemed unlikely, to take a matter closer to my heart, that Sony and Panasonic could ever regain the lead in consumer electronics that they had lost to Apple and Samsung.

I should clarify that I had never been a Japanophile in the Western mode: longing for the tea ceremony, going ape over Kabuki and Noh, or sighing about Basho's rural idyll. Nor was I a connoisseur of feather-light screens, lacquer masks, and sculptured gardens. I found nothing thrilling about either the Yakuza or ikebana. Japan, I vaguely knew, had 'won' after losing World War II. It had become part of the 'developed' West, an engine of the world economy, and a dutiful vassal of the United States, all the while retaining its unique social mores and timeless aesthetic culture. But, growing up with a national economy devoted to import-substitution, I couldn't summon much regard for the possibility that, as Claude Levi-Strauss put it, 'Japan, perhaps alone among nations, has until now been able to find a balance between fidelity to the past and the transformations brought about by science and technology.'

It was Japan's consumer products, its simple conveniences, gizmos, and gadgets that tantalized. After the war, Japanese consumers had moved quickly from cherishing the 'three treasures' of domestic living in the 1950s—a black-and-white television, a fridge, and a washing machine—to coveting higher things in the 1970s: an air-conditioner, a car, and a colour TV. The rest of us were decades away from attaining this holy trinity of consumer capitalism. In the 1970s and 1980s, Japan was, for many middle-class Indians, synonymous with Canon cameras, JVC stereos, and Sony televisions, which the luckier among us hauled back, in flimsy cardboard boxes secured with nylon strings, from trips to duty-free utopias in the Persian Gulf. Suzuki was the respectable other half of Maruti, rescuing the 'People's Car' from the fantasies of the maladroit dynast Sanjay Gandhi; Japanese expertise with Hero Honda motorcycles also helped fuel social mobility in the 1980s among the lower middle class.

Japan's economic heft was even then provoking fresh hallucinations of the Yellow Peril in the United States. And Japan itself was about to reach the limits of its peculiar model of cartelized capitalism. But Japanese philanthropy in Bihar's antique Buddhist heart, and tourists garlanded with

expensive cameras in Varanasi and Agra spoke of the lone
Asian nation that had miraculously conquered poverty, and
achieved high literacy and long life expectancy.

In Japan, however, I felt pulled back in time, surprised and
often baffled by its isolationism, over-regulated economic
regime, monopolies, and inefficiencies—visitors will find it
easier, for instance, to procure a data connection on their
smartphone in Laos than in Japan, and a SIM card for voice
calls is simply unobtainable.

The Japanese were still rich. Then why did their houses
look so flimsy, their supermarkets so poorly stocked, and
their public architecture so unprepossessing? As early as
the 1920s, Japan was introduced to the material culture of
capitalism, and its attendant phenomenon: the consumption
of cars, radio, films, magazines, the rise of the nuclear
family, the commercially motivated exaltation of youth and
romantic love, and Western mores; it was also then that a
popular culture grew around the new urban middle class,
featuring the ubiquitous so-called salaryman (*saririman*) and
the hard-working white-collared women—*moga*, or modern
girls—who were, in the overheated male imagination at
least, as prone to retail kisses as Western clothes.

But Japan's modernity, famously encrypted in neon
after the war, seem to have visibly stalled in the 1970s and
1980s. In Tokyo, the decades have petrified into buildings
of startling ugliness and vulgarity, given an interesting
weirdness only by the heavy neon in the evening and
the young men and women with stylized haircuts. The
uniformly grey commuters add to the strange impression of

homogeneity and exclusivity in a city that remains defiantly non-multicultural in the age of globalization, where very few people speak English or look foreign; the Pakistani running an Indian restaurant looks subdued by his alienness as much as by his subterfuge.

There are many signs of a still-impressive physical and social infrastructure—the serenely swift Shinkansen matched by the quick courtesy and cheerful goodwill of ordinary Japanese. The temples, shrines and gardens of Kyoto and Kanazawa rapidly eradicate all fear of disappointment; and even the careful partitions of *bento* boxes speak of an unatrophied aesthetic sense. But there is no avoiding the sense of a long malaise, the product of two 'lost' decades, when *pachinko*, a form of pinball, became one of Japan's biggest industries.

To be in Japan is to see how the intimations of decay have deepened despite its flourishing soft-power exports worldwide of manga and anime, and the insistent chirpiness of Pokemon and Hello Kitty that belie the Cool Japan sobriquet. The human toll of the slow economic implosion shows in the statistics about suicide—one every fifteen minutes; child abuse (a fourfold increase since 1999); rising domestic violence; and the stories in the press about empty rooms where salaried employees with no work are asked to spend their day until they resign. Japanese youth, surveys claimed, don't travel the way their parents or grandparents used to; nor do they show much interest in foreign languages. An estimated one million Japanese people almost never leave the house. Many of those who bother probably do so in order to indulge in the *otaku* (geek) subcultures of obsessively idle young men.

The political consequences of the long economic winter are manifest by the aggressive self-pity and sanctimoniousness of the neo-nationalists I met. They reminded me of Hindutva-mongers of the 1980s: the same revisionist energies, invocations of the 'national spirit,' claims to extended victimhood and the attempt to mask, with a bogus cultural unity, the inconvenient facts of poverty, inequality, environmental degradation, and social discrimination. The aged were everywhere, as befitting a country with a swiftly declining population, the packed subways and tiny restaurants as though designed for their small frames. The youth, deprived of the stable jobs of their parents, and languishing in cafés with their smartphones or po-facedly working up a racket at pachinko parlours remind one that Japan had pioneered what T.J. Clark calls 'the essence of modernity,' which, 'from the scripture-reading spice merchant to the Harvard iPod banker sweating in the gym, is a new kind of isolate obedient "individual" with technical support to match.' And, among the streetwalkers ready to pamper any fetish in Shibuya, the swarms of sweet-faced wide-eyed young women in schoolgirl costumes seem a dismal consummation of the moga.

The striving for innocence, or the careful suggestion of stunted development, among the neon-lit cathedrals of consumerism was oddly disturbing. In 1952 the *New York Times* marked the end of America's occupation of Japan with a cartoon depicting over-sized American hands releasing a miniaturized figure in wooden clogs on to a meandering path. On his return to the United States, the supreme commander and overlord of Japan, Douglas MacArthur spoke of how the Japanese, 'measured by the standards of modern civilization,' were 'like a boy of twelve as compared with our development.' The vendors of kinky sex in Shibuya reminded me of Japan's long and seemingly unbreakable subjugation to the United States, one symbolized most cruelly in 1995 by the rape of under-age girls by American marines in Okinawa, and now marked by Japan's continued failure to end the widely detested American military presence on the islands.

American actions have defined the country's long 'postwar' which, in many ways, has yet to end. As John Dower, the dean of American scholarship on Japan, writes in his masterwork *Embracing Defeat*, 'much that lies at the heart of contemporary Japanese society—the nature of its democracy, the intensity of popular feelings about pacifism and remilitarization, the manner in which the war is remembered (and forgotten)—derives from the complexity of the interplay between the victors and the vanquished.'

The subordination of Japan can be dated back to the arrival in 1853 of Admiral Matthew Perry's menacing 'black ships', which jolted a feudal country out of its isolation and into an audacious and lethal program along Western lines geared to catch up with the West. But true subservience began with America's punitive incineration of Hiroshima and Nagasaki in 1945, its refurbishing of Emperor Hirohito among other war criminals, and the semi-successful imposition of 'democracy.' The unquestioned dominance over Japan, or what Dower called 'total control over a pagan "Oriental" society by white men,' also shaped the self-perceptions of the world's most powerful country—among other things, it subliminally informed many fantasies in the 'American century' of remaking, through violence, various parts of the world in America's self-image.

Keen to shoulder the white man's burden, MacArthur was much less bigoted than Harry Truman, who confided in his diary a few days after ordering the nuclear ravaging of Hiroshima and Nagasaki that 'when you have to deal with a beast you have to treat him as a beast.' But MacArthur suffered from the same mistaken view of Japanese capacity as the British colonial governor of Singapore in 1942 who, when informed by an underling of an imminent Japanese attack on the island, responded, 'Well, I suppose you'll shove the little men off.' This ingrained condescension, soon to be shattered by the scale and speed of Japanese triumphs during the war, was reinstated after 1945; it was deepened by early Japanese facilitators of the Occupation, which ranged from wily politicians like Yoshida Shigeru, prime minister in both the late 1940s and early 1950s, who argued to 'let the stronger have their way' to the Japanese leftists who originally welcomed the democratic reforms of the American military. In the 1960s Charles de Gaulle could still count upon a shared contempt for Japan in the white man's world when he described the Japanese prime minister Ikeda Hayato as a 'transistor salesman.'

In actuality, Japan, measured by the standards of modern civilization set by the West, had already done extremely well without American supervision, even surpassing its former overlords briefly in the 1980s. From the time Admiral Perry 'opened up' the country with his battleships, and sundry other Westerners began to harass and bully the previously isolated country, Japan's leaders had been obsessed with becoming a first-rate power, an *itto oku*, and achieving *bunmei kaika* (civilization and enlightenment), all in double quick time. Modernization for them seemed to equal westernization. It required 'abandoning' the backward neighborhood of Asia, as the Meiji modernizer Fukuzawa Yukichi exhorted, and knocking on the doors of Europe for admittance to the elite club of nations with real power and wealth.

So much, Fukuzawa reported, had to be learned from scratch, including, literally, the meaning of words like 'competition' and 'economy' for which no equivalent words existed in Japanese. But, for a country that, as the novelist Natsume Soseki wrote in 1902, had been 'awakened by a firebell and jumped out of bed,' Japan had shown itself to be extraordinarily adaptable to the dog-eat-dog world of international relations. It had comprehensively defeated China in 1895, and annexed Taiwan (then Formosa). Then in 1905 it signalled its arrival in the modern world by vanquishing Russia, electrifying Asians everywhere with fantasies of self-empowerment. It took a bigger step towards modern-style civilization and enlightenment by turning Korea into a colony and preying on China; all these acts of aggression adorned, in the Western way, with the rhetoric of humanitarian intervention. Japan's reward was increased respect and offers of alliances from Britain and the United States. As Rabindranath Tagore's sardonic friend and art historian Okakura Tenshin pointed out, 'The average Westerner was wont to regard Japan was barbarous while she indulged in the gentle arts of peace; he calls her civilized since she began to commit wholesale slaughter on the Manchurian battlefields.'

Loyal support of the Allied effort in World War I secured Japan a permanent seat on the council of the League of Nations; but its clause for racial equality at the Paris Peace Conference in 1919 was squashed by white statesmen, who were keen not to dilute their racially homogenous populations or entertain any potentially dangerous nonsense about racial parity. Japan weathered the Great Depression well, and with the growth of its heavy industry in the 1930s, and increased exports, seemed to have also mastered the laws of the economic jungle. But, as full-fledged itto oku, it still found itself excluded from the club of 'civilized nations,' which, in a sly act of hypocrisy, censured Japan's imperial conquest of Manchuria, forcing it to abandon the League of Nations in 1933.

Militarist nationalism in the 1930s fed on paranoia about encirclement by Western powers, and the fear of rising Chinese nationalism that threatened Japan's ambitions to use China to become a first-tier nation. It culminated in Japan's invasion of China in 1937, and then a desperate assault on the United States in 1941. Japan's mission for the next eight years was to return to the Asia it had abandoned, and remake it through conquest and occupation. Accordingly, it proclaimed a civilizing mission for its anti-imperialist imperialism: conquered territories, in Japan's own Monroe Doctrine, were to be part of a new 'Greater East Asia Co-Prosperity-Sphere.'

Having articulated many of the ironies of Japan's 'progress,' Emperor Hirohito revealed himself as a master of understatement when, after the annihilation of Nagasaki, he went on air on 15 August 1945 to inform his countrymen that the 'war had developed in a manner not necessarily to

Japan's advantage.' He called on his vanquished country, now faced with a prolonged American occupation, to 'endure the unendurable and bear the unbearable,' partly so that Japan could 'keep pace with the progress of the world.'

Japan's new ruler Douglas MacArthur tried to ensure this progress by keeping the emperor and parts of the wartime bureaucracy in place. His ostensible goals were demilitarization and democratization, and while disbanding the Japanese army he proclaimed human rights and equality for all. But the emperor's titular authority was needed so that the twelve-year-old boys did not become unmanageable again; and so Hirohito was asked only to renounce his divinity.

The occupiers became even more conservative as the Cold War began, and many Japanese, dragged through hell by their right-wing leaders, looked particularly vulnerable to socialism and communism. After briefly encouraging trade unions, the American occupiers watched as they were crushed by Japanese corporate thuggery. The family-owned *zaibatsu* conglomerates—such as Mitsubishi and Nissan— that had powered Japan's industrial revolution before the war were allowed to reconstitute themselves as *keiretsus*, bank-centred industries, as ready as ever to benefit from their proximity to the state. Having insisted on disarmament, the Americans changed their mind as war erupted in the Korean peninsula. Japan was enlisted into a 'great crescent' of anti-communist states against communism in Asia; its substantial army, navy, and air force was later camouflaged with the moniker 'Self-Defence Forces' so as to preserve, in letter at least, the war-renouncing Article 9 of the new American-drafted constitution that forbade Japan from maintaining any armed forces.

American economic experts with harsh austerity plans nearly ruined the Japanese economy before the providential intervention of the Korean War. American war procurements helped launch Japan's economic growth of more than 10 per cent annually from the latter half of the 1950s. It was miraculously sustained over the next two decades by a hard-working population determined to rebuild their shattered nation, freely importing technologies from Europe and the US with industry obeying 'administrative guidance' from the government.

One of the side effects of economic growth was extensive pollution of land, air, and water; the other was the destruction of childhoods as anxious, go-getting parents forced their wards into cram schools. The position of women, despite legalized equality, remained inferior; minorities, such as the Koreans who had stayed in Japan after the war, faced discrimination at all levels. Suspected war criminals, such as Abe Shinzo's grandfather Kishi Nobusuke, who had assisted in Japan's pacification of Manchuria, were enlisted by the CIA in 1955 to help create a dependably anti-left political party: thus, the Liberal Democratic Party, which ruled Japan for the next four decades, was forged in response to the growing appeal of Japanese socialists.

The ideologues of progress—American modernization theorists in this instance—were at hand to uphold industrializing and democratizing Japan as a model for other Asian countries. As John Dower points out, 'to American reformers, much of the almost sensual excitement involved in promoting their democratic revolution from above derived from the feeling that this involved denaturing an Oriental adversary and turning it into at least an approximation of an acceptable, healthy, westernized nation.' In the idealized version of the West's own history, Japan was saved all unflattering comparisons to Western countries, which had also modernized through internal suppression at home and external violence abroad. Such thinkers as Walt Rostow and Edwin O. Reischauer, who moonlighted as diplomats and administrators, explained away their docile ward's 'aberrant' behaviour in the first half of the century as though Japan's allegedly pathological militarism wasn't deeply connected with the essentially expansionist nature of the pre-war Japanese state and economy.

American occupation ended in 1952, but the legacy of its policies remains alive to this day. The contradictions, absurdities and hypocrisies of the occupation opened up plenty of scope for conservative nationalists even as they became Japan's most staunchly pro-US force. The CIA-sponsored Liberal Democratic Party institutionalized one-party rule. The 'iron triangle' of Party politicians, senior bureaucrats, and businessmen came to underpin the country's institutional corruption; it helped secure a pliant media, and cultivate historical amnesia.

Released from postwar guilt and repentance of the kind Germany underwent, Japan was turned into America's permanently junior partner. Though barred from fighting any more wars, Japan became a source of ready cash—and, in case of the Iraq war in 2003, its personnel—for American military campaigns against communists and terrorists in distant lands. Public resentment against the tens of thousands of American soldiers stationed in Japan is limited outside of Okinawa where most are based. Japanese attempts in 2009 to relocate an American Marine base outside of Okinawa were met with contemptuous refusal; breaking with their own government, conservative Japanese diplomats actually advised the US state department not to relocate the base. The partnership continues with its ample quota of deception and bad faith as Japanese nationalists seek to turn the American 'pivot to Asia' into an encircling manoeuvre around China while promising to restore national strength and pride.

Few places in Japan encapsulate its compromised triumphs and resulting schizophrenia more vividly than the controversial Yasukuni shrine and the adjoining Yushukan Museum, which indiscriminately commemorate Japanese who died in the 'imperial cause,' a category that includes some high-ranking war criminals, and periodically provokes howls of fury among Japan's neighbours. The landmarks of Japan's desperate struggle to be modern are all here: the path-breaking defeat of China in 1895, the glorious triumphs of the Russo-Japanese war in 1905, and the pain and tragedy of the 'wars to end all wars'—Japan's anti-imperialist campaign which, by a terrible self-contradiction, came to be an imperialist war in Asia.

The shrine and the museum lie just north of the Imperial Palace, where Tokyo's promiscuous clutter makes way, briefly, for the self-conscious monumentality of the imperial city: broad avenues, parks, and vistas. It was raining heavily as I walked past the ceremonial gates, the last of the cherry blossoms sticking to the long path. But the tour buses still discharged scores of elderly Japanese visitors. Old enough to have lived through, and even fought in, World War II, or seen their fathers, husbands, and brothers consumed by it, they looked weighed down by their transparent plastic umbrellas as they stood before the Shinto shrine, and then shuffled off to the adjoining Yushukan museum.

Originally an Italianate castle, it was rebuilt in the pan-Asian style in the early 1930s, with gabled roofs. The gesture to Pan-Asianism was part of the decade's intellectual and political mood that influenced most Japanese into thinking of their country as the liberator of Asia. The exhibit remains a weathervane, reflecting the moods and sensibilities within the country, the mingled emotions of pride, defeat, humiliation, and wounded vanity.

'Oh, the militarism, the militarism, it's unbelievable,' a Chinese friend and Japan-o-phile had exclaimed to me when I brought up Yushukan. He was not wrong. National war museums or memorials are built on the intense need to grieve and mourn, and to give meaning and dignity to the sacrifices of the dead; they don't usually mention the victims on the other side. Maya Lin's moving Vietnam War Memorial in Washington, for example, has no record of the millions of Vietnamese, Cambodians, and Laotians who also died in the 1960s and 1970s in an unnecessary war. Even so, Yushukan seems to take too many liberties with historical accuracy.

A Zero fighter used in kamikaze missions dominates the lobby, and sets the tone for displays of the locomotive used in the Thailand–Burma railway, the one-man submarine, or 'human torpedo,' and the many pictures of soldiers with raised guns shouting *banzai* cries to the glory of the emperor. Japan had joined Western nations in brutally suppressing the Boxer Rising in China in 1900. But the crucial point of this appalling episode, according to the exhibit, is that Japanese soldiers 'impressed' the Chinese by their discipline. It presents the invasion of Manchuria in 1931, which inaugurated a particularly deranged phase of Japanese militarism, as an act of 'legitimate self-defense.'

There are complaints about American support for Chiang Kai-shek, but nothing about American businessmen assisting the Japanese war machinery all through the 1930s; it would have been too much to expect inclusion of Japan's military and technological tutelage to Britain and United States until the 1920s. The Rape of Nanjing in 1937 is referred to as the Nanjing 'Incident' in which 'Chinese soldiers in civilian clothes' were 'severely prosecuted.' The narrative on display portrays the attack on Pearl Harbor in 1941 as a response to America's malign bellicosity. Coerced into war, Japan kept pursuing peace but was crudely rebuffed by the Allies, and then fiendishly firebombed into submission, but not before it had 'liberated' much of Asia from Western domination.

Nothing undermines this litany of half-truths, omissions, suppressions, and outright falsehoods than the simple failure to acknowledge that Japan's pan-Asianist crusade came as a calamity to most Asians. In any case, the Burmese, the Javanese, and the Vietnamese had liberated themselves after suffering the hypocrisy of both Westerners and Japanese. For Japan the moment of self-reckoning was postponed. And no single individual assisted in this great exculpation more than an Indian: a Bengali jurist called Radhabinod Pal.

A memorial to Pal, easily the most famous Indian in Japan,

stands just outside the Yushukan Museum. Breaking the traditional Japanese reserve before foreigners, two women shot approving looks and even a faint smile at me as we stood trying to decipher through the rain these words inscribed in stone.

> When time shall have softened passion and prejudice
> When reason shall have stripped the mask from representation
> Then justice, holding evenly her scales, will require
> Much of past censure and praise to change places.

The lament of bitter victimhood was borrowed appropriately from a confederate general—the Japanese conservative Eto Jun once pointed to the confederacy as a prototype for America's relationship with vanquished Japan. Pal seems to have been in tune, too, with other Japanese grievances about their country's treatment by its victors.

He was one of the token non-Western judges at the so-called Tokyo Trials, Japan's protracted version of Nuremberg, whose proceedings were almost entirely directed by American and European jurists. In his voluminous 1235-page dissent, Pal voted to acquit all the twenty-five Japanese accused by Allied powers of the 'unprecedented' crime of 'conspiring against peace.' Pal had no time for Japanese militarism that claimed nearly 20 million lives across Asia. But he argued that thousands of Japanese implicated in atrocities during the war—the 'Class B' and 'Class C' criminals—had already been executed or imprisoned.

Pal wasn't the only one to notice serious problems with the Tokyo Trials. The Soviet Union's representative had previously served as a judge in Stalin's mock trials of the 1930s. The British, Dutch, and French presuming to judge Japan's conduct invited attention to their own much-despised imperialisms in Asia. China, with its 15 million dead in a war that began as early as 1937, or other Asian victims of Japanese imperialism would have been better placed to judge Japan than the United States.

In fact, the trial was rendered absurd from the very beginning by Douglas MacArthur's aggressive and obsessive attempt to shield Emperor Hirohito from responsibility for his country's crimes. The chief Japanese militarist Tojo Hideki was forced to recant his statement of the obvious: that he could not have done anything against the wishes of the divinely ordained emperor. The American chief prosecutor lunched with Hirohito on the day Tojo's death sentence was confirmed. Even the right-wing General Charles Willoughby, MacArthur's chief intelligence officer, privately denounced the trials as the 'worst hypocrisy in recorded history.'

Pal brought a special political edge to these denunciations. A closeted Bengali nationalist, who had rejoiced in Japan's victory over Russia in 1905, and resentfully put up with the hypocrisies and humiliations of British rule over India, Pal seems to have seized the chance to make his western counterparts feel uneasy. The Tokyo Trials, he said, were no more than a 'sham employment of legal process for the satisfaction of a thirst for revenge.' Though 'fiendish,' Pal argued, Japan's expansionism was hardly unprecedented. Like all modern imperialist and industrial powers, it had sought to advance its outsized ambitions and respond to perceived threats.

Modernization, in other words, had turned out to be inseparable from westernization. The Japanese philosopher Takeuichi Yoshimi was to remark on a similar irony about Japan's urgent mimicry of Western ways, and its inevitable lapse into imperialism: 'Europe's invasion of the Orient resulted in the phenomenon of Oriental capitalism, and this,' he stressed, 'signified the equivalence between European self-preservation and self-expansion.' Japan felt that it had to acquire colonies in order to survive—the logic also overcame many European nations, most prominently Germany, in the late nineteenth century. Other points raised by Pal also warned against an easy moral clarity about Japan's war in Asia. He argued that the Allied firebombing of nearly seventy major Japanese cities and the nuclear incineration of Hiroshima and Nagasaki should also be counted as major war crimes. These state-sanctioned atrocities against civilians, he implicitly argued, were on a greater scale than the depredations of assorted Japanese commanders in the field.

Not surprisingly, Pal became a hero to those Japanese who felt more 'victim consciousness' than guilt over Japan's brutalizing of Asia. Tojo Hideki, the wartime prime minister, honored him with a haiku shortly before being executed. Kishi Nobusuke, the employer of slave labour in Japan-ruled Manchuria, was a fan. So is his grandson Abe Shinzo, who wants to revise Japan's 1995 apology for its Asian war; Abe even sought out Pal's son in West Bengal on a state visit to India in 2007.

Japan's reckoning with its war was postponed indefinitely when the American occupation authorities went on to enlist former war criminals in their anti-communist crusade, entrenching rather than uprooting the right-wing politicians and bureaucrats who had brought Japan such misery and grief. Kishi Nobusuke was one such beneficiary of a hasty and expedient rehabilitation; as prime minister in the late 1950s, he became notorious for railroading through strong opposition a security pact with the United States that confirmed Japan's subordinate status.

Japanese leftists in the 1960s tirelessly repeated that almost all of the napalm unleashed by American bombers on hapless Vietnamese peasants was manufactured in Japan. For many of them their own country's botched attempt to remake Asia through war was reflected in the American crusade to make it safe for democracy. Certainly, Japanese writers and thinkers couldn't help but see—and the experience of defeat destroyed their illusions—that Japan, the nation state forged first by aggressive wars and then occupation, had illuminated large-scale violence and a Darwinian struggle for national existence as the clearest sign of modernity.

Early in its modern history, Japan had broken from the normatively benign account of progress in which democracy and liberalism followed, if not accompanied, the nation state and industrial capitalism. The first non-Western country to try to become modern, Japan became an economic and military power without enshrining liberal concerns for individual rights, which were subordinated to the economic and military imperatives of a country lurching very late into the modern world. Few Japanese wished to criticize the slogan *fukoku kyohei*—enrich the country and strengthen the military, or challenge the notion of kokutai—roughly translated as national polity embodied by the emperor—as their country rapidly modernized in the late nineteenth century under the not-so-benign gaze of the UK, Russia and the US. Nor did Japan embrace the Anglo-American traditions of economic liberalism, which encouraged individualism, laissez-faire economics and a fundamental distrust of state power. From the early years of the twentieth century to the present, the Japanese state has been closely involved in building up domestic industries, and giving them a competitive advantage in international markets.

Still, catching up to the West had called for an intolerable degree of turmoil, mimicry, and debasement, from the rampant Anglophilia of the 1890s to Japan's futile pleas for racial equality at the Paris Peace Conference in 1919. Unlike India or Indonesia, Japan had not been occupied by a European power. Nevertheless, the Meiji reformers had decreed Japan's surrender to the West in the inner realm of thought and values as well as outer realm of material culture and political forms. They had taken modernization as equivalent to Westernization. They had counterposed tradition to modernity, and found it greatly wanting, especially in neighbouring countries like China and Korea, which, in Japanese eyes, had yet to awaken from their backward slumbers.

The result of this internal colonialism was a wrenching social and intellectual crisis, which preoccupied and consumed some of the country's sensitive minds; the suicide of the short-story writer Akutagawa Ryūnosuke in 1927 set a grim precedent for many anguished self-extinctions by writers and artists, including Mishima Yukio and Kawabata Yasunari.

Already in the 1890s, Japanese thinkers and writers

had begun to question the Meiji model of indiscriminate mimicry, and to chafe at the intellectual dominance of Westernizers like Fukuzawa Yukichi. Did Japan, they asked, have anything unique to offer to mankind, or was it destined to be an inferior clone of the West? The greater the intensity of this self-questioning the deeper became the longing for certainty. By the 1930s, its tormented consciousness forced some of Japan's most sensitive writers, thinkers, and artists to stand behind the emperor, endorse the 'Yamato spirit,' and hail the 'war to end all wars.' They shared the vague hope that Japan, assuming the leadership of Asia after ridding it of Western imperialists, would open up the space for an Asian modernity. The Japanese words that subsequently entered international parlance—kamikaze, *hara-kiri*—belonged to that mood of fanatical self-purging.

The recent eruptions of Islamic fundamentalism, and an atavistic Western obsession with Islam in general, have distracted us from the fact that Japan had initiated the 'form of revolt that is the most modern,' which seeks to transcend Western modernity, a kind of 'political spirituality' that breaks 'away from all that marks their country and their daily lives with the presence of global hegemonies' and aims at 'another way of life, and new relations with the West … with Asia, and so forth.' The words are Michel Foucault's, writing on the Iranian revolution of 1979. But they could belong to Okawa Shumei, a scholar of Islamic studies, who provided the philosophical underpinnings to Japan's own plan to overcome modernity, and its spiritual malaise brought about by industrialization, and attendant ills of atomization, alienation and anomie.

According to Okawa, the Asia that had invented the

gunpowder and the printing press, and originated all major religions, could not be inferior to the West. It had to find its own way to a renaissance, and here the 'Japanese spirit' had a historical mission could help save not only Asia for Asians but also the West from Western modernity. This goal was to be reached by violence, if necessary.

Okawa shared his aims with a wide range of writers and thinkers recoiling from secular Western ideologies, including Miki Kiyoshi, a student of Heidegger, who spoke of a new 'co-operativism' as an antidote to atomization. Aesthetes such as novelist Tanizaki Junichiro, who in *In Praise of Shadows*, hailed the 'magic and mystery' of old Japan, and the 'silence and tranquillity' banished by the invention of the light bulb, took on the task of proving traditional Japanese culture to be the equal of, if not superior to, Western culture. Many of these culturally defensive Japanese took on the German distinction between 'civilization,' identified with vulgar material progress and human degradation, and 'culture,' spiritual and creative self-realization.

The 'father of the Chinese nation,' Sun Yat-Sen, who depended on Japanese patrons for much of his life, weighed his words carefully in 1924, in one of his last speeches: 'Japan today has become acquainted with the Western civilization of the rule of Might, but retains the characteristics of the Oriental civilization of the rule of Right. Now the question remains whether Japan will be the hawk of Western civilization of the rule of Might, or the tower of strength of the Orient. This is the choice which lies before the people of Japan.'

The militarists who committed Japan to an Asian war of conquest in the 1930s had already made their choice.

In their fantasy of an Asian lebensraum, the vast territory of China was there to be conquered and pressed into the service of Japan's industrial economy. Step by step, the dislike of the Westernization imposed by Meiji utilitarians led many Japanese into praise for their country's invasion of China in 1937. It helped that Japan was already being pushed by the depression of the 1930s into a desperate quest to commandeer Asia's markets and resources. The rhetoric grew wilder after the attack on Pearl Harbour in 1941 and the swift annexation of European-ruled Asia. Asia, it seemed, would soon be directing its own cultural destiny, free of the specialists without spirit and sensualists without heart who had ruined modern cultures and shattered the spiritual unity of Japanese culture.

The search for an unalloyed cultural past, free of the contaminations of modern materialism and individualism, culminated in a famous debate in July 1942 in Kyoto, where intellectuals were given full license to invent their own noble reasons for supporting war. History, it seemed in 1942, was finally being shaped by the Japanese and their unique 'Yamato spirit.' The world-historical meaning of Pearl Harbor could still be discussed without much self-doubt about Japan's likelihood of victory in the war. And so participants freely denounced Meiji bureaucratic modernizers as philistine and soulless. They expressed their hostility to naïve evolutionary theories of progress, including dialectical materialism, which had shaped Japan's path from the Meiji era onwards.

The literary critic Kobayashi Hideo feared that Japan was becoming a pale replica of the West, repeating the tragic modernization of the West with a pathetic comedy. Others worried more parochially about the urban fads of *mobo* and moga, and the cults of fast living (*supido*) and eroticism among other fads of mass production culture imported from the rootless immigrant society of the United States. Old values of scarcity and restraint, many participants agreed, had been damaged by a culture than sanctified possession of trivial mass-produced goods.

This anti-modern rhetoric combined with boosterish speculation about Japan's destiny proved to be an unbreakable intellectual prison; Japan miserably underestimated China's resilience and American resources in the war. Defeat and surrender in 1945 briefly put an end to the culture talk. Remarkably, it soon resumed, and actually intensified as Japan rose from the proverbial ashes, and realized the old Meiji dream: it became an economic, if not political, itto oku.

There were many critics of Japan's post-war obsession with growth, or 'GNP-ism.' Takeuichi Yoshimi believed that Japanese modernization had been catastrophically successful, and that the Japanese, recklessly westernized, had failed to appreciate the variety of Asian approaches to the challenge of Western power. Like many other Japanese intellectuals, Takeuchi wondered whether Japan's total rout would expedite a new intellectual and political awakening, similar to the one he saw occurring in China. Intellectuals such as Maruyama Masao, Japan's greatest modern political theorist, formed a 'community of repentance,' keenly scrutinizing the pre-war Japanese political model for flaws. 'National sovereignty,' Maruyama concluded, 'was the ultimate source of both ethics and power, and constituted their intrinsic unity.'

The Japanese, in this view, had failed to make essential separation between their public and private spheres. Their mindless adherence to a family-oriented polity like kokutai was why the emperor hadn't been overthrown; no resistance movement, unlike in Italy or Germany, had developed in Japan. Seeking to explain their compatriots' meekness, and their superstitious belief in the *bushido* and 'Yamato spirit,' liberal-leftists concluded that the true spirit of science and reason had been lacking in Japan, along with personal autonomy and genuine historical subjectivity. As Maruyama saw it, Japan has never achieved modernity, let alone overcome it. Japan's westernization had been incomplete, hobbled by the collectivist ethic, the family state, and the imperial system. What it needed now was true liberal democracy.

And, to an extent, democracy was what Japan did get, under American supervision, allowing a diversity of political voices to emerge. But Japan after the war was to be invigorated more by the instrumental rationality of economic growth than by the enlightenment values of reason and self-criticism. The conservative bureaucratic and business elites despised by the intellectuals remerged, sans the war rhetoric, to become the prime movers of the national economy—an 'economic general staff' in Chalmers Johnson's excellent phrase. Ironically, the claims to Japanese exceptionalism were now harnessed to explain Japan's success in defeating the West at its own game: the mass-production of consumer goods. Arguments about the nature of Japan's modernization in the past—the frequent recourse to colonialist violence and expropriation, for instance—seemed moot as the pre-teen boy of Western fantasies of domination metamorphosed into 'miracle man' with his high-tech innovations in electronics and communications.

The achievements of the Japanese economy after the war and occupation were considerable: Japan moved out of agriculture and into manufacturing; rural poverty was wiped out; the country was integrated into new global economic structures. Japan's success had knock-on effects in the region. China under Mao was closed to foreign investment. Japan signed war reparations agreements with Southeast Asian countries, largely export credits for the purchase of Japanese products. By the early 1970s, Japan and the United States became the biggest external investors in the region, extracting natural resources and investing in industrial and infrastructural development. Thus Japan became—in yet another dark irony—the chief enabler of a 'Greater East Asia Co-Prosperity sphere' under American auspices.

The success of its state-led industrialization had keen admirers and imitators across East Asia, including Singapore, Taiwan, and South Korea. All these Asian state capitalists ironically received much assistance from the US as it pursued its geopolitical interests, boosting local economies through wars in Korea and Vietnam, foreign aid, and its open markets. But Japan, weathering well the 1973 oil shocks, outgrew American patronage in the 1980s. Japanese corporates, buying up the Rockefeller Center in New York or snapping up Columbia studios, suffered fresh caricature in the mainstream Western media.

By then, GNP-ism was the regnant ideology in Japan, part not only of a quantitative mania that spread across industrial societies in the 1950s and 1960s, but also the key component of a self-congratulatory nationalism. Revisionist accounts of the war in Asia first emerged in the 1960s, on the rising tide of national pride after the Tokyo Olympics in 1964. As the Japanese novelist Oda Makoto wrote in 1965, 'The Pacific war was fought for the liberation of Asia, and it is undeniable that that many Japanese participated in the war for the sake of that principle. ... Many Japanese still sincerely believe this, and this makes our conception of peace three times more complicated.'

The national obsession with economic growth not only strengthened social cohesion; it also produced fresh imperatives of consensus and conformity. While visiting Japan, American sociologist David Riesman marvelled at how 'people refer to organizations as 'undemocratic' if there is no harmony or consensus. Thus democracy and politics would seem to be antithetical.'

Massive protests against the American war in Vietnam and environmental despoliation defined the strength of the counter-culture in Japan. But this was also the time when fresh ideas about Japan's uniqueness began to proliferate. Even the novelist Kawabata Yasunari became the purveyor of *Nihonjinron* (Japaneseness) in his Nobel lecture titled 'Japan, the Beautiful,' in which he rambled on about the tea ceremony and flower vases and Zen.

The old Meiji equation between civilization and power, which had led to a disastrous militarism, was abandoned. Pacifist and entrepreneurial Japan was the new model of modernity, its national past and traditional values— consensus and harmony—enlisted in the project of making Japan look uniquely placed to generate high GDP. The men in khaki neck flaps—the much-despised fanatical fighters of

Imphal and Manila—and the meek postwar salaryman were replaced by men in business suits, exalted by apparently Confucian company structures, mystically infused with the spirit of bushido. American sociologists helped adorn Japan with its self-image as a unique country with an organic sense of tradition: the twelve-year-old boy's skills at bonsai seemed to make him especially adept with transistors.

Never mind that the supposedly Japanese 'household' model of industrial relations household—whose three features were lifetime employment, seniority-based wages and company unions—was unavailable to most industrial workers. Or that traditional values of harmony and hierarchy were partaken of only by workers in large enterprises, and that gender discrimination was rife, and pollution in Japanese cities was unrivalled anywhere in the world.

In any case, the peace of consumerism did not satisfy all self-appointed sentinels of Japanese culture. The void of American-style materialism gaped as intolerably wide as ever for cultural conservatives like Eto Jun and Mishima Yukio. Visiting Japan and India in the late 1950s, Arthur Koestler claimed that 'lilies that fester smell far worse than weeds; both India and Japan seem to be spiritually sicker, more estranged from a living faith than the West.'

Looking to expose the charlatanry of the East, Koestler was far more revealing about Western supremacism. But his account of confusion certainly fitted Mishima Yukio. Sending his characters of his fictional tetralogy *The Sea of Fertility* to Buddhist India, dressing up in military uniforms and demanding the restoration of the emperor to divinity,

Mishima invoked the austere martial spirit of his ancestors. His dramatically staged suicide in 1970 rounded off a spectacle of aestheticized politics. But it also pointed to the failed project of combining kokutai with consumer capitalism.

Nevertheless, the vendors of nihonjinron flourished, especially after the shock of the 1973 oil prices, when American—and general Western—decline began to seem a fact. A nine-volume report commissioned by the Japanese prime minister in 1979 concluded that Japan, as international financier and high-end exporter, has surpassed the West in material progress and industrial growth; its greatest task was now to promote its unique culture. Daytripping Japan-o-philes like Claude Levi-Strauss were ready to endorse vanity projects of the Japanese: 'May they long maintain that precious balance between the traditions of the past and the innovations of the present, and not only for their own good, since humanity as a whole finds in them an example worth contemplating.'

It was as though Japan had finally overcome modernity, with high-tech exports rather than kamikaze missions. It had not only caught up with the West; it was now defining the shape and texture of late capitalism. In a commonplace postmodern vision of Japan in the 1980s, the country emerged as perfectly depthless, living in an endless present, among a plenitude of commodities and signifiers of lifestyle and status. Private and public spheres now finally seemed independent of each other—too much so, in fact. Japanese glued to their Walkmans and video games seemed to have attained the sovereign authorship of the world enjoined by modernity. Many respectable intellectuals partook of the general giddiness, presenting 'being Japanese' as a unique privilege and dispensation.

The celebration, on both sides of the Pacific, ended as the Japanese economy buoyed by inflated land values came down to earth, wiping out by the early 1990s about 3 trillion dollars, three times the size of Japan's GDP—the Japanese stock market collapse remains the world's biggest loss of wealth.

Western paranoia about an imminent Pax Nipponica, one achieved furtively through corporate takeovers and mergers, subsided as the Japanese asset bubble burst. Japan, already receding from the international stage, was pushed back deeper into itself by an earthquake in the city of Kobe in 1995 that killed more than 6,000 people, which was followed by the murderous sarin attacks by the religious cult Aum Shinrikyo on the Tokyo underground.

Damaged further by the 1997 Asian financial crisis, Japan has stagnated since then, confronted a new 'normal' of depopulation, a shrinking labour force, rapid ageing, young women forced into the sex industry, and homelessness. The decline, which has seemed irreversible since the 1990s, made plain that what had served Japan's post-war recovery and growth well—cosy capitalism, rigidly organized and protected domestic systems—had become a liability in the freshly globalized world. Pampered for too long, bankers, industrialists and stockbrokers were caught out by the new ways of doing things.

And they could not change in time. Two decades later, the Japanese economy remains hobbled by insider-dominated

labour market, irrational regulation, an underutilized female
workforce, anti-immigration policies and poor corporate
governance. The country has fallen behind in almost
every field—entertainment, tourism, medicine, software,
communications—where it had once enjoyed the initiative.
Even Japan's lead in popular culture is now being challenged
by South Korea's worldwide export of television dramas
and rock music.

The rapid turnover of governments and prime ministers
hints at problems that no politicians can resolve. And the
recourse by men within the Iron Triangle to neo-liberal
recipes (deregulation and privatization), especially under
prime minister Koizumi Junichiro, and the consequences
(extensive layoffs, income disparities, unstable jobs,
unemployed youth) have only undermined the social
compact built upon egalitarian ideas of trust, mutual
dependency and security.

Post-Fukushima, the Japanese public has even less faith
in the government. As the novelist—and Japan's social
conscience—Ōe Kenzaburō puts it, 'the structure of the
Japan in which we now live was set [in the mid-1950s] and
has continued ever since. It is this that led to the big tragedy
of Fukushima' in March 2011. This continuity was apparent
in the mutually supportive networks of government
bureaucrats, national and local politicians, and big business,
and the media that came together to avoid blame for, and
obscure the proportions, of the disaster.

Meanwhile, as Abe Shinzo promotes 'Abenomics,'
his idiosyncratic mix of reflation and heavy government
spending, capital and jobs continue to fly out of Japan.
Japan's once-vaunted income equality has eroded over the

past two decades; its poverty rate is now among the worst in high-income countries. But Japan's crisis, which began in 1989, seems existential as much as economic and political. Old myths and beliefs that gave meaning to ordinary lives lie shattered, along with secure jobs and stable families. This is more damaging than it seems because, unlike Christian and Muslim countries, Japan never had a transcendent system of religious values, as opposed to codes of moral belief and behaviour that had survived from close-knit communities in the pre-modern era.

The rural collectivity was supplanted by a national community, united in the post-war era by the shared aim of economic growth. The rapid doubling of incomes, and the impression that everyone was middle class and in the same rising boat, nurtured strong social cohesion. But the culture of postmodern individualism, not to mention neo-liberal capitalism, undermined the national community and its sense of social solidarity, creating a vacuum that reactionaries and conservatives now try to fill.

Jeff Kingston, one of the shrewdest observers of contemporary Japan, concludes that 'muddling through is probably the best case scenario.' This may sound gloomy. But Kingston is guardedly optimistic about Japan's 'quiet transformation' during the lost decades, when the media became a lot more diverse and alert, transparency and civil society blossomed and the public became more demanding and sceptical of their representatives. It is also true that Japan remains the only major economic power without an ongoing commitment to war or the armaments industry; the strong

Japanese opposition to nuclear bombs remains an example to countries desperate to build them. Japan achieved rapid economic growth without rampant inequalities, at least until the 1990s. Life expectancy remains highest among large countries; unemployment doesn't rise much above 5 per cent. Crime levels are among the lowest in the world and its social ills are the envy of other advanced industrialized societies. The Japanese thinker Kato Norihiro even argues for post-growth 'maturity.'

> The rest of the world's population is still exploding, and we are coming to see the limits of our resources. The age of "right shoulder up" is over. Japan doesn't need to be No. 2 in the world, or No. 5 or 15. It's time to look to more important things, to think more about the environment and about people less lucky than ourselves. To learn about organic farming. Or not. Maybe you're busy enough just living your life. That, the new maturity says, is still cooler than right shoulder up.

One of the signs of the new maturity is the politicization of many young Japanese by the disaster at Fukushima. In the summer of 2012 massive protests filled Japanese streets for the first time since the great anti-Vietnam demonstrations of the 1960s. But Japan's politics also displays more disquieting continuities with the past.

As Kato writes,

> the old guard—those politicians who led the charge in the heady 1970s and '80s and fought back (however pointlessly) against the economic stagnation of the '90s—still want

to compete. Those men, best represented in my view by Tokyo's governor, Shintaro Ishihara, speak as if they are under siege. They hate being beaten by China. For them, it seems, maturity only means striving to be No. 1. They won't change. They are too settled in an earlier stage of development, in a dream of limitless growth.

Indeed, China's emergence just as Japan declined, and becoming the favourite destination of foreign investors, constitutes another reversal in the long history of Sino-Japanese relations. Transmitting its Confucian cultures to its neighbours, China had been Japan's 'teacher' for centuries. In the late nineteenth century, however, Japan abruptly broke free of its stagnant neighbourhood. While the Qing Empire floundered, and foreigners blithely sliced the Chinese 'melon,' the feudal Japanese re-constituted themselves into a modern nation state. The new Japan's coming-out party, appropriately, was the defeat of their doddery old tutor China in 1895. Many Chinese flocked, or were driven as political exiles, to Japan to learn the secrets of its awesome new power. Indeed, China's political leadership and intelligentsia would be drawn from these men.

Visiting China in 1928, when a rising Japan had begun to prey on its neighbour, the Japanese poet Akiko Yosano took a surprisingly broad-minded view of anti-Japanese passion among the Chinese: 'It's surely frightful from the imperialists' point of view,' she wrote in her travelogue, 'but for the Chinese people it must be celebrated in the name of humanity.' Akiko Yosano wrote benevolently about the nascent Chinese sense of nationality, it seemed essential to the survival of a country ravaged by civil war. But prejudice and ignorance about China prevailed in Japan. Takeuichi Yoshimi, who was Japan's leading Sinologist, reported a now familiar disconnect in modern scholarship: 'When we studied Chinese history and geography,' he wrote, 'we never studied the fact that there were humans there.' The dehumanization helped the perpetrators of Nanjing massacres in 1937.

For a long time, however, 'the Rape of Nanking' was far from becoming Chinese shorthand for Japanese brutality. Mao Zedong discouraged public discourse about the Japanese invasion and waived reparations. The People's Republic of China sought diplomatic recognition from Japan Tokyo moved to restore relations with China in the early 1970s, even recognizing the latter's claims over Japan's old colony, Taiwan. The next decade witnessed ever-closer cooperation as China opened up its economy to foreign trade and investment. Japanese relocated factories to China, and showered assistance on China—massive infrastructure construction, billions of dollars in loans and grants. Japan is now the second biggest investor in the country. The basis of the relationship laid then still exists in the form of the large Chinese student population in Japan.

China's troubled history with Japan was disinterred only in the post-Mao era. This was when communist leaders, ushering their country into a market economy, first began to face the problems of uneven growth, which now included social unrest on a huge scale. The commemoration of the Sino-Japanese War is now central to the post-Cold War Chinese strategy of finding new foils internationally and fresh ideological legitimacy at home.

It is a bit unfair to expect Japan's present conservative rulers to periodically denounce their country's short-lived empire and produce apologies on demand to its former enemies while British Tories have proposed to celebrate their imperial past in revised history textbooks. A willed amnesia and self-righteousness afflicts all former empires, and many nation states, including China, which shows no signs of officially acknowledging the killings near Tiananmen Square in 1989. Japan's extreme case of forgetfulness, ignorance and self-absorption can be credited to the fact that it was long exempted from an honest reckoning with its history by its stifling embrace of the United States.

But this can no longer be an excuse as Japan searches, still confusedly, for a new identity within the Asia it once dominated. Abe Shinzo needs Chinese and Korean tolerance of the steadily devalued yen; and his growth strategy will suffer if Japan's exports to China don't recover. Japan seeks to co-operate with China in dealing with the looming threat from North Korea. And it has to reckon with an evitable Chinese hegemony in the region. Japan needs to refurbish its image in order to advance these projects. But even Japan's potential allies, such as South Korea, remember too acutely its earlier reckoning with its geographic destiny in the first half of the century. In most Asian eyes, Japan has remained, for the past six decades an American client state—unable or unwilling to alienate its former occupiers by charting an independent path. Remarkably at the same time, another formerly occupied country and close American ally, Germany, has moved to the center of Europe, and is now shaping the continent's political and economic future.

As Kato points out, right-wing Japanese politicians

are largely to blame for their country's isolation and unpopularity; a great majority of the Japanese remain wary of militarism, and firmly opposed to war. Ishihara Shintaro, Tokyo's governor, provoked the stand-off with China with his plan to buy the Senkaku Islands—barren rocks known in Chinese as the Diaoyu Islands—claimed by China. The young mayor of Osaka, a rising politician, claims that the 'comfort women' sexually enslaved by the Japanese military in World War II helped maintain discipline and morale.

Abe Shinzo also stokes bad memories of this violence, and region-wide suspicions that the Japanese remain in denial about their history of imperialism. He has already proposed to revise Japan's pacifist constitution to officially acknowledge its possession of a remarkably large standing army, navy and air force. He openly doubts if imperial Japan was an 'aggressor' in Korea. He has allowed his deputy to visit the Yasukuni shrine. A month after I left Japan, he appeared, wearing army fatigues, atop a fighter jet emblazoned with the numerals 731, the number of a notorious Japanese chemical and biological warfare unit during World War II.

More so than Ishihara, Abe is a typical representative of the old guard in Japanese politics, which gets worked up about things like the decline of the work ethic, and respect for hierarchy, flag and anthem. Abe wishes to restore the emperor as head of state; emphasize collective duties over individual rights; and, most importantly, promote veneration for the family. Speaking to the right-wing manga artist Kobayashi Yoshinori, Abe recently confided his belief that 'Conservative spirit' is necessary to build a 'healthy market system.' He says, 'Japan has been a country in which people have lived by tending the fields together and sharing the water. With the imperial family at the center, people prayed together for bountiful harvests and prosperity.'

This takes the old culture talk to a new level, enlisting it into the project of Japan's market economy as an extension of the family, one that is fundamentally benign, and in need of protection. John Dower points out that 'national pride—acute, wounded, wedded to a profound sense of vulnerability—lay behind the single-minded pursuit of economic growth that created a momentary superpower a mere quarter-century after humiliating defeat.' Abe now seeks to revive that pride through a more explicitly nationalistic program. His supporters outline his grand ambition by actually invoking the Meiji slogan 'fukoku kyohei': enrich the country, strengthen the army.

Indeed, cultural nationalism is for Abe a bigger political trump card than Abenomics as he confronts massive fiscal imbalances, public debt, ageing population, and stagnant economy. Still, Abe is unlikely to succeed. The kind of socializing that turned individuals into loyal citizens of a conservative monarchy no longer happens in a country increasingly divided, in the American way, into 'winners' and 'losers.' The social capital that underpinned post-war Japan has shrunk. The old life with its stability and promise of opportunity is gone even as older men like him cling to visions of the political and corporate collective.

Despite its much-heralded 'pivot to Asia,' the United States, or any other foreign power, is not in position to substantially shape a new national narrative for Japan. Japan must assume alone the privileges—and burdens—of its growing autonomy. And perhaps there would be some lessons for the rest of us in how Japan lives its long historical defeat.

In the last century, Japan seems to have run through a whole cycle of the modern experience, from industrialization to nihilistic militarism, from the frenzy of economic growth to the passivity of otaku. It objectified and instrumentalized nature, equated progress with technological advances, and, in its postmodern phase, individual subjectivity with sundering of social bonds; but the confusion and anomie that beset its greatest minds in the early twentieth century seems to have only deepened.

Asia's pioneering nation, the twelve-year-old boy of MacArthur's paternalist vision who briefly turned into a world-conquering businessman, can often seem lost in its dotage. Japan caught up with the West, and even surpassed it, only to find that there is now no place to go to, no new course to chart. A regressive nationalism presently carries the burden of this end-of-things fatigue and bemusement. But Japan's impasse amid a global crisis of capitalism also points to a new future—one as full of possibilities for the West as for Japan and Asia. As Kato writes, 'Japan now seems to stand at the vanguard of a new downsizing movement, leading the way for countries bound sooner or later to follow in its wake. In a world whose limits are increasingly apparent, Japan and its youths, old beyond their years, may well reveal what it is like to outgrow growth.' Whether or not Japan takes it on, it would be an appropriate task for the oldest modern country in Asia.

ACKNOWLEDGEMENTS

I am grateful to the editors—Robert Silvers, Sheila Glaser, Leo Carey, Jeffries Blackerby, Becky Gardiner, Rahul Jacob, and Mary-Kay Wilmers—who commissioned most of the pieces in this book. Shruti Debi encouraged me to put them together, and Chiki Sarkar at Penguin skilfully carved a thematically linked narrative out of them.

Many of the people who helped me find my way—logistically as well as intellectually—are mentioned in the text. But I would still like to thank John H. Bowles, Michelle Garnaut and Karim Raslan for introducing me, and then smoothing my access, to different parts of East and Southeast Asia. My first trip to China was greatly enriched by Julia Lovell's generous sharing of her contacts. There were many valuable interlocutors over the next few years, including Zhang Lijia, Eric Abrahamsen, Lynn Pan, Jeffrey Wasserstrom, Alex Travelli, and Jeff Kingston. I feel especially blessed to have had, for more than two decades, such hosts as the Sharmas at Mashobra. As always, my biggest debt is to the two Ms.

Scan QR code to access the
Penguin Random House India website